Deviance Management

Deviance Management

Insiders, Outsiders, Hiders, and Drifters

Christopher D. Bader and
Joseph O. Baker

UNIVERSITY OF CALIFORNIA PRESS

University of California Press, one of the most distinguished university presses in the United States, enriches lives around the world by advancing scholarship in the humanities, social sciences, and natural sciences. Its activities are supported by the UC Press Foundation and by philanthropic contributions from individuals and institutions. For more information, visit www.ucpress.edu.

University of California Press
Oakland, California

Library of Congress Cataloging-in-Publication Data

Names: Bader, Christopher, 1969- author. | Baker, Joseph O., author.
Title: Deviance management : insiders, outsiders, hiders, and drifters / Christopher D. Bader and Joseph O. Baker.
Description: Oakland, California : University of California Press, [2019] | Includes bibliographical references and index. |
Identifiers: LCCN 2019005363 (print) | LCCN 2019015521 (ebook) | ISBN 9780520973121 (e-book) | ISBN 9780520304482 (cloth : alk. paper) | ISBN 9780520304499 (pbk. : alk. paper)
Subjects: LCSH: Deviant behavior—United States.
Classification: LCC HM 811 (ebook) | LCC HM811 .B33 2019 (print) | DDC 302.5/42—dc23
LC record available at https://lccn.loc.gov/2019005363

28 27 26 25 24 23 22 21 20 19
10 9 8 7 6 5 4 3 2 1

CONTENTS

ILLUSTRATIONS

IMAGES

FIGURES

TABLES

ACKNOWLEDGMENTS

Deviance Management was a long-running and complicated project, and we have many people to thank for their help and support now that it is complete. Thanks to Roger Finke and Steven Pfaff for taking the time to read and comment on early drafts, and Pete Simi for informing us about research directly relevant to the project. Thanks to Jessie Arnold for providing insightful feedback on the chapter about gender and sexuality. Special thanks are due to Chris Scheitle. In early iterations of the project, Chris helped us better understand the connections between deviance management and social movements. Although we ultimately took the book in a different direction, we still benefitted from Chris's insights and knowledge.

To the many colleagues who were forced to listen to us drone on about this project, including but not limited to Paul Froese, Melissa Schrift, Andrew White-head, Ed Day, and Scott Desmond, we owe you all a drink. Thanks also to the students in our classes for their interesting questions and discussions about the ideas and research in the book. The feedback of our peers and students improved the final product in innumerable ways. Research for the book was also generously supported by a non-instructional assignment from the College of Arts and Sciences at ETSU in the spring of 2017. Thanks to Bill Duncan, Gordon Anderson, and Bert Bach for their support of this research.

Our chapter on the Bigfoot subculture would not have been possible without the help of many people. It was the North American Wood Ape Conservancy that introduced us to the world of Bigfoot research. Thank you to Brian Brown, Daryl Colyer, Michael Mayes, and other members of the NAWAC for your willingness to hang out with sociologists. Visiting the Patterson-Gimlin film site would not have been possible without the hard work of the Bluff Creek Project, including Steven

Streufert, Rowdy Kelly, Jamie Wayne and Robert Leiterman. Our thanks to the BCP.

Our research on Westboro Baptist Church would not have been possible without the cooperation and openness of the members, particularly Shirley Phelps-Roper, who agreed to let us visit on multiple occasions and interview members of the group. While we obviously do not support the hurtful public actions of WBC, they were nonetheless gracious hosts and thoughtful interviewees. Our thanks to Shirley and other members (and former members) of WBC for their time and willingness to talk about their experiences and beliefs.

We are especially grateful to Maura Roesnner at University of California Press for her enthusiasm about the project and valuable advice throughout. We must also thank six anonymous reviewers solicited by UCP for their detailed feedback. We have admittedly created a strange concoction in the world of academia: a book that combines original theory with mixed-methods research, and aims to be plain-spoken rather than prolix. While some reviewers were more enthusiastic than others about our willful deviance from academic conventions, all gave constructive feedback that improved the book.

Finally, we are grateful for the steadfast support of our families while we worked on this project for over a decade. To Sara and Amy: We couldn't have done it without you. And now you never have to hear us talk about working on this again! To John, Max, Hazel, and Eleanor: Thanks for always reminding us what is really important.

Introduction

Insiders, Outsiders, Hiders, and Drifters

One crisp fall Sunday afternoon, we stepped into the sanctuary of a small Baptist church in Kansas to attend worship. Given the prevalence of Protestantism in the Midwestern United States, this in and of itself was not particularly noteworthy. Likewise, the service was unremarkable, at first. We sang a hymn. An elder led the congregation in prayer. But then the grizzled, fiery pastor started preaching. His message was anything but ordinary.[1]

The sermon covered a host of topics: sin, hell, the American military, the Supreme Court case *Lawrence v. Texas*, "Antichrist Obama," "hordes of Sodomites," "Satanic miracles," and, for good measure, a Komodo dragon.[2] All those who were not members of the group—including us—were labeled "fag enablers." The preacher chided that we and everyone else not in the group, were "DRUNK on the bitter wine made from the grapes of gall from the vine of Sodom, which grows only on the fields of Gomorrah." The sermon ostensibly centered upon responding to a dubious text titled "The Homosexual Manifesto." Copies were distributed to all congregants. The heading read: "Reprinted from the Congressional Record." The actual original source of the text was explicitly labeled as satire, but in the pastor's jeremiad that morning, the story of the manifesto was presented as a deadly serious conspiracy of the highest order, one in which "both houses of Congress are filled to the brim with Sodomites."[3] Further, the preacher intoned, just "as leaven secretly, quietly, mysteriously, works its way throughout every particle of the bread dough, making it rise, we are told that the sinister forces of evil work, permeating society until the whole is fatally and irreversibly corrupt."

The man beseeching his followers to wage an apocalyptic battle against homosexuality and mainstream culture on that afternoon was none other than the infamous

IMAGE 1. Members of the Westboro Baptist Church, Luke Phelps-Roper, 8, left, and Seth Phelps, 9, both from Topeka, Kansas, picket outside the White House in Washington, Tuesday, October 5, 2010. (AP Photo/Carolyn Kaster. © Associated Press; Photo ID: 101005151168)

(and now deceased) Fred W. Phelps Sr. The place we were attending services was the notorious church he founded and led: Westboro Baptist Church (WBC) in Topeka, Kansas. The themes from Phelps's sermon that day were in no way an aberration from a typical Sunday there. A content analysis of more than one hundred sermons across multiple years from the group's worship services showed that homophobia, religious evil (apocalypse, Satan, hell, demons, etc.), contemporary politics, and the wrath of God were the most common themes covered, typically in conjunction.[4] As patriarch of the WBC, Phelps led his band of true believers to protest the perceived sexual sinfulness of America in ways that shocked and outraged the public. Their general strategy was to carry extremely offensive signs around in public places. Young children in the group often participated in these protests.

WBC first gained wider media attention when its members protested the funeral of Matthew Shepard, who was murdered in a hate crime, with signs declaring Shepard was in hell because "God hates fags." Although these shocking antics drew some scorn, it was not until WBC started to protest outside the funerals of American service members killed in combat that they became truly infamous.[5] During one such protest at the funeral of Marine Matthew Snyder, WBC held up signs reading, "Semper fi fags" and "Thank God for dead soldiers," among other things. This action resulted in a Supreme Court case about free speech and the right to protest, which WBC argued on their own behalf and won.[6] WBC threatened to protest the funerals of five Amish girls who were murdered after being taken hostage in their one-room schoolhouse. The group only relented from the planned protest in exchange for air time on a national radio show so they could spread their message to the public.[7]

And what is their central message? "So, earth-dweller, our message to you is this: You've sinned away your last day of grace; there is no remedy for this country and this world; God is your enemy; and America is doomed. . . . We warned you to obey, so your blood is not on our hands, but is on yours. Your duty stands constant— OBEY. You won't fulfill it, and very shortly Christ is coming through the clouds to punish the disobedient, and to destroy this earth with a fervent heat."[8] To put it succinctly: God hates you. You are going to hell.

Feel like converting yet? Neither did we. But as researchers who study both deviance and religion for a living, we were intrigued. What could possess people to do and say such things? Beyond the appalling lack of concern for others' feelings and privacy, there are puzzling paradoxes at the heart of WBC's identity and activism. Why preach to (at, really) people you don't think can be converted? Why protest ceaselessly if you do not believe any changes to governmental policy or practice will follow? And why try so hard to offend people, showing no regard for norms of tact and decency, while also meticulously avoiding the violation of legal boundaries regarding protest?

We will return to each these questions at the end of our study. But the answer, in short, lies in the group's sense of deviant identity and their related strategies of messaging about that identity to the outside world. This is a book about both. It also is about how identities rooted in social conformity conflict with identities rooted in actions or attributes labeled as socially deviant. More directly, we outline some of the basic processes of deviance management—meaning the strategies and messaging that communities and individuals use in response to being labeled deviant. We then test these hypotheses across a range of substantive examples—specifically, sex, drugs, and Bigfoot—but deviant religion, too. We use a variety of social scientific methods to look at different dimensions of deviance management, including qualitative research using ethnography, interviews, and content analysis, as well as quantitative research analyzing patterns in primary data and secondary survey and policy data. Qualitative methods allow us to look for thematic patterns in narratives, social movements, and identities focused on deviance management. Quantitative methods allow us to see if there are distinctive patterns of deviance management, how these patterns are related to subcultural conflict, whether different styles of deviance management are related to social activism, and under what conditions changes in public policy toward normalization occur.

THE PROCESSES OF DEVIANCE MANAGEMENT

Our focus on the processes of deviance management is guided by five observations about people who are labeled, or potentially labeled, as socially deviant.

1. Being Labeled Deviant Creates Role Conflict

People's daily lives are partially defined by shifting between different roles. The role of employee carries different expectations regarding behavior and use of time; what is valued or disvalued; how to achieve "success"; and sometimes even appearance, dress, and language than does the role of parent. Individuals act differently in church than they do at home, change conversational tones and choices of words when addressing close friends versus strangers, and studiously avoid discussing controversial topics in the workplace, even after attending a fiery political rally the night before. Stated simply, people tend to present themselves in the manner they believe best suits the current situation and leaves the most positive impression with their fellow interactants, within the parameters of a given situation.[9]

Problems arise when two or more roles carry "incompatible expectations for the behavior of a person," a situation known as *role conflict*.[10] An example is the competing demands placed upon women working outside the home, particularly those with spouses and children. Cultural expectations about what it means to be a successful wife and mother often are in direct conflict with those placed upon women by the workplace.[11] Devoting enough time to work to be considered a valuable employee takes time away from housework, child care, and other "second shift" duties.[12] Reducing time spent at work to meet the demands of family may lead coworkers to conclude that a woman is not serious enough about her career.[13]

Similarly, those labeled deviant face competing demands.[14] Satanists have to interact with non-Satanists, whether it be on the bus, around the family dinner table, or at the supermarket checkout. The Amish need to sell their products to the English in order to survive. Furries have parents, and white supremacists have jobs. With rare exceptions, such as hermits or entirely self-sufficient, underground communities, deviant identities are lived in continued interaction with conventional society. How individuals manage their conventionality influences how they interact with a deviant subculture—a synergistic relationship.[15] Since *deviance* refers to behavior that "violates a social norm or rule," and it is impossible to conform to every social rule at all times, it is simply not feasible for someone to be a perfect deviant (or a perfect conformist).[16] Therein lie role conflicts. Publicly and vocally committing to deviance risks conventional relationships, opportunities, and options. Likewise, taking full advantage of conventional opportunities or experiencing major conventional turning points such as marriage or having children may limit opportunities to fully engage with a deviant subculture.[17]

Clearly people labeled deviant will differ in the extent to which they experience role conflict. For those more committed to deviance than conventionality, subcultural concerns will take precedence, and vice versa. To predict responses to role conflicts between deviance and conformity, as well as who will experience such conflicts more or less acutely, we must understand the relative *salience* of both conventional and deviant identities.

2. Deviants Vary in the Relative Salience of Deviant and Conforming Identities

Role conflict can cause stress and exhaustion,[18] career burnout,[19] depression,[20] and poor health.[21] Yet not all role conflicts lead to such outcomes. The work of sociologist Sheldon Stryker proves insightful regarding the circumstances under which conflicting role demands are likely to cause negative consequences.[22] The multiplicity of roles that individuals must perform throughout their lives form larger *identities*. Enacting the identity of physician can involve performing a number of different roles, including medical researcher, surgeon, patient confidant, coworker, and boss. Should that physician also carry the identity of mother, then she also will have to play the roles of child confidant, disciplinarian, comforter, caregiver, and moral compass. The degree to which statuses are embraced or resisted varies, and the veracity with which they are emphasized or imposed by others varies by cultural and temporal context.

Roles accompanying specific status positions considered important by both an individual and others she interacts with can be understood as social identities. But people simultaneously hold multiple status identities, which must be amalgamated into a broader sense of "self."[23] When identities come into conflict, such as when a physician must choose between finishing a research project or attending her child's school event, individuals are forced to choose between them. As Stryker argues, primacy will be given to the identity with greater *salience*: "[T]he higher the salience of an identity relative to other identities incorporated into the self, the greater the probability of behavioral choices in accord with the expectations attached to that identity."[24]

We can measure the salience of a conforming identity by drawing on criminologist Travis Hirschi's social control theory. Hirschi operationalized the strength of an individual's ties to conformity, or social bond, as consisting of several elements, including attachment, commitment, and belief.[25] *Attachment* refers to the extent to which an individual has valued relationships that could be damaged by engaging in deviance. *Commitment* refers to prior investments an individual has made in conventional society or expectations of future rewards from sustained conventionality. For example, those committed to advancement within a conventional career have much to lose by engaging in deviant behavior. Finally, *belief* refers to having moral beliefs that align with conventionality.[26] Simply put, we would expect conformist identity to be highly salient when conventional attachments, commitments, and beliefs are strong.

Hirschi envisioned the elements of the social bond as measures of conformity, but they are equally useful measures of the salience of *any* identity, if we remove direct references to conventionality. A deviant is likely to have some valued relationships with conventional people *and* valued relationships with people in a deviant subculture.[27] While opportunities for advancement and high-status positions in deviant subcultures are often less stable and transposable than those in conventional systems, deviants also will vary in their status within subcultural communities and the desire to maintain that status. Deviant subcultures necessarily involve nonnormative beliefs about life or society that members subscribe to in varying degrees. Deviant identity salience, therefore, will depend upon the strength of deviant attachments, commitments, and beliefs.[28]

By conceptualizing the salience of conforming *and* deviant identities in relation to each other, we can build a framework for understanding how and when individuals will give deviant identities primacy and what strategies of action they are likely to use for managing the role conflicts inherent in deviant statuses.

3. The Relative Salience of Deviant and Conforming Identities Produces Different Deviance Management Strategies

Dichotomizing the salience of conventional and deviant identities into "high" and "low" produces four different, broad strategies individuals may use to manage deviance/conformity role conflicts. As outlined in figure 0.1, we call these ideal types "Insiders," "Outsiders," "Hiders," and "Drifters."[29] For the sake of simplicity, we often speak of these categories as types of people, but in actuality they are behavioral strategies, and individuals may use a combination of strategies to manage stigma across different situations. This follows Erving Goffman's theorizing about stigma: "[S]tigma involves not so much a set of concrete individuals who can be separated into two piles, the stigmatized and the normal, as a pervasive two-role social process in which every individual participates in both roles, at least in some connections and in some phases of life. The normal and the stigmatized are not persons but rather perspectives."[30] Likewise, Insiders, Outsiders, Hiders, and Drifters are not specific people, but *deviance management strategies*.

Identity theory predicts that people will act in accordance with their most salient identity whenever conflict occurs, which is of greatest relevance to those we label "Outsiders" and "Hiders."[31] *Outsiders* have strong and highly salient deviant identity and weaker and less salient conforming identity. Outsiders are the focus of much of the research and theory in the study of deviance.[32] When challenged by conformity, Outsiders prefer deviance to disavowal or compromise and will likely see their deviance as superior to so-called normalcy. In contrast, *Hiders* hold strong and highly salient conforming identities and weak and less salient deviant

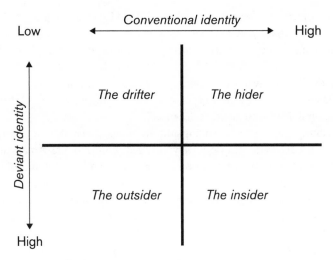

FIGURE 1. Deviance management subtypes.

identities. In other words, Hiders engage in some form of deviant behavior or interact with a deviant subculture while simultaneously facing high personal costs for discovery.[33] Here the strategy of deviance management is one of information control rather than openly combatting stigma.[34]

It also is possible for people to have conventional identities of lower salience (little interest in conventional occupations, educational attainment and few conventional attachments) and simultaneously feel little affinity with a particular deviant subculture with which they occasionally interact. We label such individuals *Drifters*. Drifters are more likely to move in, out, and between conventional and deviant identities, and also in and out of multiple deviant subcultures over time.

Of great interest to our study are *Insiders*, who simultaneously hold highly salient deviant and conforming identities. Insiders will find themselves in situations that can provoke considerable stress and potentially threaten both their deviant and conforming identities if not managed successfully.[35] The flip side of this "double consciousness" is that Insiders are integral players in attempts to normalize deviance.[36]

4. Different Deviance Management Strategies Produce Varying Pressures to Normalize Deviance

There have been many attempts to explain the dramatic softening of attitudes toward same-sex relationships that has occurred in the past few decades. Some argue that prejudice toward minority groups is reduced by interpersonal contact between majority and minority groups—the "contact hypothesis."[37] In theory, meeting members of a deviant category humanizes them, leading to greater understanding and sympathy. A number of studies have found that personal contact with sexual minorities decreases negative attitudes and homophobia.[38] Others speculate that a societal trend toward valuing individualism (independence of thought) over collectivism (obedience, favoring the group) can lead to "fewer restrictions on sexual behavior,"[39] and/or that increasing levels of education among the general public lead to greater tolerance.[40]

Such attempts to explain changing attitudes toward sexuality implicitly assume that the shift occurred because *society* changed; conventional American culture (anthropomorphized) became more open-minded, and gay men, lesbians, and bisexuals reaped the benefits. Minimized in these discussions is the key role that those labeled deviant themselves play in engendering such change by how they choose to message about themselves and the strategies of action they pursue. After all, contact with gay people might *increase* negative attitudes if that contact reaffirms preexisting biases or stereotypes. But, "If the stereotypes are false, if homosexuals as a group behave in general like others (aside from their sexual orientation), then contact with them can prove the stereotypes wrong and reduce prejudice."[41]

Normalization is a process of *negotiation* between representatives of conventional "society" and "deviants." To change minds, deviants must be willing to present themselves in a manner that is palatable to the general public—in a way that changes minds and shatters preconceptions or, at the very least, encourages some form of identification with those labeled as deviants.[42] This suggests a cyclical process whereby deviants seek affirmation and attempt to message about themselves in a more palatable manner. In response to this messaging, members of conventional society may soften their attitudes, encouraging further changes in messaging from the deviant subculture.

But it is not a given that members of a deviant subculture will *want* to change their image. If the deviants in question refuse to soften their presentation and instead focus upon differences between themselves and conventional society, attitudes among the general public are unlikely to soften. Understanding the competing pressures of deviant and conforming identities allows us to predict how people are likely to frame and message about their deviance and, consequently, which types of deviants are most likely to promote and successfully achieve normalization. Chapter 3 focuses upon these messaging differences, deriving predictions based on the relative salience of deviant and conforming identities:

- Having weak salience of both deviant and conforming identities, *Drifters* are less likely to experience role conflict and also less likely to develop a strong message about deviance.
- Having a stronger and more salient conforming identity than deviant identity, *Hiders* are more likely to avoid publicizing their deviant activities and may actively deny participation in or affinity with deviance.

- Having a stronger and more salient deviant identity than conforming identity, *Outsiders* are more likely to promote messages of difference and superiority, as well as to actively discredit deviants who promote compromise or capitulation.
- Having to manage both a strong and salient deviant identity and a strong and salient conforming identity, *Insiders* are more likely to message about their deviance as less threatening and more normal than it has been labeled, and to highlight points of similarity between deviants and conventional society.

5. Differing Deviance Management Strategies Produce Subcultural Conflict

Deviance theory and research typically focus upon the relationship between deviant subcultures and conventional society. However, it is important to also focus upon what happens *within* deviant subcultures. Throughout the book, we demonstrate how differences in the management of deviant identities can cause subcultural conflicts.

The most pronounced area of disagreement will be conflict between Outsiders and Insiders. These conflicts will arise from two very different needs. If a person holds a highly salient deviant identity *and* a highly salient conventional identity, she has much to lose from being stigmatized as deviant. Insiders must therefore perform the difficult balancing act of openly avowing their deviant identities while maintaining attachments to conventional others and preexisting commitments to a conventional lifestyle. Such concerns lead Insiders to develop narratives that present their deviance as less threatening than it has been portrayed and to magnify similarities between themselves and conventional others. Absent those concerns, or holding them to a lesser degree, Outsiders are comparatively free to enact unrepentant deviant identities in a wider variety of contexts. As we discuss at length in chapter 5, Outsiders may view Insiders as "sellouts"—people far more concerned with pleasing their conventional friends than being true to the deviant subculture. For Insiders, Outsiders are a potential source of embarrassment, threatening messages of similarity by performing deviant roles in outwardly defiant ways. As we discuss in chapter 4, it is not enough to simply know that a person is a Bigfoot believer to understand the performance of that identity, as Insiders tend to frame the search for Sasquatch as a scientific enterprise, while Outsiders view the pursuit of Bigfoot as a supernatural quest.

SYNOPSIS

This book presents a concise but novel framework that explains the paths of action most likely to be taken by individuals who are labeled deviant, as well as some of the consequences of these patterns for issues such as subcultural conflict, normalization movements and social policy reforms. Linking our five main points together reveals a longitudinal story of deviance management. Individuals with particular attitudes, attributes or behaviors are labeled deviant by conventional others. These individuals must then decide how to respond to this stigmatization (or its potentiality). The relative likelihood of different responses will be strongly influenced by individuals' levels of commitment to both conventionality and deviance. The resulting strategies vary in their level of engagement between conventionality and deviance, with Insiders' normalization efforts having the highest level of engagement and negotiation. As reform movements negotiate conflict with conventional society, differences over how best to manage stigmatization—particularly with regard to normalization—also create internal subcultural conflicts.

By conceptualizing individuals' and groups' investment in social processes of both conformity and deviance, a clearer picture of the strategies of deviance management and subcultural dynamics emerges. Empirically, we can predict with relative accuracy which individuals and groups will be most likely to hide, limit commitments and drift, separate from conventional society, or make efforts to normalize what has been labeled deviant. We use a wide range of behaviors, groups, and movements as examples and sources of empirical data to test and refine these ideas. From marginal religious groups and paranormal subcultures to same-gender sexual relations and cannabis use, all are examined to see how people manage social stigma, who chooses different strategies for doing so, when individuals join reform-oriented social movements, under what conditions such movements succeed, and how and why these processes create subcultural conflict.

We begin by specifying a framework for understanding deviance management in chapters 1 through 3, then turn to empirical assessments of these ideas in chapters 4 through 6. We will also return to the Westboro Baptist Church to see how our conceptual framework can provide insight into the group's behavior, as well as how the group's unique characteristics illustrate some of the complexities involved in studying deviance management.

The Complementarity of Deviance and Conformity

The first and arguably most foundational idea in the sociological conception of deviance is its necessity for social order. More formally, we might say: Regardless of historical or cultural context, at least one group of people within a community—real or imagined—will be viewed as evil, dangerous, and/or unacceptably different.[1] Sometimes these outgroups are relatively large and organized. Other times there is only an idea or fear that such a group is lurking among us, even with little or no evidence of an actual threat. Whether witches or sexual predators, communists or biker gangs, cultists or punk rockers, deviant outgroups are perpetual features of social life. Since we always seem to have, nay, create, "deviants," social theorists have gotten considerable mileage out of the counterintuitive question: What purpose do deviants serve for communities?

THE "FUNCTIONS" OF DEVIANCE

Early sociologists analogized social systems to physical bodies.[2] Just as the heart, lungs, brain, muscles, and bones work in concert and serve vital functions, so must each part of society serve some vital function for the larger organism. Those phenomena that do not (or no longer) serve an important function eventually wither away by being "selected against" and removed from the system. From this perspective, there *must* be some utility for the constant recurrence of deviance and its accompanying processes of punishment—including those with imaginary foci such as witch trials—otherwise they would not continue to occur.

Initially, it might be difficult to see a purpose in horrific events such as witch trials, but this is the approach sociologist Kai Erikson took when analyzing the witch trials in Salem, Massachusetts. He argued that in England, the Puritans' collective identity centered on criticisms of the normative and dominant religion in that context, and thus their identity was secured through the fact that they were *not* typical Anglicans.[3] The group's boundaries were solidified by having the Church of England as an ever-present, negative example. After moving to the New World, the Puritans were forced to reconceptualize their collective identity. Who are we "Puritans" now that our previous enemy is no longer present? Like all interpretive communities, the Puritans needed to continually reestablish who they were, especially as previous cultural distinctions were blurred or called into question in New World communities.

To compound the cultural crisis, the revocation of the Massachusetts Bay Colony's royal charter, which established its system of governance, made the legitimacy of the community's official order even more uncertain.[4] Applying demonic paradigms of misfortune, the Puritans reasoned that the threat of supernatural evil was ever present and, worse, had even infiltrated the group. Community survival and cosmic struggle required violent expiation. The witch trials powerfully reestablished that the group's identity was founded on combating evil.[5] At the expense of already peripheral group members (relative to more powerful factions), the community reaped a collective return on violent persecution by shoring up its sense of collective identity, explaining its misfortune, and definitively delineating the cultural landscape, even if only temporarily.

Drawing on the legacy of structural-functional theories shorn of the overzealous biological metaphors, Erikson argued that the execution of twenty accused witches and the baseless accusations and prosecutions of hundreds of others bolstered the social order. Although problematic in some ways, a worthwhile takeaway from functionalism is that *deviance* can be defined as the product of the social processes surrounding the punishment and control of behavior, ideas, or conditions that violate cultural norms.[6] In other words, the response to deviance is as important for analysis as the deviant acts themselves, if not more. Because punishment requires social power for enforcement, cultural boundaries are generally buttressed by ideologies of morality and policed by those authorized to use physical coercion by the extant power structure. But like all social processes, boundaries of deviance and punishment can change over time and thus require continual reproduction through enforcement and punishment.

In short, demonizing a deviant group clearly marks cultural boundaries. Symbolic boundaries are maintained by scripts of acceptable behavior and justified by the values espoused by the powerful within a community. In essence, the clearest way to define cultural boundaries is to point out and punish those who have violated expectations.[7] Consequently, collective identity crises tend to produce scapegoats and the righteous infliction of pain and shame.

Having a common enemy to fear, despise, decry, defy, or ridicule is a powerful force for solidarity. Enemies work at all levels of collectivity, for "families as well as whole cultures, small groups as well as nations."[8] In contemporary American culture, politicians and pundits utilize the threat of terrorism, whether it be from ISIS or al-Qaeda (or Islam in general), to rally public support behind American foreign policy.[9] In the previous century, communism fulfilled the role of arch villain. On a more local scale, politicians have little to lose and much to gain by raising the specter of sex predators or street gangs when trying to win an election. With its appeal to fear and emotion, the claim of being "tough on crime" is one of the safest positions any candidate can take.[10]

While pedophiles and terrorists serve as generalized enemies for many contemporary Americans, other perceived enemies are only demonized by particular social groups. Religious conservatives define themselves against "godless liberals." Environmentalists define themselves against "SUV-driving planet killers." Anti-immigration advocates define themselves against "illegal aliens." Every us requires a them.

If demonizing enemies bonds members of a group to one another, a necessary corollary is that boundary maintenance is equally important in deviant subcultures. To the extent that cultural codes strengthen internal ties by demonizing deviants, those labeled as deviant can likewise strengthen their own resistance identities by collectively dismissing conventional culture.

THE FUNCTIONS OF DEVIANCE FOR DEVIANTS

Albert Cohen's classic criminological study of gangs examined this process of collective resistance to societal norms. Cohen's key initial observation was that much of the deviant behavior engaged in by youth gangs appeared to serve little useful purpose. This observation was somewhat at odds with the work of other scholars such as Robert Merton, who argued that deviant behavior was an attempt to achieve mainstream goals (such as wealth) through the use of "innovative" means, such as theft.[11] If youth crime served a purpose, Cohen argued, it was a less obvious one than the acquisition of wealth. In fact, much of the youth crime he observed was decidedly anti-utilitarian; its only purposes seeming to be to destroy, vandalize, or injure. To Cohen, it seemed as if youth gangs were purposefully rejecting the "American dream" by expressing outright contempt for conventional culture and reveling in the opportunity to act out against it. Unable to see a means by which to achieve middle-class standards, youth rejected the system that had rejected them, a phenomenon Cohen labeled "reaction formation:" "[W]e would expect the delinquent boy who, after all, has been socialized in a society dominated by middle-class morality and who can never quite escape the blandishments of middle-class society, to seek to maintain his safeguards against seduction. Reaction-formation, in his case, should take the form of an 'irrational,' 'malicious,' 'unaccountable' hostility to the enemy within the gates as well as without: the norms of respectable middle-class society."[12]

By encouraging its members to act in potentially illegal ways, the gang exposes its members to risk, but not without potential benefits. Cohen argues that the shared experience of breaking rules bonds youth together. Further, gangs provide an alternative status system by which lower-class youth can hope to succeed.[13] By strongly rejecting unreachable goals, gang members justify their choice to engage in deviant activities. In the language we outlined in the introduction, the lack of stakes in conformity combined with deep investment in a deviant subculture generates the strategies and actions of the Outsider.[14]

We can draw a general principle from Cohen's work. Just as individuals aligned with conventional groups have powerful motivation to reject deviants, those labeled deviant have powerful motivation to reject conventional society.

Example: Rejection of the Mainstream in Amish Communities

Deviant religious groups are well known for their tendency to reject the dominant culture in which they exist. For example, the Amish quite explicitly separate themselves from mainstream society. Although exact rules and regulations vary by settlement, Amish groups reject the use of many modern technologies. Visitors to Amish areas can easily spot members in their horse-drawn buggies or tending fields without the aid of tractors or electricity. Photos should be avoided, however. Posing for a photograph is considered an act of insolent pride by most Amish. All glory is due to God and not to the individual, so actions and behaviors that draw attention to the self are to be avoided.

This philosophy extends to outward presentation of self. Amish men wear their hair long in an unfashionable, unparted bob. Married men must let their beards grow, but may not have a mustache. Belts also are taboo, requiring men to wear suspenders to hold up their black trousers, which are frequently worn without zippers or buttons on the fly. Men's coats also are black and without collars. Topping off the distinctive Amish uniform is a wide-brimmed hat; its style closely regulated. Amish women face similar style restrictions. Jewelry is taboo, as are cosmetics and makeup of any kind. Women wear long dresses of a single color and keep their heads covered at all times.[15]

While the "English" (as Amish call the non-Amish) struggle to be fashionable and purchase the latest gadgets to keep up with the ever-changing flow of popular culture, the Amish proudly and permanently maintain an old-fashioned manner. Living by rules that are at odds with mainstream cultural norms may be too high a price to pay for the average person, and the relatively low conversion rate to the Amish indicates that the lifestyle is, purposefully, not for everyone.[16] What is important to remember is that the Amish lifestyle serves what sociologists term *manifest* and *latent* functions.[17] Manifest functions refer to the intended purposes or outcomes of a given action or behavior. For example, the manifest function of anti-gambling legislation is to curb gambling. Latent functions refer to the *unin-*

tended outcomes or results of an action or behavior. Latent functions may be positive or negative in nature. Criminalizing gambling, unfortunately, has the latent function of creating an "illegal empire for the gambling syndicates."[18]

Amish lifestyle restrictions have an obvious manifest function—to keep members focused on giving glory to God rather than on bolstering their personal pride. The Amish diverge from the norms of the rest of the world because their theology, activities, and rules of etiquette constantly remind them to do so. But Amish lifestyle restrictions also have powerful latent functions. Like any public good, religious groups are forced to deal with the problem of "free riders." Given the choice, a "consumer" of religion would prefer to have all the benefits of belonging—such as the promise of otherworldly rewards as well as more earthly benefits like community; social support; holiday festivities; and access to birth, marriage, and death rites in a church—without having to tithe, spread a religious message, attend worship services frequently, or restrict one's behavior or ideology in any way. Just as a person who jumps subway turnstiles still gets to enjoy the ride that everyone else has paid for, a member of a religious group who rarely attends services and gives little to his congregation still gets to enjoy the same benefits as everyone else.

One way a religious group can reduce the number of free riders is to make strict demands.[19] Strict groups force members to choose: "participate fully or not at all."[20] Requiring members to dress or act in certain ways or placing prohibitions upon behaviors serves the important *latent* function of making the cost of low-level participation outweigh its potential benefits. Why would anyone *want* to be Amish and undergo the comprehensive lifestyle restrictions membership requires if they are not truly dedicated to the group's ideals? Current members who are less committed will tend to leave, and potential joiners who have not fully "bought in" will stay away. At the end of adolescence, a period called Rumspringa allows Amish youth a chance to defy the rules of the group and briefly live "English" lifestyles before deciding if they want to become full members of the group as adults, thus helping to ensure full buy-in from those who choose to stay in the group.[21]

As a consequence of this latent function, the Amish and similar groups are left with a committed core and a strong sense of in-group identity. It is easy for the English to spot an Amish person in a crowd. It is equally easy for two Amish to spot one another in that same crowd. The costs of rejecting the world are offset by the benefits of a strong collective identity—that incomparable, primal feeling of "us."

THE NECESSITY OF INTERACTION

The social processes surrounding deviance thus serve vital functions for the conventional social order, as well as for groups labeled as deviant. Rejecting and demonizing nonmembers helps those on both sides of a cultural divide create and reinforce their identities, increase commitment, and maintain members. But the issue becomes more complicated when we move away from groups that revel in their deviant status. Groups or acts previously considered deviant might eventually become conventional. Communities defined by same-gender sexuality, for example, have made significant progress in moving from being seen as decidedly deviant to being viewed with ambivalence and often even acceptance, with intolerance now concentrated more in specific subgroups among the wider population.[22] Such normalization presents a paradox for the concept of the "functionality" of deviance. Why should normalization ever occur if agents of conventional social order have so much to gain from demonizing deviants and those labeled deviant have something to gain from reciprocally demonizing conventional society?

We would not expect a form of deviance to change its normative status if the so-called deviants and conformists could truly keep each other at a distance to ensure that greater levels of mutual understanding never occur. Despite the benefits for deviants and conformists in remaining separate, it is virtually impossible to actually do so. The Amish survive by selling their goods and labor to the outside world, producing food, furniture, and quilts and building homes and barns. Even deviant groups that may appear independent from conventional society, such as isolated polygamist communities, must still interact with it, although those interactions may be limited to law enforcement and other government agencies.[23]

The results of contacts between deviants and conformists will vary, of course, with some heightening prejudice, some reducing prejudice, and others simply reaffirming preexisting notions. But the key point is that the lives of deviants *also* are necessarily the lives of conformists. What varies is the salience of each role. Unfortunately, theories of deviance largely focus on the deviant side of this equation, even though, as sociologist Erdwin Pfuhl emphasized, most deviants actually conform most of the time: "People are not committed *either* to deviant *or* to nondeviant values or behaviors. As we have noted, few persons, including the most dedicated delinquent, engage in rule-violating behavior at each and every opportunity. 'Severely disturbed' mental patients conform to most rules most of the time. And even among the most dedicated professional offenders, violation of the law is occasional. Rather than being unique, this same observation may be made of anyone. Realistically then, commitment to legitimate values is a modality, a condition characteristic of most people most of the time."[24]

Without a hypothetical deviant community that provides for all of one's needs, the necessity of balancing deviance with conformity becomes imperative. Deviants need to earn money, pay bills, maintain relationships with people of a variety of backgrounds and opinions, be aware of their neighbors, interact with relatives, take the bus, and walk down the street.

In their influential studies of gay men and lesbians, sociologists William Simon and John Gagnon show how the lives of homosexual men were quite similar to that of heterosexual men in terms of major concerns such as earning a living; levels of career commitment; the consequences of aging; and relationships with family, friends, and religion. Where homosexual men differed, Gagnon and Simon argued, was in how they were forced to negotiate their sexuality *while* addressing these shared concerns.[25]

Gagnon and Simon found that occupational considerations influenced the expression of gay identity in many ways. First, to the extent that a job was considered gratifying and required extensive commitment, it limited the time men could devote to gay subcultures if they expected to make a successful career in that occupation. Some jobs require late hours, others early mornings or long shifts. The men discussed how the need to be well rested or work long hours often required them to make a choice between joining the late-night gay bar scene or doing well in their occupations. This balancing act led some men to greatly limit the time spent in "gay spaces," while others sought out less professional occupations in order to facilitate subcultural participation.

Of greater concern than time commitment, especially at the time of the study, was the prospect of being publicly exposed as "a homosexual." Although there had been some liberalization toward same-sex sexuality at the time of Gagnon and Simon's research in the 1970s, being outed as a gay school teacher, minister, or politician would still have had disastrous consequences for one's life and career. In other occupations, sexual orientation was of little concern, and in a small minority of jobs, Gagnon and Simon note, being gay might have a "positive consequence."[26] Understandably, the likelihood and anticipated consequences of exposure greatly influenced the "outness" of the gay men in the study.

The desire to maintain relationships with immediate family members also constrained expressions of gay identity. As with occupation, Gagnon and Simon argue that "[t]here is no substantial evidence to suggest that the proportion of homosexual men having significant relationships with relatives differs from that of heterosexuals," but rather that, "[t]he important differences rest in the way relationships are managed . . . and . . . the consequences they have for other aspects of life."[27] The dynamic nature of family relations and the fact that some family members might be more accepting than others can lead to great variation in interaction patterns. Some relatives will reject a man entirely if they learn he is gay. Others will fully accept him. Many relatives will fall somewhere between these two extremes— being willing to accept some *version* of homosexuality. A lesbian at a large family reunion may find herself with the unenviable task of navigating a complex web of conversations with relatives of differing levels of awareness and acceptance of her sexual identity.

In addition to managing the awareness and acceptance of others, Gagnon and Simon found it was equally crucial for a gay man to "accept himself" by developing a worldview in which homosexuality is an acceptable and moral choice. Religion can provide such a moral framework, but the frequent condemnation of homosexuality in religious texts leaves many gay men and lesbians "caught between dominant Christian culture and gay subcultures."[28]

In their study of gay and lesbian Christians, psychologists Eric Rodriquez and Suzanne Ouellette summarized the identity work involved in resolving the conflict between traditional religious and sexual identities.[29] Some simply reject one identity or the other. Those with weak religious identities dealt with the conflict by rejecting religion altogether or by switching to one with less negative views of homosexuality. Others were too strongly committed to a particular religious identity to reject it, leading instead to the rejection of homosexuality, which might be accomplished via "conversion therapy" or attempts at abstinence. When rejecting one identity is too difficult, sexual minorities may choose to compartmentalize their religious and sexual identities; keeping their homosexuality out of church and their church out of homosexuality. Alternately, some people develop an entirely new identity that integrates their gay/lesbian and Christian identities into a new, syncretic self.[30]

Of greatest interest, for us, is not *how* sexual minorities reconcile sexuality with religion, but the fact that they must do so. To fully understand deviant identities, we must understand that most deviants also must conform most of the time. Gagnon and Simon chastised scholars for focusing almost exclusively upon the "deviance" of homosexuality, ignoring the importance of more common and conventional acts in shaping gay identity: "Similar to the larger society's reaction, there has been a tendency to be too exclusively preoccupied with the manifest deviance, and a failure to observe or report upon the conforming behavior which frequently accounts for the larger part of a deviant's time and energy—and provides the context for deviant performances as well as often giving meaning to such performances."[31]

Put simply, it is difficult to understand how individuals manage deviant identities (and therefore, how, when, and to what intensity they will engage in deviance) without reference to their conventionality. Two people who share the same deviant identity or predilection for a certain deviant behavior are likely to engage in that deviance differently depending on the extent to which each must simultaneously manage the role of a "normal" person. Social psychology provides tools for better understanding the management of such competing roles and identities.

IDENTITIES, ROLES, AND ACTING NORMAL

When the gay men Gagnon and Simon studied chose to act one way in front of coworkers and another when at a gay bar, they were, in essence, displaying two different expressions of their selves. They, like all of us, were treating the self as a performance, to be played differently in front of different audiences. This is not to say that these men were liars or inauthentic, nor is this behavior unique to either gay men or those labeled deviant. To the contrary, an influential school of social theory running through Georg Simmel, Charles Cooley, George Herbert Mead, and others frames all human interaction within a dramaturgical perspective, wherein the *self* is largely a social construct, developed and enacted via interactions with others.

This perspective found its most persuasive proponent in Erving Goffman, whose seminal book, *The Presentation of Self in Everyday Life*, outlined theatrical metaphors for understanding human interactions.[32] Humans are actors, and all the world's a stage.[33] Every person plays multiple roles. These roles may be tied to social relationships, such as spouse, parent, employee, student, or friend. They also may be dictated by the situational environment in which a person is acting, such as commuter or bus rider, diner at a restaurant, customer at a store, and so on. Each role has different expectations about how one should act in order to perform that role successfully. To successfully play the role of friend, one must be willing to talk, joke, listen to others' problems, and socialize. To successfully play the role of college student, one must sit quietly, avoid socializing and joking, and (at least appear to) carefully take notes. Playing the role of a customer requires forms of interaction different from those of acting as a commuter. For Goffman, the existence of a permanent self is questionable, given that people may have to act out so many different roles in different settings, particularly over time.[34] Social life is about "acting" and presenting a version of one's self that best fits the current situation.[35] Actors engage in a successful "performance" if the audience agrees with and accepts their self-portrayal. At work, we will engage in expected tasks, dress accordingly, avoid situationally improper language, use the lingo (argot) inherent to that job, and maintain an appropriate level of social distance. Our lingo, dress, behavior, and level of social distance will change somewhat between "playing" family member, friend, churchgoer, Elks Club member, or whatever other role we may be required to perform.

Dramaturgical theories of human interaction have led to an abundance of research on how people manage the many different roles they must play and the distinctions between the concepts of *role, identity,* and *self.* The definitions of *role* and *identity* vary between theorists and are sometimes unfortunately used inconsistently.[36] We use *role* to refer to situational, socially constructed expectations for appropriate behavior. The occupation of teacher qualifies as a role. Once a person is identified as a teacher, others hold certain expectations of that person. Consistently failing to meet those expectations would result in sanctioning or removal of the status and accompanying role.

Identity is a broader concept, referring to the "meanings that persons attach to the multiple roles they typically play in highly differentiated contemporary societies."[37] Identities partially determine *how* we play required roles within the broader constraints society places upon us. For example, two men may both hold the roles of spouse, politician, and churchgoer. The expectations associated with those roles produce somewhat predictable behavior (assuming adequate performance of the roles). Both men will provide emotional support for their spouse and contribute to their household finances. As politicians, they will (presumably) follow the law and keep the best interests of their constituents at heart. Each man will sit in the pews on Sundays to learn about God's will and donate to his church. But if one man holds a political self-identity of "extremely conservative" and the other an identity of "extremely liberal," we can expect considerable variation in how they play these roles beyond the minimum expectations. They may have different views on gender roles, leading to differential sharing of household chores and spousal employment. They will pursue vastly different agendas within the confines of the political system, and they will attend churches with strikingly different interpretations of the same scriptures.

People do not possess a single identity. Rather, it is possible to hold as many identities as there are distinct groups of people with whom we interact or distinct roles we must play.[38] The line between a person's role and identity may be quite blurry, depending on the individual. For some, identity is strongly tied to occupation. Being a professor requires such a large commitment of time and energy that it tends to become an important part of the self-identity of most professors we know, in addition to being a role they play. Others may perform the role of employee without the job affecting how they view themselves. For them, it's just work. In other words, there is great variation in the salience of status identities between individuals.

Each semester, we ask students to list their identities on a whiteboard. These lists vary widely in the number of identities listed and their level of abstraction. Some list political orientations (liberal, conservative, moderate), others specific political parties or candidates. Some do not find politics important enough to put such a designation on their list. Students who belong to racial, ethnic, sexual, or religious minority groups often include these as identities on their lists. Religious affiliations, if they appear, may be broad, as in "Christian," "Buddhist," or "atheist," or more specific, such as "Southern Baptist" or "Episcopalian." Types of relationships (boyfriend/girlfriend, son/daughter) often make the lists, as do memberships (fraternity member, Greenpeace) and occupations or desired careers (artist, architect, politician).

We conceive of the *self* as the larger narrative by which individuals understand themselves and integrate their varying statuses and accompanying roles and identities. This makes the self both a singularity and a multiplicity. It is achieved through personal, subjective evaluations of a hierarchy of identity salience, ranking the relative importance of different statuses as a way to organize a coherent self-narrative.[39] This story of one's self is then told to other people. Metaphorically, the self is perhaps best understood as a soliloquy—a story you tell about your self to yourself, as well as to audiences.[40] The self is fundamentally narrated as a moral story. As social psychologist Steven Hitlin defined the concept: "The self involves reflexivity, the capacity to use second-order concepts to judge first-order reactions. Reflexivity is at the root of our ability to be moral beings. The self includes elements necessary for understanding the moral actor: identities, personal identity, and time."[41] In this book, then, we focus our effort on examining how individuals manage deviant and conventional identities simultaneously and attempt to resolve the inevitable conflicts between such identities into a larger self-narrative, as well as how this narrative guides future actions.

ROLE CONFLICT AND DEVIANCE

After writing their identities down, students easily comprehend how they alter their performances of self throughout the day, guided by their identities and shaped by the requirements of the audience(s) and role. They also easily provide examples of being confused about how to act in particular situations, due to competing demands. A devout, conservative Christian described instances in which she withheld her opinions about social issues, fearing that doing so would anger other students at her liberal college campus. The assistant manager at a sandwich shop vowed to never hire a friend again. It proved impossible to drink with his friend on the weekends and be treated like a boss at work.

All self-aware people will face some form of role conflict in their lives, whether it be in dividing time between home and work, the competing demands of different people or groups, or expected behavior as a member of a particular social group (e.g., race, gender, religion, profession) and desired actions. Such conflicts are of interest to us as social scientists because they cause stress, tension, and poor health outcomes if individuals cannot find a way to resolve them.[42] As a result, role conflicts can be used to document dysfunctions in social systems or to explore how individuals react to these conflicts.

Role conflicts are of special import to those labeled deviant, in terms of how they behave, how they construct their selves and how they message about their identities to others. As we noted, because they comprise multiple identities, selves are necessarily "multifaceted, composed of diverse parts that sometimes are independent of one another and sometimes interdependent, sometimes mutually reinforcing and sometimes conflicting."[43] In the case of deviant and conventional identities, interdependent, mutually (negatively) reinforcing, and conflicting all apply, as deviant labels always have direct implications for the level of conventional identity those aware of the stigma are willing to grant deviants. Prevention from regaining stakes in conformity is often a central form of punishment for deviance.[44] Stigma is, after all, "spoiled" conventional identity, resulting in a gap between how individuals are perceived by others and how they perceive themselves.[45]

Goffman is not alone in observing this connection. Theorist Talcott Parsons tied the genesis of a deviant motivation to role conflict: "Exposure to role conflict is an obvious source of strain and frustration in that it creates a situation incompatible with a harmonious integration of personality with the interaction system. Indeed . . . exposure to conflicting expectations of some kind may be presumed to be the generic situation underlying the development of ambivalent motivational structures with their expression in neuroses, in deviant behavior or otherwise."[46] For Parsons, the strains produced by role conflicts play a key role in causing deviance. We view the relationship between role conflicts and deviance as cyclical in nature. The strain of experiencing role conflict could potentially lead to deviant acts or to the development of a deviant identity as a way of resolving or avoiding such conflicts.[47] Our focus, however, is on how a preexisting deviant identity or motivation might lead someone to respond to situations of role conflict, particularly situations where the need to play a role associated with conventional society is in conflict with the expectations of a deviant identity. Within this framework, paths and strategies of action are the phenomena to be explained, using as predictors identity salience and psychological centrality, which are understood as products of the level of commitment individuals hold toward particular social statuses, roles, and identities.[48]

Example: Role Conflict among White Power Movement Members

How deviants respond to role conflict would not be interesting if the responses were invariant. In fact, research into deviant subcultures has found considerable variation in how members balance subcultural needs with the necessity of playing conforming roles. A recent study of the White Power Movement in the United States conducted by sociologists Pete Simi and Robert Futrell illustrates this point well.[49]

The U.S. White Power Movement (WPM) refers to an ideology shared among groups such as the Ku Klux Klan, neo-Nazis, Christian Identity religious groups, and skinheads that espouse virulently anti-Semitic views and argue for the superiority of the "white race."[50] As Simi and Futrell note, the popular image of WPM members is that of extremely vocal, hostile, and confrontational fanatics who take advantage of every opportunity to disrupt polite society. In reality, "[i]n many everyday settings it is difficult to determine who is an Aryan and who is not."[51] Drawing upon in-depth interviews with WPM members, content analyses of their websites, and participant observations of the subculture, Simi and Futrell found that white supremacists recognized the costs of enthusiastically expressing their views in public and actively attempted to "pass" as conventional in many settings.

WPM activists spoke of the conflicts they experienced, with friends cutting off ties and parents and other relatives expressing concern, anger, and disappointment. Members of such groups respond to this conflict in various ways. Some choose their Aryan views over family and friends, disengaging from those who express disapproval and creating a social world where all or most of their close associations are with other racists. But for most WPM members the cost of such isolation is too high. Some cannot afford to take such an approach, particularly if they are living with relatives or otherwise relying on them for financial support. Many Aryans consequently search for ways to maintain a self-identity as a WPM member while avoiding open conflict with others. They actively avoid political conversations with relatives and friends so that sensitive subjects do not come up. Social life becomes about "seeking a balance between deception and disclosure"; as one of Simi and Futrell's informants said: "I'm pretty selective in revealing all of my views. The best I can explain is like a compromise that helps me sustain my personal beliefs without compromising my relationships. I show some of who I am and hide other parts."[52]

The problems of balancing a blatantly racist identity with everyday requirements of living are further complicated by the need to play the role of student or employee. More than half of Simi and Futrell's informants believed that they had lost a job in the past due to their expression of white supremacy beliefs, and students knew they could face severe sanctions for being outed as racists. Many learned to hide their beliefs. They worked with employees of other racial and ethnic groups without complaint and some even espoused liberal values while at work or school; "fooling others" was rationalized as a form of resistance. They learned how to manage racist tattoos, white power flags, and other popular signs of Aryan devotion. Activists with conventional occupations and concerned friends and relatives placed tattoos on parts of their bodies that were easily hidden, as expressed by "David," who said, "I think it's better to avoid getting tattoos you can't cover with a suit. I know some people might think I'm being hypocritical, trying to hide my beliefs but not everyone can make it in this world with a ton of tats; it can make finding work pretty rough."[53]

IDENTITY SALIENCE AND RESPONSES TO ROLE CONFLICT

The gay men studied by Gagnon and Simon and the white supremacists that were the subject of Simi and Futrell's work may not share much in common in terms of worldview, but they faced similar concerns: how to manage the role conflicts inherent in maintaining a career and relationships while also holding a deviant identity. And both exhibited variance in their responses to this role conflict. Some gave deviant identity preference and left occupations or ended relationships that conflicted with that identity. Others, being tightly constrained by conventional concerns, gave preference to convention and either hid or sublimated their deviance. Most tried to find a balance between the two by choosing when and to whom to be open about their deviance or finding subtle ways to express themselves.

"William," a Southern California Aryan interviewed by Simi and Futrell, provided a succinct description of this compromise: "We can't all move to a compound in Idaho. . . . We've got to deal with what we have in front of us."[54]

From the standpoint of studying deviance, this raises an interesting question. Can we predict variation in responses to role conflicts produced by participating in a deviant subculture? After all, while most find ways to fit in, some white supremacists *do* move to a compound in Idaho to fully embrace their beliefs. Why do some deviants choose compromise, others concealment, and still others defiance? Research on role conflict provides an answer.

In addition to documenting the various stresses and strains caused by role conflict, Sheldon Stryker developed the concept of *identity salience* to answer a fundamental question: "Given situations in which there exist behavioral options aligned with two (or more) sets of role expectations attached to two (or more) positions in networks of social relationships, why do persons choose one particular course of action?"[55] Stryker and colleagues proposed that the various identities people hold can be organized in a hierarchy of salience.

Salience in this context refers to the likelihood that a given identity will be enacted across a wide variety of circumstances. Should two women hold the same series of identities, such as "professor," "mother," "Republican," "Evangelical Christian," and so on, we would expect their reactions to social situations to vary based on how they rank order these identities in terms of importance to their respective self-images. Should a controversial social issue arise in class, such as abortion, someone with a highly salient identity of professor and an identity of "Evangelical Christian" of much lower salience will likely conform to the norms of classroom discourse, discussing the issue in relation to trends, changes in attitudes, and impacts of public policies. Given the same circumstance, an individual who favors the identity of Evangelical far more than the identity of professor may insert views about the morality of abortion into classroom discussions. This effect will be amplified or attenuated by the setting in which it occurs. Should the Evangelical Christian who happens to be a professor work at an explicitly faith-based university, she may be actively encouraged to bring moral concerns into the classroom. Should she work at a public, nonreligious university, she may find herself sanctioned for doing so.

Of course, this discussion simplifies these matters considerably. Many other contingencies will come into play. Sometimes people will act in ways not consonant with their own ideas, as when a person desperately wants to stop using drugs but persists out of habit and the pain of withdrawal. And sometimes people act out unconscious desires or unrecognized motivations. But these important caveats notwithstanding, we should expect that self-identities and the manner in which people rank-order them will influence how they play the many different roles we all face navigating life. Indeed, researchers have found that the salience of identities predicts a wide variety of behaviors.[56] Stryker provided further guidance regarding *how* individuals will rank-order their identities. The salience assigned to an identity is related to the commitment an individual has to performing certain roles: "Commitment refers to the degree to which persons' relationships to others in their networks depend on possessing a particular identity and role; commitment is measurable by the costs of losing meaningful relations to others, should the identity be forgone."[57] A distinct, but interconnected aspect of commitment is one's level of emotional connection to an identity—the sense that "this is really who I am."[58]

So not only do people have a variety of different roles that they must play and a variety of different identities that guide their performances, they also have varying levels of commitment to each of those roles and identities.[59] Failing to perform certain roles as per expectations potentially threatens one's livelihood if that failure might result in losing a job, being overlooked for a promotion, or failing to achieve high grades at a school or university. Other failures may alter the strength of one's social connections, potentially resulting in broken friendships, estranged relatives, breakups, and divorces.

The potential costs of deviant behavior are, obviously, the province of criminology and deviance studies. At the same time, the conceptual framework we have laid out is entirely consistent with recent theoretical advancements in other fields of study, such as economics, where the paradigm of "identity economics" has helped explain oft-ignored considerations in economic models, for example, preferences, motivations, and seemingly "irrational" behaviors.[60] Articulated by Nobel Prize–winning economist George Akerlof and his former student, economist Rachel Kranton, identity economics posits that

1. identities are based on the social positions individuals occupy;
2. social identities are bound to accompanying norms and ideals that create cost/benefit structures based on whether behavior aligns with or diverges from such norms; and
3. people consider the gains or losses in "identity utility" when creating and maintaining "preferences," as well as when making decisions about future paths of action.

Akerlof and Kranton have shown that this concise theoretical model has high utility for explaining economic and social behaviors.[61] The three foundational assumptions of identity economics theory sync well with our own assumptions about the social sources of identity, the norms and expectations of accompanying roles, and the likelihood of specific behaviors based on relative levels of identity commitment and salience.

Yet deviance represents a special case of social identity by going against the grain of social norms. Further, for extending the ideas of social identity into considerations of deviance, it is critical to recognize and account for a basic fact: Any person who holds a deviant identity also will be expected to perform conventional roles at times. Consequently, all deviants necessarily hold deviant *and* conforming identities. How individuals perform these identities will depend upon the relative salience assigned to each, which will be a function of respective levels of commitment to these competing identities. Those with a more salient deviant identity will tend to make decisions and manage relationships guided by subcultural expectations. Those with a highly salient conforming identity and deviant identity of low salience should be expected to perform and act in line with conformity more often and to hide their deviance when necessary. Those who hold deviant and conforming identities of equal salience will find themselves in a difficult situation, forced to balance the demands of incompatible ideologies and expectations.

All of this suggests we can answer many interesting questions about how those labeled deviant manage their stigmatized identity, but only if we pay equal attention to the fact that all deviants must play some conforming roles or else face costs for failing to do so.[62] To fully understand the conundrum faced by those labeled (or potentially labeled) deviant, we must conceptualize and analyze the relative salience of conforming and deviant identities. To do this, we must measure how committed deviants are to the relationships and roles they play in deviant subcultures and to their conventional relationships and roles. Synthesizing the central expectations of two competing criminological theories provides a way forward in conceptualizing and measuring how conventional and deviant identities intersect, a task we undertake in the next chapter.

2

Deviance and Conformity

The Pressure of Dual Identities

Groups like the Amish are fully committed to their deviant status and thrive as outcasts from mainstream society. This requires wholehearted, collective belief that the Outsider group is actually "normal" and all others are the true deviants. But not all groups labeled (or potentially labeled) deviant are fully committed to their deviant status. Many so-called deviants have at least some investment in or connection to conventionality. Indeed, we can think of all individuals, whether they are currently seen as deviant or not, as constantly balancing their lives between at least two potential identities: conventional and deviant.

Most of us work very hard to maintain a conventional lifestyle and identity that will gain us recognition as a part of mainstream society, but even people who are generally conventional dance with the devil every now and then. The staid businessperson or schoolteacher might get a tattoo in a place that most people cannot see. With an otherwise conventional appearance and lifestyle, one tattoo would not significantly shift the balance between a person's conventional and deviant identities. On the other hand, people who have multiple highly visible tattoos, piercings, and other body modifications have increased their investment in a deviant identity.[1] Importantly, this does not necessarily mean that they have abandoned their commitment to a conventional identity. But it does mean that they might have to fight to make others recognize that commitment. When simultaneously holding an attachment to deviant and conventional identities, people will struggle to get others to treat them as normal. If they do not want to lose their conventional standing, those labeled deviant will have to fight for a status of "normal."

In the next chapter, we will examine how the struggle to maintain dual identities produces different messaging and framing strategies among individuals and causes factions within deviant subcultures. But before we do that, we must examine how a person develops an attachment to conventional identity in the first place and, conversely, how a person develops an attachment to deviant identity. Why are some people more committed to one over the other? And what happens to those stuck in between? In this chapter we build a new framework for understanding the origins, intersections, and expressions of conventional and deviant identities.

STAKES IN CONFORMITY

It is tempting to focus on those engaging in deviant or criminal behavior by asking a basic and intuitive question: Why do people do these things? This is indeed the starting point for positivist criminology and sociological theories about crime.[2] But we should also ask: Why *don't* most people do these things? Why do people conform at all? Why are most people committed to a conventional identity and lifestyle? After all, deviance can be quite profitable and enjoyable, especially if you can avoid punishment. Accordingly, other social scientists have approached the question of deviance by asking: What leads people to conform? The answers proposed are generally known as social control theories. Control theories argue that deviant behavior is part of human nature. Consequently, they assume that people will naturally deviate if not restrained in some way. In short, control theories detail some of the most important forces that *prevent* people from engaging in deviant behavior. These forces can come from both within and outside of an individual.

Although the ideas can be traced to the works of other theorists, criminologist Travis Hirschi outlined the most influential version of control theory.[3] Hirschi built upon earlier conceptualizations of control to develop what has remained the most influential version of the theory, positing that delinquency is the result of a weakened or broken bond to conventional society. Control theory details the elements that make up this social bond.

As noted at the beginning of the book, Hirschi proposed different elements that create a bond to conventional society: commitment, attachment, involvement, and belief. *Commitments* of money, energy, or time made by a person in order to obtain a conventional lifestyle, compose an integral part of stakes in conformity. Someone who has worked hard and achieved material and social success will be more likely to avoid deviant behavior that might threaten investments they have made and achievements they have obtained. Future expectations of achieving conventional rewards are also a form of commitment. *Attachment* refers to an individual's affection for others and sensitivity to their opinions. Someone who has strong attachments will, presumably, not want to risk the disapproval of these significant others by engaging in deviant behavior. *Involvement* refers to the extent to which individuals engage in conventional activities. An individual who is frequently involved in activities such as religious groups or social clubs will, presumably, be too busy doing conventional things to find the necessary time to engage in deviant behavior. *Belief*, the final element of the social bond, assumes that individuals will be less likely to engage in deviant behavior if they believe the rules governing deviance are legitimate and should be obeyed.

Researchers have used several empirical measures to assess conventional identity within the context of control theory. Regarding commitment, we can assume that individuals who currently hold conventional jobs or are engaged in educational programs designed to secure such conventional employment will be, on average, more tied to conformity. The constraining effect of such employment will be magnified to the extent that an individual considers the job to be part of a lifetime career with hopes for advancement. A junior lawyer or a medical resident should be less likely to deviate in ways that may threaten their careers compared to a person who is temporarily working as a cab driver to make ends meet until something better comes along. The cab driver, in turn, has more to lose from deviant behavior than does a person who currently does not have employment. Both the removal of income from losing a job and the derailment of chances for advancement or educational opportunities should increase the pressure on an individual to remain committed to conventionality.

Attachments to others further enhance the development of a conventional identity, but here we diverge from Hirschi's original formulation. Hirschi suggested that attachments, in and of themselves, should promote conformity, regardless of the character of the people to whom one is attached.[4] In other words, any valued relationship should promote feelings of responsibility and concern about disappointing others, which Hirschi argued would spur conformity. Thus, a person who has a valued relationship with a deviant person should, theoretically, be no more or less likely to engage in deviance than a person who has a valued relationship with a conformist. However, we would expect that individuals will only be likely to conform to the extent that the people with whom they have strong relationships value conformity.[5] Indeed, there is a vast amount of theoretical and empirical literature on differential association theory pointing to the tendency for relationships with people who have pro-deviance attitudes to result in deviant behaviors.[6] Only if people's relationship partners would find their deviance to be disgusting, immoral, or dangerous can we expect those interactants to impose costs upon its discovery. Those costs can range from minor, such as expressions of disapproval or disappointment, to severe, such as ending the relationship entirely.

Where commitment and attachment have been found to be strong depressors of deviant activity in empirical research, Hirschi himself questioned the importance of involvement after his initial tests. Although the free time and boredom that results from having few conforming activities does allow more time to explore deviance, most deviant behaviors themselves do not necessarily entail a large time commitment. Further, "time spent" is something we prefer to explain as an outcome. We would expect that people who have a stronger conventional identity via commitments to a conformist career and attachments to conforming others will spend more time in conforming activities as a by-product and expression of their social networks and associated roles. So, while the amount of time spent in either conforming or deviant activities will, no doubt, be related to deviance, we frame this as an outcome of other factors and do not treat involvement as a separate measure of stakes in conformity.

Belief in conformist values, however, proves vitally important to understanding deviance management. To the extent that someone responds in the affirmative to questions asking about conformist attitudes, that individual has a stronger conventional identity. Here we are not concerned with whether or not the individual has given socially desirable responses. In many ways, that is the point. Indeed, innovative field research has found that some deviants express hyper-conventional attitudes when around conformist others.[7] An individual who feels compelled to express conformist beliefs and values must feel an external and internal pressure to conform, or at least to appear to conform.

Together, Hirschi's elements of the social bond essentially outline potential indicators of the salience of one's conventional identity. Using control theory as a starting point, we use the following definition of conventionality identity:

> **Conventional Identity:** The salience of a *conventional identity* is stronger to the extent that an individual is engaged in conforming lines of action, holds attachments to others with conventional identities, and expresses conformist beliefs and values to others.

While social control theories focus on "stakes in conformity," a person can have "stakes" in any identity or line of action. Where those stakes lie will guide behavior in a corresponding direction. Stakes in conformity channel behavior toward conventional or "normal" behaviors and identities. But to fully understand the dynamics of deviance, we must also consider "stakes in nonconformity."[8]

STAKES IN NONCONFORMITY

Control theories raise interesting and relevant points for understanding the origins of deviant behavior, and perhaps more importantly, also for understanding conforming behavior. Nevertheless, there are substantial shortcomings in these general formulations. Most importantly, Hirschi and other control theorists built on a basic, often unstated assumption: humans are inherently prone to actions that would be labeled deviant. As a result, control theories tend to assume a one-dimensional and prototypical individual who is driven by animalistic impulses and kept in check only by the social order—a caged animal, as it were. This idea represents a considerable under-theorizing of social identity and assumes that humans do not have proclivities toward both selfishness *and* sociality.

Conceptualizing humans as only self-interested, as control theories do, over-simplifies human complexity. Similarly, conceptualizing humans as only social, as some cultural theories of deviance do, is also too narrow. It is reasonable to assume that people have an innate capacity for self-interest *and* consideration of others. This dual nature is evident in young children, who tend to be self-interested yet simultaneously responsive to and dependent upon other humans for protection and provision. Survival requires both. And as can be seen in sibling behavior, children seek friendship and inclusion, but they are also more than willing to selfishly exclude and demean others, depending on the situation. While this dual nature makes tidy theorizing about deviance difficult, accuracy must take precedence over simplicity for foundational assumptions. Complex assumptions can still generate parsimonious theories.

Interaction theorists have long noted that deviance is not simply the spontaneous behavior of the "uncaged animal" portrayed in control theories.[9] If it were, we would expect deviant behavior to be entirely disorganized, random, and unpredictable. Instead, deviant acts often require the existence of a deviant subculture with some level of organization. To use marijuana where it is illegal an individual must interact with an underground dealer, who, in turn, must get the product from a supplier or grower. Obviously, there are varying levels of direct contact in such a purchase. One might purchase drugs from a friend of a friend, who purchased from a dealer or grower; but, short of self-sufficient production, the existence of a supply chain is still required. To engage in acts of consensual sexual deviance such as BDSM, an individual must be able to locate willing partners and learn the norms and expected behaviors before, during, and after sex acts. Even the individual deviant who does not interact with members of a deviant subculture in person may benefit from the existence of a subculture through various forms of mediated communication. For example, pedophiles find photographs of underage children in online forums or may even consult child molestation "manuals" written by other pedophiles.[10]

Therefore, a key point of variance among individuals is the extent to which they interact and identify with a deviant subculture. Some will avoid interaction with subcultures related to their preferred area of deviance as much as possible. This might be due to concerns about discovery, fear of or distaste for members of the subculture, or simply because the individual drifts between different types of deviance and feels no connection to any one particular form. At the other end of the spectrum would be individuals who, through pursuing their deviant interests, come to strongly identify with a deviant subgroup. A person may become friends with others who engage in similar forms of deviance, begin sharing "trade secrets" in online forums, or even join related organizations.

We can also use Hirschi's elements of attachment, commitment, and belief to conceptualize a person's "stake in nonconformity."[11] Counting deviant friends is an imperfect measure of interpersonal attachment to deviance, to be sure.[12] If two individuals are hiding their behavior from one another, they may actually express conforming attitudes and have conforming expectations of the one another. But if a person is indeed attached to others who deviate and those peers expect or permit similar behavior, such a relationship will clearly promote deviance, not deter it. The stronger the attachments someone has to individuals with deep investments in a deviant subculture, the more we should expect the individual to (inter)personally identify with that subculture.

We also can consider commitment and belief in regard to deviance. For some, deviance is merely a temporary flight from normalcy; a spur-of-the-moment act involving little consideration of the subcultures supporting that act of deviance. For others, deviance becomes a "career."[13] As with conformist culture, deviant subcultures often include levels of formal or informal "membership," leadership positions, and advancing levels of expertise that follow a long-term commitment. Just as we can consider an individual as having a commitment to conventional lines of action, we can also consider a person as having a commitment to deviant lines of action. To the extent that people desire to gain status, acceptance, and expertise within a deviant subculture, they have commitment to that subculture. Consequently, leaving the subculture may incur high social and psychological costs, to the point of being akin to addiction withdrawal.[14]

Belief should work in a similar manner. Deviants vary in the extent to which they believe in the "rightness" of their behavior. A pot smoker who believes that marijuana should be legalized and that the government has no right to control its use has a high level of belief in the moral justification of cannabis use. A pot smoker who looks on the behavior as a shameful or distasteful vice has a much lower level of belief in deviance. Both individuals may hide their behavior, but for very different reasons. The first hides for fear of being arrested or otherwise sanctioned. The second hides because of shame.

Linguistic strategies that people commonly use to manage beliefs about their deviant behaviors have been termed techniques of neutralization, which consist of excuses, justifications, or rationalizations used to explain deviant behavior and release a person from societal expectations surrounding an action. For example, a person might deny that engaging in the deviant practice harms anyone (*denial of injury*), that a victim deserves what he got (*denial of victim*), that situational factors forced a deviant act (*denial of responsibility*), that those who condemn the deviant act are hypocrites who have no right to judge (*condemnation of condemners*) or that loyalty to a deviant subculture or a higher power requires the act (*appeal to higher loyalties*). Others have suggested that deviants also may rationalize their actions by arguing that certain impending needs have left them with no choice, such as stealing food to curb hunger (*defense of necessity*), that the deviance in question is justified because the individual is a good person in other ways (*metaphor of the ledger*), or by claiming that a law or norm against a particular form of deviance is antiquated or no longer needed (*denial of the necessity of the law*).[15] We can assume that the techniques of neutralization temporarily release individuals from conventional beliefs, but it is also reasonable to assume that these techniques lead to more stable beliefs in the "rightness" of a deviant action. Those who continue to argue that their behavior is not wrong for one of these reasons—aside from denial of responsibility—may come to truly believe that the behavior is justifiable, or even righteous.[16]

Taken together, just as attachments, commitments, and beliefs may tie someone to conformity and result in the development of a conventional identity, they also may tie someone to deviance and result in the development of a deviant identity:

> **Deviant Identity:** The salience of a *deviant identity* is stronger to the extent that an individual is engaged in nonconforming lines of action, committed to gaining status or expertise within a deviant subculture, holds attachments to others with deviant identities, and expresses beliefs and values that justify deviance.

THE PRESSURE OF DUAL IDENTITIES

People simultaneously hold and alternate between conventional and deviant identities. This is not easy to pull off. Everyone who engages in actions deemed deviant faces an acute form of role conflict. One role requires one set of behaviors and beliefs, while the other requires an entirely different set. The level of this conflict depends upon the relative salience of *deviant identity* compared to *conventional identity*. At an extreme, a person can choose to only play one role (i.e., absolute, committed deviant), but this means that they are giving up their ability to play the other (i.e., upstanding citizen).

Importantly, deviant labels are "stickier" than normative labels. It is much easier for a person to move from being labeled normative to being labeled deviant than the inverse; however, unless the deviant behavior involves the most intensive forms of social control, individuals still exert at least a modicum of agency by choosing the extent to which they will internalize (and alter) deviant labels, transforming them into deviant identities.[17] Those who engage in deviance but maintain weak deviant identities will play the role of deviant differently than those who strongly and openly identify as deviant. Those who have weak conventional identities should feel little pressure to justify their behaviors to others compared to those who have strong conventional identities. Thus, the desire for gaining acceptance from the wider culture for a deviant presentation of self should depend upon the extent to which a person feels the need to play the roles of conventional society member and, simultaneously, the role of deviant subculture member.

As noted in the previous chapter, there is a rich history of theoretical work examining the reasons why and the conditions under which representatives of conventional society label others deviant. Here we are more concerned with the outcome—how individuals react to their status as social deviants, or the potential of being so labeled. While those who have strong commitments to deviant subcultures but not conventionality should feel little pull or desire to sanitize their behavior for others, those who live predominantly conventional lives while also having subcultural commitment will feel a strong need to reconcile these two roles (and therefore identities). This may include efforts to push subcultural narratives in directions more palatable to the mainstream and efforts to reform conventional society to be more accepting of subculture members.

As detailed in the introduction, dichotomizing the salience of conventional and deviant identities into "low" and "high" produces four different, archetypal ways that individuals will respond to their status as deviants. Over the course of a deviant "career," an individual may move from category to category, and may at any given time, fall between or at the extremes of these categories. Although there have been many attempts to typologize the varieties of deviant behavior, our proposed schema differs by focusing on understanding the variety of potential *responses* to labeling. Where other typologies have focused on the differences between rule-breaking and conformist behavior, severity of the norm violation in question, or the social organization of deviance, we instead place emphasis on the management techniques used by those engaging in acts deemed deviant.[18]

While we use a different approach to get there, it is worth noting that the deviance management strategies that arise from our formulation are compatible with sociologist Bruce Link's modified labeling theory.[19] Link and colleagues argue that labeled individuals may respond to the labeling process with secrecy (hiding their status from others), withdrawal (limiting one's social interactions to accepting others), and educating (attempting to enlighten others to have less negative attitudes).[20] Clearly secrecy is the response we expect of the Hiders of our formulation. Further, we expect Outsiders to favor deviant over conventional attachments, suggesting some form of withdrawal. And, as discussed at great length in the next chapter, we expect Insiders to be highly motivated to try to educate others that their deviant subculture deserves normative status.[21] Although focusing on the management of deviance is not new, by connecting this concept with that of conventional and deviant identities we are better able to conceptualize responses to deviant labeling from the "ground up."

In essence, we: (1) employ an interactionist perspective on deviance to conceptualize how deviant labels (and their threat) are imposed from the "outside in," then (2) posit a schematic for understanding sociological patterns in the management of such labels and threats, and (3) use this conceptualization as a theoretical tool for understanding how different management strategies can produce conflict within deviant subcultures and lead to reform-oriented social movements. To do this we begin by delving deeper into our ideal types of deviance management.

OUTSIDERS

We're not like everyone else.

The *Outsider* is the classic conceptualization of deviant individuals, around which most of the research on deviance has been focused. An Outsider has a stronger deviant identity than conventional identity. In other words, Outsiders prefer deviant subcultures to normative society. As the above quote, from an open letter titled, "Queer Kids of Queer Parents against Gay Marriage" makes clear, some individuals labeled as deviant are not interested in trying to be "normal."[22]

The development of a strong deviant identity frequently accompanies the absence or erosion of conventional identity. For Outsiders, the rewards and costs of maintaining deviant identity and the rewards and costs of "fitting in" will be tipped toward continued deviance in a wide variety of situational contexts. For example, in subcultures of lower-class gang members, economic conditions block most opportunities for achievement by middle-class standards. Faced with this circumstance, an oppositional subculture of "smartness," defined as the ability to outwit or con others while avoiding punishment, may develop.[23] Similarly, in-situation respect, commanded through a readiness to use physical violence and coercion, may be emphasized over more conventional forms of status.[24] Such behavioral codes provide a set of beliefs that justify deviant actions and downplay the importance of convention. In truly countercultural contexts, those who do pursue a conventional education or job opportunities will be viewed with disdain.

Consequently, true Outsiders are not likely to be deeply involved in an occupation, committed to advancing in a normative career, or pursuing a line of conventional credentialing, such as education. The time ordering of the loss of a conventional identity and the development of a deviant replacement varies. A deviant identity may emerge due to a lack of opportunities to achieve by mainstream standards: Merton's innovators.[25] Appropriately, the process may result in a self-fulfilling prophecy. Individuals may begin to develop an identity due to blocked opportunities or social strains, but that emergent identity further segregates them from mainstream opportunities, leading to additional investment into a subculture or counterculture. A lack of conventional opportunities provides the freedom to pursue a deviant identity, along with an ego-sustaining explanation for the lack of conventional success.

Outsiders' strongest attachments will be to other members of a deviant subculture. This process is reflexive. Those who share a similar set of deviant beliefs may find one another and bond over their shared ideals, a "birds-of-a-feather" model of attachment. Alternately, an individual may become attached to members of a

deviant subculture and then learn beliefs that support the subculture as a consequence, as frequently occurs in cases of conversion to deviant religious groups.[26]
Both common sense and empirical research suggest that ideology and social network composition act upon one another reciprocally over time; thus, individuals
receive and internalize feedback on their identities from those whose appraisals
they value.[27]

As subcultural participants know quite well, individuals also vary in their levels
of commitment to a subculture.[28] For instance, there are four distinct levels of
involvement in the survivalist/prepper subculture.[29] Level-1 survivalists are only
loosely affiliated with the subculture, perhaps buying a few guns or other supplies,
taking classes or attending conferences. More committed (level-2) survivalists
increase their expenditures on supplies and spend more time attending survivalist
courses. Level-3 survivalists find themselves balancing the requirements of conventional culture and the survivalist subculture. These survivalists maintain their
conventional jobs and attachments, but they have established ties to a survivalist
subculture and tend to visit their "retreats" at every opportunity. The most committed (level-4) survivalists have largely forgone their ties to the outside world and
retreated entirely to a survivalist community or shelter.

Likewise, sociologist Kathryn Fox found that members of "punk" subcultures
internally distinguish themselves by level of commitment to the lifestyle, with
hard-core punks having the strongest countercultural identification.[30] Hard-core
punks tended to be on the margins of conventional society. Many were "desperately poor" and did not have much to lose from fully embracing a deviant identity.
As full converts to the subculture, hard-core punks gained status by clearly signaling their identity commitment to others via Mohawk haircuts, piercings, or other
visual markers that made it difficult to interact with conventional people: "By
doing something out of the ordinary to their appearance, the punks voluntarily
deprived themselves of some of the larger society's coveted goods."[31] Such visual
markers are an important signifier of cultural allegiance. When forced to choose
between the values of conventional society and the antiestablishment values of a
counterculture, the loyalty of the hard-core punks rested with the latter. They
expressed open disdain for convention and viewed their scene as a permanent way
of life, not as a temporary fashion statement. As one hard-core punk described
those who try to split time between the punk scene and the mainstream: "They
think they can have their nice little jobs and their semi-punk hairdo and live with
mom and dad and be a real punk, too. Well, they can't."[32] Other researchers of the
punk scene have detailed the same phenomenon, wherein "authentic" punks continually draw boundaries between themselves and inauthentic poseurs.[33]

True Outsiders can select from a limited array of strategies for managing stigma,
although it should be said that, in one way or another, claiming agency is itself a
central rallying cry for Outsiders. The most common behavioral and collective

strategy for Outsiders is to retract from and create subcultural boundaries with conventional society in the manner of sectarian religious groups, as was evident in the example of the Amish. There is an alternative strategy for Outsiders, though.

Rather than retreating, Outsiders can actively resist conventional structures of power. Here, however, relatively lower levels of investment in conventional sources of social capital restrict the options for resistance. Whereas Insiders can use accrued conventionality to push for reform within existing power structures, Outsiders are more likely to be forced into high-risk forms of resistance, such as direct-action protests, where one's bodily rather than social well-being is at stake. Violence and incarceration loom as sanctions for Outsiders seeking change, rather than the protracted bureaucratic battles awaiting Insiders. As a result, Outsiders also may align with other rejected groups for the sake of resistance. In chapter 5 we provide an in-depth example of such an alliance with the story of Fed Up Queers (FUQ), a sexuality-based activist group that was a catalyst for widespread protests over police brutality against racial minorities in New York City in 1999. Outsiders are often forced to be the "leading edge" of social movements of resistance, particularly in contexts of greater oppression. Unfortunately, success also holds potential peril, as bringing about greater social equality in some areas may result in mainstream co-optation of Outsider style and ideas. Inevitably, the true Outsider who strives for change must reckon with both the existential perils of failure and the cultural ironies of success.[34]

HIDERS

These false allegations hurt me deeply.

By all appearances, Bishop Eddie Long was a model citizen.[35] Born in 1953, the muscular, exquisitely groomed, and eloquent pastor earned a bachelor's degree in business administration from North Carolina Central University before completing theological training in Atlanta. At the age of thirty-four, Long took over the New Birth Missionary Baptist Church (NBMBC) located in Lithonia, Georgia, a small bedroom community of Atlanta. Under his watch, the NBMBC grew from a few hundred members to approximately twenty-five thousand; a true mega-church. The NBMBC's $50 million New Birth Cathedral opened as part of a sprawling 240-acre campus in the spring of 2001, with enough seating for ten thousand at a service, a large library, a retail-sized bookstore, a computer lab, and an abundance of programs and ministries available to members. In the meantime, Long became a pillar of the black community. He authored several books and audio sermons on the topics of personal religiosity, morality, the family, male-female relationships, and ministry and personal growth, receiving three honorary doctorates (including one from his alma mater NCCU). He was selected by the family of Martin Luther King Jr. to officiate at the 2006 funeral of Coretta Scott King.

New Birth Missionary Baptist Church is a part of a long, rich tradition of Black Protestantism in the United States. Black Protestant denominations hold many similarities to Evangelical Protestants, but are sufficiently different in their history, membership composition, and theology to merit distinction.[36] Both Evangelicals and Black Protestants tend to be theologically conservative, affirming the infallibility of the Bible and the reality of Hell. Where they differ is in political views. Whereas Evangelicals are typically politically conservative on both moral and economic issues, Black Protestants tend to be more progressive than Evangelicals on economic issues (such as supporting social programs), but are similar on "moral" issues of sexuality (such as abortion and homosexuality).[37]

Long's congregation fit this model well. The NBMBC was supportive of the George W. Bush administration's faith-based initiatives program and received a $1 million grant from the U.S. Administration for Children and Families in 2004. The church also is conservative on issues of sexual politics, particularly homosexuality. The same year that the NBMBC received its grant, Long led a march through Atlanta to protest same-sex marriage. Among Long's available works is the sermon "God Is After Himself," which claims to provide the "truth" about homosexuality.[38] Long argues that God created man in His image and that reproduction is God's attempt to reproduce Himself.[39] Since God has placed His "seed" in humans, any form of sexual activity that does not have the potential to result in reproduction, including cloning and homosexuality, constitutes a "spiritual abortion," and children raised by gay or lesbian parents will grow up "off balance." According to Long's public ministry, homosexuality was a disorder—the product of being raised by an effeminate father.[40] In 2006, Long invited gay men and lesbians to attend a "Sexual Orientation and Reorientation" conference at NBMBC, which offered to "deliver" them from their homosexual urges. Such exploits led the Southern Poverty Law Center to label Long as one of the "most virulently homophobic black leaders in the religiously based anti-gay movement."[41]

Given his very public stance against homosexuality, many of Long's supporters and admirers were, no doubt, shocked by charges leveled against him in 2010, when Anthony Flagg filed a lawsuit claiming that the pastor had coerced him into a sexual relationship.[42] The NBMBC offered a tuition-based program for young men between the ages of thirteen and eighteen called LongFellows Youth Academy (LYA), which purported to train boys in life skills as they progressed in their "masculine journey."[43] The program's website stated: "In the LongFellows Masculine Journey, God uses Bishop Long and his qualified staff to intentionally guide these boys through a journey of masculine initiation. The LongFellows Youth Academy walks them through the stages of masculinity; from Son to Rough Rider, from Rough Rider to Gladiator, from Gladiator to Ishmen and finally to becoming a real man, 'A LongFellow.'"[44] The Bishop was a constant presence in the LongFellows program, acting as a counselor, mentor and confidant to the participants.

Flagg's complaint asserted that Long targeted the often troubled young men who joined LYA and used his "authority as Bishop over them to ultimately bring them to a point of engaging in a sexual relationship."[45] Flagg joined the academy at the age of sixteen. After an arrest for simple assault, Long suggested to Flagg's mother that the youth move into a church-owned home, where Long could more closely monitor him. Long then allegedly performed a ceremony that involved a discussion of Bible verses, the exchange of jewelry, and the lighting of candles to bestow the title of "Spiritual Son" upon Flagg, creating a "God-like connection between himself and the young man."[46] Over time, Long's control over and enticement of Flagg increased. Flagg was placed on the church payroll and Long gave him a Ford Mustang convertible, jewelry, and clothing, and arranged visits with celebrities. In exchange, he was expected to keep regular contact with Long and avoid sexual contact with women.[47]

Not long after Flagg moved into the church-owned house, Long started spending the night, sleeping in the same bed. Soon Flagg and Long were exchanging "sexual massages," which eventually increased to "oral sodomy."[48] Flagg was then asked to join Long on out-of-town trips. The two would share a room, where Flagg alleges: "During overnight trips, Defendant Long shared a bedroom and engaged in intimate sexual contact with Plaintiff Flagg including kissing, massaging, masturbating of Plaintiff Flagg by Defendant Long and oral sexual contact."[49]

Three other young men, Maurice Robinson, Spencer LeGrande, and Jamal Parris filed similar complaints in September 2010. Long vehemently denied the allegations but ultimately settled the claims out of court via third-party mediation.[50] Settling the allegations in this manner allowed Long to continue proclaiming his innocence, avoid public disclosures of information at a trial, and place restrictions on what could be publicly discussed about the accusations. The tactic proved relatively successful. After Long's death in 2017, the Georgia Senate approved a resolution honoring the bishop, calling him "a person of magnanimous strengths with an unimpeachable reputation for integrity, intelligence, confidence, and kindness."[51]

If the claims of his accusers are true—they have promised a tell-all book in the future—then Long fits a long line of public figures who have decried homosexuality, only to be caught engaging in same-sex affairs.[52] This company includes Ted Haggard, former leader of the National Association of Evangelicals, who supported a constitutional amendment to outlaw gay marriage, only to be caught having a long-term affair with a male masseuse; former Republican senator from Idaho and staunch moral conservative Larry Craig, who scored a zero rating from the Human Rights Campaign for the support of gay rights, only to be caught soliciting sex from an undercover agent in an airport bathroom notorious for being a tearoom; and former Florida congressman Mark Foley, who voted for a bill to ban the legal recognition of same-sex marriages and was chair of the Congressional Missing and

Exploited Children's Caucus, but was then caught sending sexually explicit emails and text messages to underage male congressional pages.[53]

This seemingly bizarre pattern of behavior, acting publicly against the very form of deviance in which one is secretly engaged, is an important aspect of Laud Humphreys' landmark study *Tearoom Trade*.[54] Tearooms are public, but sufficiently secluded locations, where men can engage in anonymous sexual relations with one another. Humphreys was able to gather in-depth information on the dynamics of tearoom interactions through participant observation as the "watch queen"—the one who keeps lookout for anyone who might breach the clandestine encounters.[55] Anonymity is a central feature of tearoom subcultures, and the participants are careful to avoid idle conversation or activities that would lead to more interpersonal commitment than absolutely necessary. In lieu of talking, participants develop a wide range of nonverbal cues to indicate their knowledge of, and experience with, tearoom subcultures. These practices serve as an effective method for identifying fellow members of the subculture and allow for engagement with less fear of recognition from the outside world.

Rather than being content with merely describing the patterns and activities of tearoom encounters, Humphreys controversially supplemented this information with covert investigations of the men participating by attempting to determine who they "really were" in everyday life. To gather such data, Humphreys recorded the license plate numbers of participants, had a friend at the Department of Motor Vehicles retrieve information on the owners, and then disguised his appearance before visiting their homes under the guise of conducting a health survey. While this type of methodology is widely considered unorthodox and ethically impermissible in the social sciences, the findings are nevertheless fascinating.[56] *Tearoom Trade* provides a rare glimpse into the social processes involved in secretive deviance, information that could not actually be attained without deceptive tactics.

Humphreys's controversial methodology allowed him to see what individuals engaging in deviant acts were like outside of the context of the activity itself, as well as to compare their "frontstage" and "backstage" behavior.[57] Some of the men he interviewed worked persistently to keep others from noticing their hidden deviance, adopting an interactive technique he labeled the "breastplate of righteousness." Specifically, these men publicly espoused vehemently *anti*-gay attitudes, not knowing that Humphreys had, in fact, personally witnessed them engaging in sexual activity with other men. He argued that the purpose of such rhetoric and attitudes was to deflect suspicion. By presenting a "red herring" public version of their selves, the men were attempting to preemptively derail any suspicions about their private deviance.

Other men that Humphreys interviewed, however, were not prone to such diversionary displays. For individuals who were already leading lives as openly gay men, there was simply no reason to erect such a façade. Although they wanted to

keep their clandestine activities secret and anonymous (like all tearoom participants), they did not have the same motivation to protect their identities from any
and all hints of suspicion. Those without openly gay identities were the most likely
to take drastic interactional measures to protect their secret activities.

Another key factor in predicting diversionary tactics was the extent to which an
individual held a strong conventional identity. Men who held conventional jobs,
had wives and children, and lived in staid suburbs stood to lose a considerable
amount of social face by having their deviance disclosed to a disapproving public.[58] Indeed, they stood to lose much more than "social face." Should their deviance be discovered, they would likely lose their families and possibly careers. In
essence, holding a conventional identity meant that these men had much to lose if
discovered, which led them to exaggerate their conventionality, sometimes by
publicly attacking the very behavior that they were secretly engaging in. Not only
did these men appear conventional, they presented "a protective sheen of super-
propriety," to the extent that "[o]ne of the early impressions formed from research
among these men was the remarkable neatness and propriety of their style of
life. . . . 'Impeccable' was a word frequently used in description: well-tailored suits,
conservative ties, clean work clothes appear to be almost mandatory for tearoom
activity. . . . New awnings, a recent coat of paint, or an exceptionally well-trimmed
yard became trademarks that enabled me to single out the home of a respondent
from others down the block."[59]

Mark Foley, Ted Haggard, Larry Craig, Eddie Long, and the homophobic men
in Humphreys's sample all share certain identity characteristics of what we term
"Hiders." All of these men had very strong conventional identities. They were married; held jobs that commanded respect and social status; had high educational
attainment; earned at least an above-average income; ascribed, often quite publicly, to a religious practice; and espoused very conservative values. Prior to being
"exposed," none of these men had a strong identification with the deviant subculture they nevertheless interacted with. None of them would have proudly told others outside the subculture of their behaviors. When holding low commitment to a
deviant identity and high commitment to a conventional identity, an individual
will likely engage in a hiding strategy to manage their deviance. Successful hiding
ensures that conventional identity is not threatened. Lack of a strong commitment
to a deviant identity frees individuals to ignore, deny, minimize, and sometimes
attack a deviant subculture whenever they are not in direct interaction with it.

Playing the role of the Hider is not necessarily a permanent state of affairs.
Should conventional identity strengthen or weaken, or deviant identity be more
widely revealed, individuals will accordingly change how they manage their deviance. For example, a person who developed strong attachments to members of a
deviant subculture or developed a leadership role over time would likely become
less ashamed of that subculture and possibly advocate for it. On the other hand,

events that weaken conventional identity, such as the loss of a job or divorce can reduce the potential costs of deviance, freeing the individual to openly identify with a deviant subculture. And of course, disclosure, the event Hiders fear most, may drastically change commitment to relative identities. If Hiders are discovered, they will be labeled deviant, unless they manage to resist the imposition of that label. Hiders then have a set of choices: (1) admit an indiscretion and fully reject the deviant identity, (2) continue to deny deviant actions and identity, or (3) avow the deviant identity. Ted Haggard chose to admit to some of his actions and seek counseling to "cure" himself. Larry Craig denied all allegations, even though his actions were consistent with those of someone who had the requisite interactional knowledge of how tearooms work. Likewise, Eddie Long denied all wrongdoing and remained pastor of NBMBC until his death. Since resigning from Congress, Mark Foley has embraced an openly gay, but still politically conservative, identity.

The pressure Hiders feel to divert attention from their behavior depends on how severely the wider culture views the perceived immorality. If the behaviors in question are considered a serious moral transgression (e.g., sinful, perverted, dangerous), there will be great pressure on Hiders to divert attention from themselves. If the deviance in question is minor (quirky, strange, eccentric) or at least morally debatable in public discourse, Hiders should not feel the need or pressure to entirely hide their behavior, even if conventional identity still requires "passing" as normal when outside of subcultural situations.[60]

Returning to Fox's observations of the punk scene, some members only had a "quasi-commitment" to the subculture, such as "Preppie" punks. These members generally fit a certain profile:

> Preppie punks did not lead the lifestyle of the core members. The preppie punks tended to be from middle-class families, whereas the core punks were generally from lower- or working-class backgrounds. Preppie punks often lived with their parents; they tended to be younger, and were often in school or in respectable, system-sanctioned jobs. This quasi-commitment means that preppies had to be able to turn the punk image on and off at will. . . . For example, a preppie punk hairstyle, although short, was styled in such a versatile way that it could be manipulated to look punk sometimes and conventional at other times.[61]

DRIFTERS

I had about as much chance of controlling my desires to drift with the current of the underworld as the canoe had of braving the storm.[62]

A popular image of criminals or deviants is that of a specialist or professional. Television shows and movies frequently portray bank robbers as highly trained specialists who, through years of practice or uncommon brilliance, have developed the ability to bypass sophisticated security systems, fool suspicious guards and tellers into thinking they are maintenance workers, and drill into seemingly impenetrable vaults with futuristic equipment. The film *Entrapment* is an example of this genre. In it, Sean Connery's character trains his apprentice (Catherine Zeta Jones) to dance around laser sensors and hack into sophisticated computer systems. Serial killers have perhaps received the greatest image upgrade from popular media. Research on serial killers has found that they often are of middling IQs and sloppy in their methods. They also have rather varied criminal records, including both violent and nonviolent offenses. However, innumerable movies, television shows, and novels depict FBI "mind hunters" matching wits with a hyper-intelligent, savvy monster who has meticulously perfected a killing routine over many years.[63]

As is often the case in matters of crime, quality research runs counter to popular stereotypes. Indeed, one might sum up criminological research with the simple statement: "Criminals tend to diversify."[64] A criminal act often is the result of boredom or a coincidence in time and place of someone willing to engage in a criminal act and the presence of an emergent opportunity—such as an unlocked door, an unmonitored purse, or a suitable victim walking alone at night.[65] This criminal type may be seen in "opportunist" robbers, who do not plan their activities, are relatively inexperienced, and "have no long-term commitment to robbery or other crimes as a way of life."[66] Although such activity may evolve into more commitment to deviant identity in the long run, at the time of their opportunist crimes these individuals exhibit little commitment to a subculture of professional thieves. Consequently, the typical criminal often holds a mixed record of different types of offenses and responds to new opportunities as they arise; rarely achieving the status of a "super criminal" who specializes in only one form of activity.

While research on specialization in non-criminal deviant careers is exceptionally limited, we expect many deviants to act in the same manner—to "drift" back and forth between deviance and normalcy and between various acts of deviance, without explicitly attaching to any particular one. This is the image portrayed by "Stanley," whose quote began this section. He is the central figure of *The Jack-Roller*, a canonical study of juvenile delinquency that relied on Stanley's first-person narrative accounts of his exploits in deviance and crime. Indeed, Stanley may be the most studied and influential individual case study in criminality.[67] While later scholars have disputed the extent to which *The Jack-Roller* is truly a representative account of both delinquency and Stanley's character, as well as the unexamined assumptions embedded in author Clifford Shaw's framing of Stanley's story, the study's influence on criminology is unquestionable.[68]

However, there is an addendum to *The Jack-Roller* that has import for criminological theory. The original study ends by presenting Stanley as reformed by virtue of external changes to his surrounding environment and stakes in conformity. But a follow-up study interviewed Stanley nearly fifty years later, when he was in his seventies, about what had happened since his experiences as the young mugger at the center of *The Jack-Roller*, and it told a much different story. Rather than a reformed life of conventionality, Stanley returned to a life a crime soon after the original book was published and the conclusion of his rehabilitation program. He was arrested and imprisoned after a failed armed robbery attempt and was institutionalized in the violent offender wing of a psychiatric hospital. There he received electroshock treatments—twice. He broke out of the mental hospital and fled on foot, escaping to nearby cities—twice. He gambled and drank extensively throughout his life and had a sordid history of violent episodes and spousal abuse. He worked short stints as a salesman, an industrial laborer, and a cab driver, but he never sustained a career. He married, divorced, remarried, separated, then remarried his second wife again.[69] As his second biographer, social psychologist Jon Snodgrass summarized, "Stanley's basic personality seems to have remained essentially the same, regardless of the social setting in which he was placed," and further that his "history fits the criteria of 'Antisocial Personality Disorder' so closely that his case might serve as a model for the category."[70] While we will leave the clinical diagnosis of Stanley to qualified psychiatrists, his story clearly fits closely with our ideal type of the Drifter.

The Drifter has long been a theoretical archetype in theories of both deviance and psychopathology.[71] Attempting to turn the metaphor into quantitative data, a recent study found that approximately 3.5 percent of non-institutionalized American adults could be classified as Drifters, using the rather literal criteria of saying yes to the question: "In your entire life, did you ever travel around from place to place for a month or more without making any plans ahead of time or not knowing how long you would be gone or where you were going to work?"[72] Consistent with how we have outlined stakes in conventional identity, the study found Drifters were of lower socioeconomic backgrounds, had lower rates of marriage and had higher rates of divorce.

Criminologist Jeff Ferrell conceptualizes "drift" as encompassing four dialectical dimensions: presence/dislocation, dependence/autonomy, together/apart and hope/despair.[73] He argues that modern political economic systems necessarily create a forgotten underclass of individuals forced to live on the margins of society: the homeless, street kids, gutter punks, and others disintegrated from conventional political and economic systems. People in such roles are perpetually displaced, and they must adapt accordingly to survive. Ferrell provides an in-depth look at the identity and mind-set of Drifters, noting their distinctive characteristics:

> "[T]he drifter can in turn be thought of as a cultural stranger. . . . [D]rifting tends to produce at least one sort of transformation: that which results from the sequenced

experience of exclusion and alienation. . . . As this drifting continues across time and space the exclusions accumulate, and in doing so reinforce the drifter's identity as always outside the frame—an outsider many times over."[74]

Thus, we can think of Drifters as *perpetually* outside and socially disintegrated, even in relation to deviant subcultures. It is worth noting that in some cases a particular form of drifting such as train-hopping can generate subcultural identity, as people may band together as Outsiders, although any related community will be highly unstable. For our study, we define Drifters as those holding low stakes in both conventional and deviant identities. As such, the ideal Drifter does not have strong attachments to conventional people, who would look upon deviance with disfavor. If such attachments previously existed, they have been severed by deaths, breakups, estrangement, disappointments, or degradation ceremonies. Drifters are necessarily separated by social and often also physical distance from others—both deviant and normative. Simply put, Drifters are not particularly concerned with what people—of any socially defined category—think of their behavior.

To the extent that Drifters work, they have jobs, not careers. Work is merely a means to achieve the money necessary for survival. Losing a job will be stressful and require finding a new one, but that loss will not result in the reorientation of a career or a long-sought opportunity for advancement. Compared to others, Drifters' beliefs will be unconventional. They do not believe that "society" should tell others what to do and may think that societal rules do not apply to them. Given their low commitment to conventional identity, Drifters' behaviors are not motivated or constrained by the need to play the role of a "normal" person. They are comparatively free to deviate, having less concern for the potential costs, especially informal sanctions.

However, unlike Outsiders and Insiders, Drifters are not well integrated into particular deviant subcultures either. This ideal type is closer to the classical sense of normless anomie found in functionalist theories of deviance. In Humphreys's study of tearooms, he delineates "closet queen" participants, who were committed to neither conventionality nor the subculture. These participants in the sexual encounters of the tearoom were characterized by "social isolation," finding "little solace in association with others who share their deviant interest," effectively making their actions a "desperate, lone-wolf sort of activity."[75] These individuals engaged in tearoom activity for a solitary, if ultimately personally unsatisfying, thrill. Likewise, Drifters may engage in same-gender sexual relations during confinement in homosocial settings, such as prison or the military, while meticulously avoiding the label of "homosexual" through an enactment of traditional tropes of masculinity and aggression coupled with resorting to same-gender sexual relations merely as a recourse in circumstances of heterosexual deprivation.[76]

Drifters also may engage in solitary acts of deviance such as self-injuring, although the internet has facilitated more mediated subcultural engagement among such individuals.[77] Still, self-harm tends to be practiced more as solitary attempts to symbolically and physically address loneliness and pain, although many self-injurers maintain enough commitment to conventional identity to be classified as Hiders rather than Drifters.

In general, we expect Drifters to engage in deviant activities by a combination of impulse and opportunity.[78] The diversity of deviant activities in which Drifters engage is a function of exposure and situational determinants more than a high level of commitment to subcultural belief systems. While such individuals may not be completely disconnected from deviant subcultures, if they do participate it will be on the periphery, due to their low level of investment in the group. That is not to say that we expect the other types of deviants (Hiders, Insiders, and Outsiders) to be complete specialists in a particular form of deviant behavior. All deviants have the potential to engage in multiple forms of deviant behavior concurrently. However, the behaviors and risks that Insiders, Outsiders, and Hiders are willing to endure in order to participate in their preferred form of deviance suggest a certain level of commitment; if not to the fate of the subculture, at least to the act itself. Drifters, on the other hand, will be characterized by the *lack* of commitment to a particular deviant *or* conventional identity.

How other members of a deviant subculture react to such uncommitted participants varies. For some, Drifters will be viewed as annoying "free riders" who take from the subculture, but never give in return. The opportunistic, party-based pot smoker may annoy others by joining in on those occasions when he is in the mood without engaging in the riskier work of securing marijuana. But for some subcultures, Drifters will be a necessary evil. In Fox's research among the punk subculture, she found that a large proportion of the crowd at punk concerts consisted of those who were simply sampling the subculture or who thought that it would be fun to see a punk show. Such newcomers made "no pretense of commitments to the scene at all."[79] They tended to sample the punk world and drift away at the first sign of risk or difficulty. Even if they might view such spectators with derision, hardcore punks *need* these spectators to survive. The bigger the crowd that attends a punk show, the more money serious punks gain to support their cause. If only the most serious punks were willing to attend shows, the subculture would die out from a lack of resources. Further, many committed members of a subculture likely begin as Drifters, happening upon a scene and then realizing that they like it enough to increase commitment.

If Drifters can sometimes be counted on to provide occasional indirect support to a subculture, their low level of deviant identity precludes them from helping the subculture mobilize in other meaningful ways. Drifters are quite simply unconcerned with what ultimately happens to a deviant subculture because they do not feel deeply connected to it and also have little concern for how non-deviants feel about the subculture.

INSIDERS

It is important to recognize that while differences in theology exist between the churches in America, we share a common creed of moral convictions.[80]

Mitt Romney, a businessman and governor of Massachusetts from 2003 to 2007, attempted to win the Republican nomination for president in 2008. During the campaign, Romney secured 280 delegates but ultimately lost the nomination to Arizona Senator John McCain. McCain lost to Barack Obama in the 2008 presidential election and Romney tried again for the GOP nomination in 2012. This time he was successful and ran against Obama's bid for reelection. Ultimately Obama defeated Romney, securing 332 electoral votes to Romney's 206.

Of course, presidential elections are complicated events with a variety of factors influencing vote distributions. But a basic key to victory is shoring up one's "base," those people who typically vote Democrat or Republican. Romney faced a clear challenge in this regard as a member of the Church of Jesus Christ of Latter-day Saints (or Mormonism); an issue that conservative columnist Hugh Hewitt labeled the "Mormon problem."[81] Evangelical Protestants, who constitute an important part of the Republican voting base, are suspicious of Mormonism, as revealed by the findings of the 2012 American National Election Study (ANES).

The ANES asked respondents how they felt about several groups using a "feeling thermometer." Respondents could provide a score anywhere from 0 (quite cold or unfavorable feelings) to 100 (very warm or favorable feelings). When asked about Mormons, the average score among Evangelical respondents was about 50, or "no feeling at all," with over one-fourth (27 percent) scoring below 50. Further, nearly 60 percent of Evangelical Protestants said that Mormonism is "not Christian," and more than one-third said that their beliefs had "nothing at all" in common with Mormonism.[82] Perhaps most damning, however, is that about 14 percent of Evangelical Protestants reported that Mitt Romney's religion was a factor that led them to vote for Barack Obama.[83]

The LDS church does not reciprocate this level of antagonism. As stated on their website: "Members of The Church of Jesus Christ of Latter-day Saints unequivocally affirm themselves to be Christians. They worship God the Eternal Father in the name of Jesus Christ."[84] Indeed, LDS teachings draw upon the Old and New Testaments of the Christian Bible, so they obviously share a significant amount of religious culture with mainstream Christianity. The Church itself has worked hard to highlight its connections to Christianity, even to the point of telling the public: "We ask that the term 'Mormons' not be used." Instead: "When a shortened reference is needed, the terms 'the Church' or the 'Church of Jesus Christ' are encouraged. The 'restored Church of Jesus Christ' is also accurate and encouraged."[85]

Although the Church regularly highlights its connections to Christianity, the conflict for other Christian groups does not lie with LDS members' use of the

Bible, but their addition of novel teachings beyond it. The Church's prophet and founder, Joseph Smith, claimed to have been led by the angel Moroni to a set of golden plates buried on a hill near Manchester, New York, which he translated with the help of "seer stones." The *Book of Mormon* was the result.[86] An in-depth overview of Mormon beliefs is beyond the scope of this volume, but among the most controversial teachings, as far as other Christians are concerned, are the claims that a resurrected Jesus visited the Americas and the belief that the Father, the Son, and the Holy Spirit are three separate entities rather than one.[87] For some Christians, the shared belief in the divinity of Jesus is sufficient to qualify Latter-day Saints as part of the Christian family. For others, further revelations about Jesus are heresy and Mormon beliefs about the Trinity are seen as a form of polytheism.[88]

The hostility and sometimes ridicule certain segments of Americans direct at Latter-day Saints placed Mitt Romney in a tenuous position.[89] How could he become president when a significant number of the most ardent base of voters for the Republican Party found his religion heretical? Clearly the deviance management strategies of Drifter, Hider, or Outsider would not work for Mitt Romney. He could have tried to downplay or hide his faith. But it was evident that Romney was very devout. He spent two and a half years as a missionary for the Church in France and graduated from Brigham Young University. All five of his sons also attended BYU and went on their missions. Romney was a bishop in his ward and president of the Boston stake from 1986 to 1994, in which he administered ten wards with approximately three thousand members.[90] Romney's record as a life-long, unwavering member of the Church clearly differs from what we would expect of a Drifter. His publicly available record as an active Mormon and his willingness to take on leadership roles in his religion also make being a Hider impossible. Besides, there is no indication that Romney actually wanted to distance himself from his faith in any way. In his "Faith in America" speech, which Romney delivered at the George H. W. Bush Presidential Library in 2007, he directly addressed those who wished he would downplay his ties to the Church: "They would prefer it if I would simply distance myself from my religion, say that it is more a tradition than my personal conviction, or disavow one or another of its precepts. That I will not do. I believe in my Mormon faith and I endeavor to live by it. My faith is the faith of my fathers—I will be true to them and to my beliefs."[91]

Romney could have played the role of the Outsider, emphasizing the superiority of the Mormon faith without concern for how nonbelievers would react, but such a tactic would have worked against his political interests. As a successful business-man and candidate for the nation's highest office, Romney needed the American public to see him as someone whose religion did not disqualify him from the pres-idency. To reject Mormonism would go against his personal, deeply felt religious identity and potentially alienate his Mormon supporters. Conversely, to emphasize Mormonism too strongly might alienate the rest of the general public.

Romney obviously qualifies as an Insider. When individuals hold a strong commitment to a culturally deviant identity and simultaneously hold a strong commitment to maintaining a conventional lifestyle, they must find a way to balance the two. We discuss the specific strategies used by Insiders in greater depth in the following chapter. Stated simply, Insiders have much to lose by being perceived as weird, dangerous, or immoral. Therefore, they must find a way to convince conventional people that their deviance is not as strange as people might assume.

Political scientists David Campbell, John Green, and Quin Monson reached a similar conclusion about Mitt Romney's approach to his candidacy. They argue that the approach Mormon candidates (or any religious minority for that matter) might take toward discussing their faith in the political arena depends upon two factors. First, Mormon candidates could be categorized as either *active* or *inactive* with regard to their personal religiosity. Second, the electoral context (or political atmosphere) could be categorized as either *congenial* or *noncongenial* to Mormonism. In most cases, religiously inactive candidates will avoid talking about religion in political contexts that are open to their religion, lest they turn off believers, but they will attempt to stay away from religious issues entirely in contexts that disdain religion (or their religion in particular). Deeply religious Mormon candidates react differently. In situations or contexts that are favorable to their religion, they will deeply affirm their unique faith. When facing a hostile or uncertain public, however, they will utilize a strategy of *alliance*. In other words, the candidate will "downplay the distinctiveness of the sacred tabernacle and play up its nondistinctive features."[92]

Mitt Romney attempted to normalize his faith by emphasizing the similarities between Mormonism and conventional Christianity, by equating his struggles with those of others seeking religious tolerance and by downplaying (and in fact ridiculing in some cases) Mormonism's more distinctive historical features.[93] The "Faith in America" speech strongly emphasized these first two themes. As scholar of presidential rhetoric Martin Medhurst noted: "By emphasizing religious liberty, free exercise of various religious faiths and the grand tradition of American civil religion, Romney clearly invited the audience to think of his Mormon faith as simply one among many American faiths."[94] Early in his speech, Romney compared Mormon beliefs to the central tenets of Christianity, while calling upon Americans to forgive the differences: "There is one fundamental question about which I often am asked. What do I believe about Jesus Christ? I believe that Jesus Christ is the Son of God and the Savior of mankind. My church's beliefs about Christ may not all be the same as those of other faiths. Each religion has its own unique doctrines and history. These are not bases for criticism but rather a test of our tolerance. Religious tolerance would be a shallow principle indeed if it were reserved only for faiths with which we agree."[95] In the same speech, Romney equated his struggle to that of John F. Kennedy, saying that, "Almost 50 years ago another candidate from Massachusetts explained that he was an American running for president, not a Catholic running for president. Like him, I am an American running for president. I do not define my candidacy by my religion. A person should not be elected because of his faith nor should he be rejected because of his faith."[96]

As the speech drew to a close, Romney placed the "Mormon problem" in the context of a founding principle of the United States, the struggle for religious liberty:

> Today's generations of Americans have always known religious liberty. Perhaps we forget the long and arduous path our nation's forbearers took to achieve it. They came here from England to seek freedom of religion. But upon finding it for themselves, they at first denied it to others. Because of their diverse beliefs, Ann Hutchinson was exiled from Massachusetts Bay, a banished Roger Williams founded Rhode Island, and two centuries later, Brigham Young set out for the West. Americans were unable to accommodate their commitment to their own faith with an appreciation for the convictions of others to different faiths. In this, they were very much like those of the European nations they had left.[97]

At the same time he tried to draw connections between Mormon history and core American values, Romney also faced the challenge of distancing himself from the most controversial aspects of Mormon history, such as polygamy. The LDS church has not endorsed polygamy since 1890, but several breakaway groups still practice "the principle." In recent years, polygamy has received increasing attention through television shows such as the fictional *Big Love*, reality shows such as *Sister Wives* and *Escaping Polygamy*, and criminal cases against powerful polygamists, including Fundamentalist Latter-day Saints leader Warren Jeffs.[98] Given the costs of appearing deviant, Insiders will need to separate themselves from the more controversially perceived aspects of their subculture.

Romney distanced himself from polygamy in two main ways. First, he always made sure to inform those who questioned him about polygamy that the practice is no longer part of mainstream Mormonism. He did so in a 2006 interview for the MSNBC show *Hardball*, in which host Chris Matthews asked him about the new (at the time) TV show *Big Love*. Romney also turned the uncomfortable question into an opportunity to show affinity with conservative Christians regarding opposition to same-sex marriage:

Matthews: You know, what I'm getting at don't you? The issue of multiple wives and polygamy. That's obviously a question that comes because this new TV show about a Mormon family and how many wives, three of them I think in the movie.

Romney: Actually it's not a Mormon family. My church has long ago given up
that practice in the 1800s, but putting that aside for a moment. It's real
clear that Americans, myself included, believe that marriage is a
relationship between a man and a woman and not more than that and
also not same-sex couples.[99]

This effectively allowed Romney to simultaneously distance himself from negatively perceived aspects of his faith and shore up his conservative, religious bona
fides.

Romney further distanced himself from polygamy by joking about and sometimes ridiculing the practice. At a 2005 St. Patrick's Day breakfast in Boston,
he joked, "I believe marriage should be between a man and a woman . . . and
a woman . . . and a woman," a line he repeated a year later on Don Imus's 2006
St. Patrick's Day show.[100] Romney's balancing act of trying to remain true to his
subculture, perceived by many of his potential voters as deviant, while simultaneously promoting its affinity to the mainstream and whitewashing its most controversial aspects, is the charge of the Insider. Consequently, as we will discuss in the
next chapter, Insider messaging is the most likely to promote the normalization
of a deviant group. Such messaging is difficult to perform successfully because of
the need to navigate between a subculture and mainstream culture without alienating either.

THE COMPOSITION OF DEVIANT SUBCULTURES

It is important to note that we do not expect every subculture to contain each
typologized deviance management strategy in equal parts and that the relative distributions will be influenced by the punishment regimes of specific contexts. Further, our typology represents ideal types, and specific individuals will be unlikely
to embody our idealized presentation of deviant and conventional identities. The
classifications we have developed can be best understood as existing along continuums of conventional and deviant identity, and individuals may straddle seemingly definitive lines we have imposed on complex realities. However, there is no
question that identities matter. From an interactionist perspective, the idea that
identity is something concrete and unwavering is a highly suspect claim. What is
not suspect is that individuals *perceive themselves as having fixed identities*, which
substantially shapes perceived situational definitions and therefore the appropriate
lines of action from which individuals select. In this way the proposed typology of
deviance management is useful for understanding reactions to deviant behavior
from the perspective of the "accused." The many ways these factions interact to
produce subcultural narratives and the social conditions under which particular
strategies are more or less likely is the focus of the next chapter.

3

Fighting for Normal?

Those labeled deviant vary in their collective level of coordination, ranging from isolates to full-fledged, formal organizations.[1] But the mere presence of a highly organized deviant subculture is no guarantee that individuals will choose to identify with it. A person may fear members of the subculture, view other deviants as a temporary means to an end, or fear that extended interaction will result in discovery. Some engaging in acts deemed deviant choose to operate solely as individuals and "do not associate with other deviants for purposes of sociability. . . . Rather, they must supply themselves with whatever knowledge, skill, equipment and ideology their deviance requires."[2] The possibilities of loner deviance are greater than ever before with advances in, and increasing accessibility of, mediated communication, especially the internet. Information that used to be obtained in direct interaction with others or from newsletters can now be acquired via websites, blogs, and anonymous chat rooms. Yet, even if individuals do not have a choice and must interact face-to-face with a subculture, they still have a choice about how to present their behavior.

So how and why do Drifters, Hiders, Outsiders, and Insiders shape, explain, and justify their deviant behavior in different ways? How do conflicts over deviance management strategies influence the public face subcultures attempt to present? Building on our conception of deviance management as a response to the relative salience of conventional and deviant social identities, this chapter outlines the different emotional and subsequent narrative responses of individuals to their own deviance. In turn, we consider how these different strategies and narratives facilitate or hinder normalization efforts, as well as create subcultural conflicts.

Before we build onto our basic assumptions about deviance management, consider an illustrative example of the different ways individuals may engage with deviant subcultures. As we detail further in the next chapter, we have conducted extensive research on subcultures devoted to Bigfoot in the United States.[3] To believers, Bigfoot is an undiscovered, upright-walking, ape-like, hair-covered creature. Thousands of Americans claim to have seen a Bigfoot and approximately 14 percent believe that such a creature exists.[4] The last two decades have witnessed a dramatic increase in the number of available Bigfoot-related television shows, movies, books, and websites, making it possible to consume a vast array of Bigfoot information anonymously.[5]

Some Bigfoot enthusiasts are satisfied, or prefer, to remain isolated from others, but there are many benefits to coordination and subcultural engagement. Meeting with people of shared interests can provide emotional support, facilitate the development of resources that are beyond the abilities of an individual to produce, and allow the sharing of information that is not available to the general public. Since Bigfoot witnesses face skepticism and often outright ridicule, subcultures can provide a protective social barrier from those outside the group and a sense of solidarity for those inside. Sociologist Howard Becker wrote about this feature of subcultures in his classic study of deviants, "Members of organized deviant groups of course have one thing in common: their deviance. It gives them a sense of common fate, of being in the same boat. From a sense of common fate, from having to face the same problems, grows a deviant subculture: a set of perspectives and understandings about what the world is like and how to deal with it, and a set of routine activities based on those perspectives. Membership in such a group solidifies a deviant identity."[6]

Given such obvious benefits of coordination, we naively expected to encounter a strong "we-feeling" once we finally gained entrée into the Bigfoot subculture. Bigfoot enthusiasts should band together, strong in their conviction about the existence of a creature that skeptics liken to a unicorn or a fairy. And we did find some sense of camaraderie. The vast majority believe that Bigfoot exists and take comfort in the fact that others do as well. But beyond that, disagreements are heated and commonplace. People argue about Bigfoot's appearance (apelike or more human-like), its disposition (shy or hostile, peaceful or predatory), the morality and necessity of killing a specimen in order to prove its existence, what constitutes valid evidence, and whether Bigfoot is a terrestrial creature or a visitor from outer space or even another dimension. These arguments are readily apparent during occasions when members of different camps of believers find themselves at the same event. When we attended meetings or conferences populated by a specific faction within the subculture, they often defined themselves in opposition to those factions that were not present.

Our experiences in the Bigfoot subculture highlight one consequence of individuals labeled deviant coming together. Subcultures allow members to share their passion for a particular subject, but those same passions often lead to vehement disagreements. Such infighting is well documented in the research literature on social movements.[7] In contrast, with their frequent focus upon deviant subcultures in relation to conventional culture, deviance researchers often overlook internal debates and their importance in the development and operation of subcultures, which are often less organized and goal-oriented than full-fledged social movements.[8] Organized deviant groups may develop philosophies and rationalizations regarding their behaviors, but there is no guarantee that all similarly labeled individuals will *agree* regarding those rationales.[9]

ON THE PRESENTATION OF DEVIANCE

Erving Goffman noted that stigma was necessarily social, representing a "spoiled" conventional identity and consequently "a language of relationships, not attributes is really needed."[10] In other words, the consequences of stigma, or being potentially stigmatized, are social. Those labeled deviant may be expected to "cover" and downplay their stigma in some circumstances, or to make "normal people" feel more comfortable about their differences.[11] While some will submit to the incessant indignities of stigmatization or find ways to overcome them through reform, others will form resistance identities and fight back. For still others, such as Hiders—who are discreditable, rather than already discredited, in Goffman's language of relationships—hidden deviance will "cast a shadow" into relations with conventional others, as well as onto interactions with people who have already been labeled deviant.[12] A key source of friction within deviant subcultures will be variance in the relative saliences of conforming and deviant identities among members and the different deviance management strategies that follow from different combinations of social identities.

Sociologist Krista McQueeney's research on Christian lesbians highlights some of these different strategies in practice. In her ethnographic study of gay-affirming churches in the American South, McQueeney found that members varied in the extent to which they placed primacy upon the identity of Christian versus the identity of gay or lesbian. Some members of "Faith Church," which was comprised primarily of sexual and racial minorities, placed primacy on their identities as Christians over their identities as lesbians.[13] Using a *minimizing* strategy, they defined sexuality as separate from the Christian faith. Indeed, the pastor of Faith Church "deemed sexuality irrelevant, urging members to emphasize their faith in Jesus over all other identities."[14]

Most of the gay and lesbian church members McQueeney interviewed also utilized a *normalizing* strategy at times. Normalizers attempted to present themselves as "[j]ust your average Christian," despite their sexuality.[15] Normalizers highlighted aspects of their personal lives that suggested an affinity with normative, heterosexual identities and relationships. For example, members emphasized the monogamous nature of their same-sex relationships and actively distanced themselves from the perceived promiscuity of others in the wider LGBTQ community. At the time of the study, same-sex marriage was not legal, so the churches offered holy union ceremonies to reinforce the idea of gay and lesbian relationships being akin to heterosexual marriage.[16]

Other members of gay-affirming churches in McQueeney's study actively resisted calls to minimize gay/lesbian identity or smooth out the identity's more controversial edges. This *moralizing* strategy placed primacy upon sexuality, arguing that holding a gay or lesbian identity blessed individuals with a "special calling as Christians."[17] For moralizers, the marginalization and stigmatization they faced as sexual minorities gifted them with an understanding of oppression and a mission to spread God's word of love and acceptance. Instead of being Christians for whom sexuality was an afterthought, moralizers were "lesbian Christians."[18]

Moralizing messages caused controversy among members who preferred the focus to be placed upon their identity as Christians first. McQueeney notes an incident where an openly gay guest minister argued from the pulpit that homosexuals have been specially "chosen" by God. After the sermon, some members characterized it as "too gay," and hoped that the reverend would "tone it down a few notches" in future sermons, lest the focus upon "gay, gay, gay" detract from worshipping God.[19]

McQueeney's study highlights some of the conundrums that face any member of a stigmatized subculture. Challenged with balancing a Christian identity with the well-known antipathy among many Christians for their "deviant" sexual identity, gay and lesbian Christians must choose how to balance the two. Some will focus more strongly on their Christian identity and minimize. Others will focus upon their sexual identity and moralize. Finally, some will feel equally attached to both identities and express identity through normalization. The paths and outcomes of this process are directly tied to the relative salience of each identity.

Certainly, use of different deviance management strategies will often be situationally motivated. Someone labeled deviant who is interacting only with others so labeled will be more likely to employ a strategy that highlights deviant identity. When interacting with those outside the subculture or with known negative attitudes about the deviance in question, that person will be more likely to employ a strategy that attempts to minimize or to present a sanitized version of deviance. However, per identity theory, the relative salience of these dual identities should produce more stable, preferred methods of messaging about one's deviance to others.

Table 1 presents the different emotional responses that we predict deviants will have based upon the relative salience of their conventional and deviant identities. These emotional responses will, in turn, impact how different types of deviants

TABLE 1 Emotional Responses and Desire for Normalization among Deviance Management Types

	Outsiders	Hiders	Drifters	Insiders
Salience of Conventional Identity	Low	High	Low	High
Salience of Deviant Identity	High	Low	Low	High
Emotional Response to Deviant Identity	Pride	Shame	Apathy	Appeasement
Desire for Normalization	Low: seek establishment of different order	Low (outwardly); internally varying	Low; indifference	High; seek alteration of existing system
Engagement with Conventional Society	Low	High	Low	High
Example: Gay Subcultures	Openly gay man submerged in LGBTQ subculture and unconcerned about reactions of those outside his subcultural community.	Closeted gay or bisexual man married to a woman, hiding same-sex relationships.	A gay or bisexual man who has little attachment to LGBTQ subcultures, drifting in and out of contact over time.	Openly gay man who carefully manages his sexual identity and argues that sexual minorities are contributing, worthy members of society.
Example: Cannabis Subcultures	Individual submerged in drug subculture. Holds little influence or power in mainstream society.	Well-respected businessperson, politician or community leader that hides cannabis use from conventional friends and family.	Cannabis user who also uses other drugs and engages in a range of deviant behaviors. Holds little influence or power in mainstream society.	Well-respected businessperson, politician or community leader that does not hide cannabis use and argues that users are contributing, worthy members of society.

will attempt to message about their deviance to others. We explore each type in greater detail below.

Outsiders: Pride

While no individual will perfectly match an ideal type, Outsiders are the easiest to readily identify. They identify themselves. Given the high salience of deviant identity and low salience of conventional identity, Outsiders typically view their deviance with pride and perhaps even righteousness. Outsiders may co-opt and internalize deviant labels as a master status, whether the label is self-applied or externally imposed. If forced to explain their behavior, Outsiders often use an "appeal to higher loyalties," noting how the concerns of the subculture outweigh the concerns of society. Likewise, Outsiders are likely to "condemn the condemners" and argue that members of conventional society have no right to judge members of the subculture. Outsiders are seen as the truly moral group.[20]

In its purest form, Outsiders will be unapologetically deviant and feel no need to justify their behavior. Deviant subcultures are superior to the wider culture for Outsiders. "They" understand something "we" do not, perceiving themselves as braver than those who feel the need to conform. As a consequence, Outsiders view "normals" with disdain and purposefully distance themselves from them. This distance may be visually expressed by an unconventional appearance but will also be accompanied by linguistic cues. Outsiders comfortably inhabit and casually employ subcultural language (argot). When it comes to labeling themselves, Outsiders will not be concerned with mainstream palatability. Indeed, as an act of defiance and as a further sign of contempt for those outside the subculture, Outsiders may reappropriate negative labels placed upon them, such as "queer," "thug" or "freak," as marks of pride.[21] Outsiders may judge other non-Outsider members of their subculture as harshly as conventional society. People who interact with the subculture but refuse to fully participate will be viewed as weak, uncommitted poseurs.

Hiders: Shame

Even if they are engaging in the same form of deviant behavior, Hiders and Outsiders have inverted deviance management techniques. Hiders are concerned that they will be labeled as deviant and endeavor to avoid that possibility. In ideal-typical form, Outsiders strive to *ensure* that people know that they are members of a deviant subculture and may fear that others fail to recognize that commitment. Hiders are often ashamed or at least afraid of the discovery of their deviance.[22] A true Hider will avoid developing strong attachments to people in deviant subcultures, as anonymity protects against discovery. In contrast, Outsiders' strongest attachments will be within deviant subcultures. Thus, despite sometimes needing one another for the sake of deviance—the furtive marijuana smoker needs someone from whom to buy pot just as the drug dealer needs customers—Outsiders will typically loathe Hiders.

Hiding, and therefore passing, requires "code switching" depending on situational cues, such as where an interaction takes place and the relationships between the individual and the other interactants.[23] Proficiency at code switching provides an individual with alternative scripts, schema, and language depending on situational constraints. Thus, youth in impoverished, countercultural areas who desire conventional success by doing well in school may hide their accomplishments from peers and act "street" when situationally called for.[24] Similarly, users of illegal drugs or those with addictions to legal vices such as alcohol, gambling, and pornography may hide their habits from other people, especially those holding more conventional views.[25] In order for the Hider to maintain a passing identity in certain social circles, effective code switching is essential.

Drifters: Apathy

As discussed in chapter 2, Drifters are the proverbial "free riders" of a deviant subculture. Having interactions within subcultures that tend to be opportunistic, situational, and often fleeting, we would not expect Drifters to have a strong, core message about specific forms of deviance. Given their lack of a salient conventional or deviant identity, we also can expect their messaging to be more situationally variable. When in the company of Outsiders, Drifters may attempt to fit in and express a message of pride. When in later interactions with conformists, they may deny their connections with deviants, attempt to normalize the group, *or* express pride, depending upon the perceived desires of the conformists with whom they communicate and any related social benefits or punishments that may follow. Although difficult due to their lack of conventional or subcultural social capital, over time Drifters may, of course, become more committed to a conforming or deviant identity and find themselves moving into the role of an Outsider or Hider. Likewise, loss of either conventional or subcultural commitment can turn today's Outsider, Insider, or Hider into tomorrow's Drifter.

Insiders: Appeasement and (Attitude) Conversion

Insiders are individuals who, more than Hiders and Outsiders, feel the cross-pressure of competing identities. Insiders have lines of commitment in (culturally) contradictory identities. Depending on the salience of these identities, an individual may be pushed toward finding a resolution to these cross-pressures. Someone with a strong conventional identity who also has commitment to lines of action deemed deviant is forced to reconcile this inconsistency through being a Hider or by adopting the stance of the Insider.

Thus, much like Hiders, Insiders face an acute form of cognitive dissonance.[26] They are externally defined as deviant for performing certain roles, but the majority of the roles they embody are perceived by themselves and others—if separated from their perceived deviance—as normative. However, the stickiness of deviant labels threatens to invade other social spheres that would otherwise be deemed normative. Faced with this set of circumstances, Insiders must find a course of action that actively combats not only the deviant label being applied, but the legitimacy of the label more generally. Insiders conceive of their own actions as normative in order to maintain cognitive consonance. The challenge lies in convincing enough initially non-sympathetic, powerful and already normative others that this is in fact the way the moral universe should be reordered. To do so requires a message of appeasement and attitude conversion, wherein Insiders attempt to convince conventional others that their deviance is not as immoral or distasteful as it has been portrayed, while facing the equally challenging task of convincing others within a deviant subculture to downplay the Outsider elements most likely to challenge images of conventional order. Consequently, Insiders play key roles in successfully mobilizing *normalization movements.*

ON NORMALIZATION

By normalization movements, we mean the processes through which an entire category of people or behavior moves from being considered culturally deviant by a majority of a population to, at the least, tolerable by a majority of the population.[27] In successful cases of normalization, a formerly deviant group can come to be considered valued members of society.[28] The seismic shift in attitudes toward same-sex relationships discussed in chapter 5 would constitute an example of this form of normalization. This is not to say that gay men and lesbians do not still experience prejudice and discrimination—as they certainly do—but rather to indicate that some social change toward acceptability has occurred.

Although a deviant group may aspire toward normalization, agents of conventional culture necessarily hold the power. Mainstream culture may "not be ready" to accept a particular act, belief, or identity as normal. Perhaps the practice or persuasion in question is still viewed as decadent, immoral, or even dangerous. Or perhaps a normative collectivity still needs the deviant subgroup to help maintain its boundaries. Acceptance will only happen if powerful members of the mainstream are willing to advocate on a deviant subgroup's behalf, or at least ignore or forgive its perceived transgressions.

However, the softening of conventional attitudes is not *sufficient* for normalization to occur. Deviant groups must play starring roles in the drama of their own normalization by engaging in a negotiation with representatives of conventional culture. First and foremost, members of a deviant subgroup must desire acceptance. If the representatives of both conventional society and the subculture have more perceived gain from demonizing the other than from normalization, the group's status will remain unchanged.

Some deviants will be more amenable to such a process of negotiation than others. Hiders who react to their deviant status with shame and go to great lengths to disguise their deviance will be unwilling to push for normalization, at least publicly. Such a push would "out" them, which they are attempting to prevent. A critical mass of attitude and punishment change is a prerequisite for getting large numbers of Hiders to voluntarily out themselves. Conversely, true Outsiders will prefer to maximize their distance from convention due to their beliefs that the subculture is superior, which are in turn reinforced by that distance. However, to the extent that a deviant behavior or identity has a significant number of individuals who react with concern to being labeled deviant, there is potential for a normalization movement. Because reform arguments and efforts are much more likely to succeed when voiced by those with high levels of conventional status and credibility, Insiders are a *necessary*, but not sufficient, cause of normalization.

The Insider Narrative

By virtue of their simultaneous commitment to normalcy and a deviant subculture, Insiders are compelled to take positions that outwardly challenge conventional definitions of both normative order and deviant labels. Being an Insider requires more than simply resisting a deviant label at the individual level; instead, it represents an effort to politicize the definition of the label in question. Certainly, most individuals labeled deviant have a desire to resist or neutralize these efforts, but only those with perceived "legitimate" claims to a normative identity will have the material and cultural capital necessary to effectively politicize the moral definitions disputed in stigma contests. It is one thing to resist a deviant label, and quite another to argue successfully that the label being applied is an *incorrect category designation*. Insiders are likely to respond to their competing identities by challenging the appropriateness of the classification of the issue in question as deviant, arguing instead that it should be considered conventional. Depending on the cultural salience of the norm in dispute and the power held by those who affirm it, this may indeed be a tall order.

So what techniques might Insiders use to try and facilitate a change in the status of their deviant label? Communications scholar Walter Fisher's narrative paradigm provides insights into the techniques people use to persuade skeptical others. Fisher argues that because humans are story-telling creatures, the art of persuasion involves telling a compelling narrative more than it does a recitation of facts.[29] When presented with a story, recipients judge its believability based on two factors: *narrative fidelity* and *narrative coherence*. A story has narrative fidelity when listeners are able to connect it to their own experiences. The more listeners can personally relate to a narrative, the greater its fidelity. Narrative coherence refers to whether or not the story "makes sense." To the extent that a story is internally consistent, has a logical structure, and aligns within its cultural context, it has narrative coherence. Whether by accident or design, narratives with strong coherence and fidelity are more likely to convince listeners. The daunting task facing deviants who aspire for normalcy is to convince conventional, powerful others that they can somehow personally relate to deviants' stories and that the behavior in question is logical and internally consistent within prevailing normative cultural frameworks.

On the Fidelity of Deviance

Theories of deviance provide insights into how behavior becomes stigmatized. "Moral entrepreneurs" work to extend preexisting symbolic boundaries of deviance by framing the actions to be stigmatized as associated with all manner of ill repute, as well as categories of individuals already defined as deviant. The more culturally repulsive the category linked to the action, the better the chance of extending the boundaries of deviance. This is done by appealing to political bodies using representatives of conventional institutions, especially if they maintain a high ranking in the "hierarchy of credibility."[30] Success or failure in these endeavors hinges on making persuasive claims about the actions in question, which is in turn dependent upon the ability to mobilize resources (time, money, and people) toward that goal. This process is also facilitated to the extent that the people mobilized have access to conventional forms of social power.[31]

Although normalization has received far less attention from scholars than deviantization, studies of the extension of symbolic boundaries of deviance can inform our understanding of how such boundaries are retracted. If linking actions to socially reprehensible categories of people and utilizing agents of conventional social institutions are the typical methods for boundary extension, then by corollary, linking behaviors to conventional categories of people and appealing to agents of conventional institutions promotes narrative fidelity. This allows conventional people to feel a sense of connection with those labeled deviant and make the offending deviance appear less exotic.

This phenomenon is at work among successful new religious groups. Novel religions are more likely to succeed (numerically) to the extent that they can claim at least some continuity with the conventional religions in a given society.[32] In the United States, deviant religious groups framing their movement as having a shared heritage with Christian traditions will make more headway into symbolic spaces of conventionality than those actively framing themselves in a manner incongruent with a large share of the population's preexisting religious views. Put another way, maintaining some ties to Christianity provides skeptical outsiders with a "foothold" into the novel claims made by the new religion, making it appear less strange.

Latter-day Saints are an excellent example in this regard. Although the religion is heavily focused upon the Book of Mormon, which claims to include the writings of prophets who lived in the Americas, it also utilizes the Christian Bible. Mormonism, therefore, can claim to be an extension of Christianity, rather than an entirely different religion. The ability to draw upon existing culture and frame itself as within the Christian tradition provides Mormonism an advantage in seeking converts over other novel religions, such as Scientology, which does not claim affinity to Christianity.[33] As discussed in the previous chapter, having cultural continuity did not remove the challenges of Mormonism for Mitt Romney's president candidacy, but his challenges would have been far greater if his "deviant" religion did not have claims of affinity with Christianity.

Deviant groups will be able to promote narrative fidelity by producing "rhetorical packages that explain . . . claims within extant, culturally legitimate boundaries."[34] Such efforts will focus on reframing the deviant behavior in question as *consistent with other, pre-existing conventional norms.* The goal, then, is usually not one of redrawing the entire moral universe of the culture in question, but one of directly embedding the behavior in question within already existing normative moral structures. The persuasiveness of such arguments will be bolstered to the extent that those within a deviant subculture can cite recognized experts in relevant fields that support their claims; a tactic utilized by Bigfoot hunters (see chapter 4) and the Prohibition repeal movement (see chapter 6).

The contemporary debate over same-sex marriage and the culturally conventional forms of family in the United States offers an instructive example of attempts at promoting narrative fidelity. Both sides in this dispute lay claim to the rhetoric of family, effectively trying to define what constitutes the normative form(s) of "the family." Opponents of gay rights employ religious language in an effort to continue defining currently "alternative" forms of sexuality as deviant.[35] LGBT organizations promote fidelity by attempting to outline a link between the lifestyles of members of the movement and more conventional dimensions of sexuality and family, such as monogamy, marriage, and parenthood. As we detail in chapter 5, this strategy becomes a point of conflict between Outsiders and Insiders.

Put simply, Insiders will be motivated to make appeals linking their behavior to normative institutions, as these constitute broader moral (and therefore cultural) constellations of conventional norms, roles, and behavior. The most general strategy in this form of claims making is arguing that the behavior in question has been mislabeled and would be more accurately classified as conventional. Such appeals will be the most likely to receive a receptive ear from those outside a deviant subculture.

On Narrative Coherence

Making the claim that something labeled deviant holds commonalities with accepted societal institutions requires a deviant subculture to consistently present itself in an idealized form. To the extent that subculture members diverge from that presentation, the plea for acceptance is threatened. Given the costs faced by Insiders if they remain stigmatized as deviant, they will be highly motivated to present "sanitized" versions of the behaviors disputed in a stigma contest. Insiders will be threatened by subgroups within a deviant subculture that do not fit this narrative and will emphasize conventional identities, both personal and collective, as salient features of the subculture. Often this involves shunning a more radical part of a larger movement. For example, in contemporary movements to normalize lesbian and gay identities, "[m]any accounts of lesbian and gay politics document how bisexual and transgendered people, as well as the leather community, are shunned by lesbian and gay political leaders, in an effort to make the movement appear 'normal' and nonthreatening to government and the public."[36] By abandoning parts of broader movements, the normalizing factions can make gains toward conventionality

An individual or group can threaten narrative coherence even if they are only tangentially related to a subculture. For example, the Fundamentalist Latter-day Saint (FLDS) church proves extremely embarrassing to the mainstream LDS church.[37] The FLDS's continued practices of polygamy, as well as allegations of child abuse and welfare fraud, can lead to negative opinions about Mormonism in general, even if the LDS church disavows them. This can further distance Mormonism from the Judeo-Christian family to which it aspires among a general public who often do not recognize or care about the distinction between LDS and FLDS. As discussed in the previous chapter, Mitt Romney was well aware of this problem, and actively distanced himself, and even ridiculed, the history of polygamy within the Mormon Church and its sectarian movements on many occasions. In a similar vein, public figures found engaging in homosexual activity in public places, including politicians like Senator Larry Craig, can promote an image of homosexuality as promiscuous or clandestine, even though Craig does not consider himself gay and the gay and lesbian community would certainly not claim him, either.

In sum, the argument that a form of deviance has been mislabeled and deserves a new designation will be successful to the extent that Insiders can claim that the behavior is akin to an accepted societal institution or behavior (narrative fidelity), and it will be bolstered if a subculture can successfully present itself in a manner consistent with that claim (narrative coherence). Consequently, Insiders will be highly motivated to define what constitutes being a valid member of the subculture and may attempt to marginalize people who do not fit this image. This motivation, and resistance to it, is a key source of friction within stigmatized subcultures.

INTERNAL CONFLICT

One factor that deserves more focus when attempting to understand the transition of a behavior or identity from culturally deviant to normal is the *composition* of a deviant subculture. Within any movement there may be conflicts about goals and strategies, which can result in competing organizations and efforts.[38] To the extent that individuals with similar deviance management strategies organize, they may attempt to push the subculture in a particular direction, emphasizing a particular narrative about the form of deviance in question, including, possibly, normalization. The timing of a subculture's normalization campaign and its likelihood of being successful are, in part, functions of the relative strength of deviance management strategies within subcultures.

As sociologist Steven Epstein noted in a comparative historical overview of LGBTQ organizations and movements in the United States, the primary axes of internal conflict have been about: (1) identity politics vs. politics of difference, (2) whether aspects of sexuality and desire should be foregrounded or backgrounded, and (3) debates about the overlap between public and private actions. Further, he argues that LGBTQ rights movements have been characterized by periodic undulation between short-lived but culturally influential bursts of radicalized politics of difference movements and longer-term organizational efforts using a strategy of liberal identity politics to appeal to the mainstream. Mirroring church/ sect schisms in religious groups, Epstein summarized the dynamic this way:

> As the historical record suggests, when the mainstream lesbian and gay rights movement advances these politics, it tends to present itself in hegemonic fashion as "the movement," almost insuring the periodic eruption of dissent from within lesbian and gay communities: hence the oscillation between the dominance of pragmatic, quasi-ethnic identity politics and the powerful surges of utopian alternatives that either insist on the instability of identities; or argue that it is dangerous to make identity the fundamental organizing principle; or assert the centrality of internal differences based on race, gender, or other characteristics that are suppressed by the hegemonic model; or reject the goal of assimilation and integration; or proclaim some combination of these views.[39]

To the extent that a deviant subculture is composed primarily of Drifters, Outsiders, and Hiders, the likelihood of normalization movements will be very low. Still, in rare cases, Hiders may secretly work on behalf of a deviant subculture by covertly facilitating normalization. An example is the book *The Homosexual in America: A Subjective Approach*, which argued that gay men were an unrecognized minority group deprived of basic civil liberties, and also gave voice to the lived experiences of stigma faced by those with same-sex attraction, behavior and identity.[40] The book was a landmark study, because "of 'insider' nonfiction; there was almost nothing before Cory's 1951 book."[41] The attributed author, Donald Webster

Cory, was a pseudonym adopted so the researcher/writer could avoid the repercussions from outing himself at the height of the Second Red Scare and political McCarthyism. He was also married with children. The legacy of the book is oft debated, but it nonetheless became "the cornerstone for what has come to be called 'identity politics,'" and contained seminal ideas whose implications pointed toward more radical queer theories.[42]

Such examples notwithstanding, most Hiders are unlikely to engage in advocacy on behalf of their deviance, and may even actively work *against* mainstream acceptance of the deviant subculture as a form of cover, the "breastplate of righteousness" strategy Laud Humphries discovered.[43]

While less radical Outsiders will be willing to support some normalization efforts, within the limitations of subcultural values, true Outsiders who have either failed to acquire status within conventional culture or chosen not to do so also will often hinder normalization movements. As noted in the previous chapter, Outsiders view their deviance as *superior* to conventional behavior and are unwilling or uninterested in "selling themselves" to conventional others. Outsiders are proud of their deviant status, just as Hiders are ashamed of theirs, but both subtypes may ultimately work *against* normalization. As alluded to in Epstein's quote about gay rights movements, Outsiders may occasionally act as the "leading edge" of a social movement during times when repression is extremely high, but as normalization efforts progress, they will likely fight against assimilation into the mainstream.

Drifters also are unlikely to contribute to normalization—but out of apathy or impotence rather than active resistance. Although there are some rare possibilities for mobilization among the displaced, usually Drifters cannot be counted on to contribute consistently to a social movement, as they oscillate freely back and forth between conventionality and deviance and between different forms of deviance.[44] Further, even if Drifters do participate in collective activities, they will not have accumulated conventional or subcultural social capital to apply toward movement goals.

Insiders hold the most potential for normalization, as they are wedded to conventional society but also sufficiently invested in a deviant subculture, so they will not (or cannot) entirely hide stigmatized identities out of fear or shame. Insiders risk a heavy loss of cultural capital from being branded as dangerous or a "nut," "slut" or "pervert," so it is in the best interests of Insiders to work to convince "normal" others that they are not a threat.[45] Should a group of Insiders coalesce within a deviant subculture, they are likely to mobilize toward normalization. They also will place pressure on the subculture to sanitize its behaviors and present a consistent, normalized image.

The greatest challenge facing deviant subcultures in terms of developing a coherent normalization message is in-fighting between Insiders and Outsiders. Insiders will be highly motivated to develop a narrative about the subculture that presents it as less threatening than previously assumed and more normal than previously thought. Insiders will magnify the *similarities* between themselves and the dominant culture. Outsiders, on the other hand, are comparatively free from concerns about how the dominant culture perceives them and are likely to magnify their *differences* from the mainstream and, in the case of true Outsiders, present themselves as superior to "normals." For highly motivated Insiders, Outsiders are potentially an embarrassment and likely to hold them back from achieving reformist goals; particularly since the most ostentatious members of a subculture typically receive the greatest media coverage. For true Outsiders, Insiders are soulless sellouts, who would choose the repressive, dominant culture over the needs of their subcultural brethren.

Even when the debate is not as fundamental as choosing between normalization and separation, significant conflicts can result from different aims and strategies within a movement. For example, sociologist Edward Sagarin argued that there are two types of "organizations of deviants."[46] First, there are organizations that look to "conform to the norms of society." These organizations and their members affirm existing moral orders, but plead for mercy and understanding as they attempt to reform themselves as much as possible. Often these organizations take the form of a self-help group and their dominant frame or narrative is one of accepting their behavior or identity as pathological and wanting to be rehabilitated. An example is Alcoholics Anonymous. Such organizations are not aimed at changing prevailing norms defining their members as deviants, but they still can be successful in changing attitudes toward members from one of anger and hostility to at least sympathy and resigned tolerance.

The second type of deviant organization aims to "change [society's] norms to include acceptance." These organizations aim not to earn sympathy, but to "convince the world . . . that their particular deviance . . . is normal, natural, moral and socially useful." Because these goals for change are beyond those of the first group, such organizations have a more difficult path to success.[47] In some cases movements may be divided between such organizations and their respective narratives. This could result in hostility, as the frame of the former undercuts the larger goals of the latter.

Yet Sagarin noticeably neglected an important third type of organization: Outsider-oriented deviant subcultures, which can facilitate early, but then may undermine later, normalization efforts. Sagarin's omission of this third type of "organization of deviants" is unsurprising given that he was none other than Donald Webster Cory, author of *The Homosexual in America*. Sagarin earned a doctoral degree in sociology writing about the Mattachine Society in New York, but his research failed to mention that he was Cory, or that he was a participant in bitter infighting about the future direction of the "homophile" movement, as it was then called.[48] As he began publishing under his given name, resentment grew among Outsiders in the nascent gay community toward Sagarin's continued Hider status and his increasingly conservative views, particularly when he began advocating for a version of the "sickness" theory of homosexuality—adopted from influential psychoanalyst Albert Ellis[49]—a position he had originally repudiated in *The Homosexual in America*.[50]

Within the New York Mattachine Society, in which Cory was an influential, if often unenthusiastic member, there was growing resistance to the sickness framing of homosexuality. As conflict within the group came to a head over whether to adopt a stance of pride and actions aimed at civil rights, gay rights pioneer Franklin Kameny wrote to Cory:

> You have justly earned the title of "The Father of the Homophile Movement." . . . [But] you have become no longer the vigorous Father of the Homophile Movement, to be revered, respected, and listened to, but the senile Grandfather of the Homophile Movement, to be humored and tolerated, at best; ignored and disregarded, usually; and to be ridiculed, at worst. . . . You have become alienated from the movement which you fathered; most of us feel that the alienation is, essentially, of your doing. I find that alienation deplorable. . . . However, the clock cannot be turned back, either keep up with the movement, or you will be dropped by the wayside—as is indeed now in the process of happening.[51]

After resoundingly losing a contested election for president of the group in 1965, Cory left the organization and political activities in general. Kameny recalled that "the vote seemed to represent a clear mandate for our views, and a clear defeat for the conservatives, the 'closet queens, and Cory's sickniks.'"[52] But Cory-cum-Sagarin continued to use his academic position to write about homosexuality.

As an example of how Hiders can try to undermine normalization movements—and simultaneously yet another validation of Laud Humphreys's theory and findings about the breastplate of righteousness—Sagarin used his now higher position in the hierarchy of credibility to undermine the work of more recent scholars and activists advocating for gay liberation, preaching an increasingly negative vision of homosexuality. In 1973, he published a scathing review in an academic journal about recent research on homosexuality. He not only derided a new generation of sexuality scholars, he also used the platform to argue that "the evidence is strong that homosexuality arises in most instances from faulty childhood development, is often accompanied by poor sex-role identification, and is overwhelmingly concomitant with compulsivity, inability to relate to others, poor self-image, low feeling of self-worth, and a great deal of . . . 'injustice collecting.' I am unwilling to exclude biology from this scene: the anatomic misfit, which may be the source of difficulty in building a sustained and repeated sex-love relationship with one partner."[53]

More scintillating was Sagarin's conclusion of the essay where he offers a thinly veiled reference to his own history and conflicted status as both legitimate academic and Hider:

As for the secret deviants among these writers, I deeply respect their right to self-protection in an atmosphere of continued hostility. But as they call on gay people to accept and assert themselves, blatantly to proclaim themselves, they may be proceeding on the road to their own undoing. For if the scene should change and such people do remove their masks (the obvious masks, those that the selves are most conscious of), then writers caught up in their own rhetoric may be compelled to pursue the strategy they had advocated. No longer, however, could they be quoted and cited as scholars in whatever their area of specialization, protected by the mantle of objectivity, for their vested interest would place their work under a shadow. It would be a bittersweet irony if the success of homosexual liberation for which they were fighting should deprive them of their only value in that struggle. It would not be the first time that a revolution has devoured its leaders.[54]

Laud Humphreys—whose recent work was summarized in Sagarin's review essay thusly: "His analysis would be unconvincing even if the observations were correct"—resolved to confront Sagarin's hypocrisy.[55] At a meeting of the American Sociological Association the following year, Humphreys was a panel discussant in a session on theories of sexuality. Sagarin presented a paper that repeated his controversial positions, reiterated his denunciation of liberationist scholars encouraging people to come out, and suggested that next-generation sexologists such as Evelyn Hooker and John Gagnon falsified their data. Humphreys used the discussion time to publicly out himself as gay. He accused Sagarin of homophobia, alternatingly referring to him as "Professor Sagarin" and "Mr. Cory." Then, "Humphreys moved in for the kill and sardonically asked, 'And where did you get *your* data? Sagarin's hands clenched and his voice choked up: 'I am my data.'"[56] When the session ended, Sagarin "sadly shuffled off the sociology of homosexuality stage forever,"[57] although he continued to chide other academics for "'hiding behind' the safety of their wives and children while advocating that lesbians and gay men come out of the closet," and "he refused to identify himself as Cory" for the rest of his life.[58]

The Cory/Sagarin saga features many facets of the strategies of Hiders, Insiders, and Outsiders—complete with a transition to a breastplate-of-righteousness strategy of publicly labeling one's own hidden deviance as a sickness, met by a humiliating public reckoning performed by none other than the very progenitor of the concept. Sagarin's conflicts with others inside the early gay rights movement, as well as within the burgeoning studies of sexuality and social movements, illustrate how subcultural conflicts can arise between Hiders, Insiders, and Outsiders. It also illustrates some of the fluidity of these identities and strategies over time.

TRANSITIONS IN DEVIANCE MANAGEMENT

Although transitions of all types are possible, we can outline some of the more common types of transitions between strategies of deviance management. Hiders

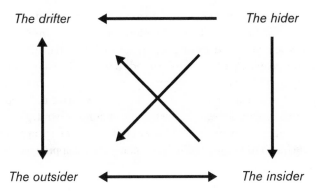

FIGURE 2. Most common pathways of transition between deviance management types.

are a starting place for deviance management, to the extent that theorists have emphasized the importance of "primary deviance" (engaging in deviance and not getting caught) as distinct from "secondary deviance" (engaging in deviance after one has already been labeled deviant).[59] Thus, otherwise conventional people typically begin their deviance careers as Hiders. In a sense, we may say that everyone begins as a Hider, except for those caught and labeled during their very first foray into deviance. From this position as a Hider, individuals can transition into all the other types of deviance management: to a Drifter, if the Hider is revealed and loses conventional stakes in conformity; to an Outsider, if the Hider finds an affinity with a particular subculture and reduces conventionality; or to an Insider, for those who out themselves and successfully fight to keep their conventional status. In contrast, those using other styles of deviance management are unlikely to transition into being Hiders, although it deserves note that Drifters may use hiding to regain stakes in conformity.

Meanwhile, Insiders who lose faith in negotiating about deviance through conventional systems transition into Outsiders with primary allegiance to a subculture. Conversely, Outsiders may make compromises with conventionality over time and become Insiders. And Insiders who lose social face due to calamity or scandal may find themselves as Drifters. Likewise, Outsiders may become Drifters if they lose commitment to or are rejected from a particular subculture. In effect, Outsiders or Drifters can come from any of the other management styles. After all, loss is easier than gain when it comes to social status, both conventional and subcultural. Figure 2 outlines the most common pathways of transition between different types of deviance management over time.

To be clear, transitions of all types are possible, these are simply the most common. Further, individuals in the real world are unlikely to use a single strategy for managing deviance but rather a combination of strategies deployed across a wide range of social relationships and situations. As a result, "pure" deviance management types are rare, and most people use multiple management strategies simultaneously. People may be Hiders around some and Outsiders among others. Examining combinations of deviance management strategies stands as one of the most important extensions of the basic framework we have outlined for understanding deviance management. Likewise, the fluidity of strategies of deviance management and accompanying social identities over time speaks to the importance of using qualitative, longitudinal, and comparative approaches when studying deviance management.

FIGHTING FOR NORMAL?

For normalization movements, framing and rhetorical persuasion are even more important than in other movements. This is because other types of movements may be able to win support through coercion or bargaining. For stigmatized groups, coercion, such as violent and disruptive activities, will likely only result in increased stigmatization.[60] Further, deviant groups are unlikely to have much to offer for bargaining. Even if they did, members of conventional society may avoid bargaining "with social movements whose followers they have stigmatized as dangerous social degenerates."[61]

The potential for a normalization movement to mobilize depends upon having individuals invested in both a deviant subculture and conventional society. Although an increasing percentage of Insiders within a subculture should be predictive of future attempts at normalization, it is not simply a matter of numbers. Even small numbers of Insiders can have a transformative effect on a subculture if they are charismatic leaders. Insiders will tend to have more social capital and connections than Outsiders, which provides a comparative advantage in controlling group resources and accessing mainstream media sources that allow for more effectively advancing normalization narratives. So even if others within a subculture disagree with and outnumber Insiders, they will still be highly influential members. These types of disputes over movement strategy are likely to result in organizational schisms.[62] The antagonistic strategies can succinctly (if crudely) be summarized as respective attempts to say to mainstream society: "We're just like you" / "Fuck you in the face!"

Nevertheless, it is not a given that Insiders, even if they constitute a majority, will "win" debates about how to frame a deviant subculture. But such debates *will never get started* until individuals who have more to gain from normalization hold sufficient power within a subculture. To reiterate, the presence of Insiders is a necessary, but not sufficient condition for normalization movements.

Now it is time to put these ideas about deviance management to the test. To do this, we examine the cultural dynamics between conventional and deviant social identities in different subcultures. We will also look at how these dynamics are related to subcultural conflict; participation in reform movements; and the identity narratives of Insiders, Outsiders, Hiders and Drifters. The sex, drugs, and Bigfoot have arrived just in time, led by the elusive Sasquatch.

4

Bigfoot

Undiscovered Primate or Interdimensional Spirit?

Understanding a deviant subculture requires an appreciation of the different inter-ests and identities of its members. Two people may share a heartfelt, passionate commitment to a subculture but have widely divergent ideas of how it should operate and message about itself to conventional society.

This chapter focuses on a subculture devoted to the study of an undiscovered creature known as "Bigfoot," "Sasquatch," and more recently the "Wood Ape." Big-foot is reportedly a very tall, hairy, upright-walking, humanlike creature that roams wooded areas. While most members of the Bigfoot community share an ardent belief that the creature is real, with many claiming personal encounters, the subculture is split into two major camps. Some believe that Bigfoot is "merely" an undiscovered form of higher-order primate and therefore that the Bigfoot subcul-ture should attempt to mimic previous efforts by naturalists to document undis-covered species. In contrast, an equally enthusiastic camp believes that Bigfoot is *not* merely an animal, but some form of spiritual being that has telepathic powers, the ability to slip into other dimensions, and perhaps even hitches rides on UFOs. These contrasting explanations for Sasquatch are mirrored with contrasting styles of deviance management.

We begin with our ethnographic observations of a group that takes a naturalis-tic approach to Bigfoot, the Bluff Creek Project. We then discuss the divide within the Bigfoot subculture and hypothesize that naturalistic and paranormal orienta-tions toward Bigfoot should align with being an Insider and Outsider, respectively. With primary data collected from attendees at conferences about Bigfoot, as well as a large UFO conference, we use measures of deviant and conventional identity to classify people according to our typology of deviance management. In this way, we show how being a Drifter, Hider, Insider, or Outsider directly relates to an individual's beliefs about the nature of Bigfoot and related practices such as attempts to capture or communicate with these mysterious beasts.

FINDING BIGFOOT

In the summer of 2017, I (Bader) found myself deep in the woods of Northern California digging away at the decomposing remains of a fallen log that was blocking a gravel road. My companions and I were the first to enter the remote area since the previous October, when Forest Service Road 12N12, outside of the tiny town of Orleans, closed for the winter. As we progressed down the narrow, twisting road, with mountains to the right and perilous drops to the left, we frequently had to stop and roll large boulders from the path, take a chainsaw to limbs that could break windshields, and kick away sharp rocks that could pop tires. Near the end of this exhausting drive, our group encountered a fallen tree. At first, it seemed we might have to turn back, despite being less than a mile from our destination. But after some vigorous shoveling, chopping, pushing, and pulling, we finally cleared the road sufficiently and continued to Louse Camp. Situated on the banks of Bluff Creek, Louse is arguably the heart of the Bigfoot/Sasquatch subculture in the United States. Although nearly every culture has folklore about "hairy men" living on the outskirts of civilization, the modern American legend and the name, "Bigfoot," originate from Bluff Creek.[1]

Bigfoot at Bluff Creek[2]

In 1958, workers on a road construction project near Bluff Creek reported a series of strange experiences. On the morning of August 27, a worker named Jerry Crew found a series of large, human-like footprints in the mud around his tractor; as if an enormous person had investigated the equipment. Similar tracks appeared about a month later. In September, the wife of a crew member wrote a letter to the *Humboldt Times* discussing the events. The paper printed a series of stories over the next few months. On October 14, the paper ran a story that featured a picture of Jerry Crew holding a plaster cast he had made of one of the giant footprints. It also named the interloper: "The big foot, as cast, was 16 inches in length, with the wide seven inch width. Crew said that the men refer to the creature as "Big Foot." . . . Who and what is Big Foot . . . the maker of those 16-inch tracks? Surely there must be an answer. Maybe someone will succeed in finding it."[3]

In October 1967, nearly fifty years prior to our arrival in Bluff Creek, Roger Patterson and Bob Gimlin set up at Louse Camp with their horses. The previous year, Patterson had self-published a book on Bigfoot that recounted the events in the Bluff Creek area.[4] He hoped to follow his book with a documentary. With its frequent reports, Bluff Creek seemed an ideal place to try to capture the beast on film.

Each morning, Patterson and Gimlin left Louse Camp to ride up and down Bluff Creek and its surrounding areas, hoping to encounter a Bigfoot. Around 1:30 in the afternoon on October 20, they rounded a fallen tree and spotted a large, hairy creature crouching on a sandbar in the creek.[5] Patterson pulled a camera from his pack. The Patterson-Gimlin film, as it came to be known, consists of fifty-three seconds of 16 mm film of the figure Patterson shot as it swiftly walked away from the men toward the tree line.

The Patterson-Gimlin (or PG) film remains of immense importance in the Bigfoot subculture. The vast majority of Bigfoot enthusiasts are convinced that the film is authentic.[6] Most Bigfoot books discuss the encounter, with several entirely focused upon it.[7] The creature depicted in the film has affectionately become known as "Patty." Frame 352, in which "Patty" turns to look at Patterson, is iconic and the most recognizable symbol of Bigfoot. Websites, books, T-shirts, and bumper stickers with this indelible image abound.

Finding Patty: The Bluff Creek Project

Given its centrality to the Bigfoot subculture, it is surprising that the exact location where Patterson and Gimlin shot their film was lost for many years. A combination of factors, including Patterson's death in 1972, Bob Gimlin's retreat from the Bigfoot subculture, the regrowth of foliage that was washed away in a 1964 flood, and the simple fading of memories rendered the exact film location uncertain.[8] In 2009, Steven Streufert and Ian Carton formed the "Bluff Creek Project" (BCP) in an effort to recover this lost piece of Bigfoot history. Over the next two years, Streufert, Carton, and other members visited the area Patterson and Gimlin were known to have traveled and carefully examined each of the varied sites other researchers had identified as the film location. At each location, they attempted to match trees, stumps and other markers to the film footage. After two years of work, the group believed they had successfully located the original film site.[9] Other influential members of the Bigfoot community soon sanctioned the proposed location as legitimate.[10]

By the time of my visit, the Bluff Creek Project was regularly taking interested visitors down to the film site.[11] After setting up at Louse Camp, Robert Leiterman and Rowdy Kelley of the BCP took our group to a trailhead leading to the PG film location. We hiked down a steep trail, over a creek and had a close encounter with a black bear. An hour later, we finally arrived on the shores of Bluff Creek.

As we wandered the site, Leiterman and Kelley explained the painstaking work involved in identifying the location. Leiterman pulled out a dossier of laminated photos and charts and dropped them on the ground. In stills from the film, he pointed out distinctive trees and stumps, many of which had received names over time, particularly those "Patty" walked in front of or behind. He pointed out the "Big Tree" in a photo, then to a tree in front of us. He talked about the "two brothers," thin

IMAGE 2. Rowdy Kelley holds an image of frame 352 in front of its marked location at the Patterson-Gimlin film site. (Photo by Mark Hopkins)

trees that slumped into each other behind and to the right of Patty in a photo he showed us. He then directed us to two trees in a similar formation, much larger now with the passage of time. A few minutes later, we stood in front of the "smiley face stump," a distinctively grimacing stump near Patty's path. The reverence of the team bore a resemblance to religious pilgrims encountering a holy site.

At the same time, there was a scientific feel to their efforts, as the BCP team had conducted extensive measurements at the site and determined the trajectory between various objects based on the perceived position of Patterson's camera. The site now resembles a forensic crime scene, with flags marking key locations. A flag shows where Patty first appeared in the camera's view and where "she" exited. The exact spot of frame 352 is flagged, as is the place where Patterson stood filming. Using these markers, Leiterman reproduced the film for us, walking through the site, mimicking Patty's distinctive gait as we reverently stood in the place where Patterson did fifty years before.

The Bluff Creek Project represents an attempt to bring science, at least amateur science, into the realm of Bigfoot. Members believe that the best path toward solving the mystery of the PG film is to assume that "if Bigfoot exists it is a physical, biological animal."[12] The BCP's work "can now be used to exact dimensional data from the film and make accurate measurement of the creature's pathway and size."[13] This raises the possibility that a group of researchers could re-create the PG film using a suit that matches the characteristics of "Patty," the same camera and film used by Patterson, and the same location, in an effort to, perhaps, lay to rest the status of its subject.

If Bigfoot *is* an undiscovered animal, then it is possible to catch it on camera again. Accordingly, a large portion of the group's efforts have turned toward installing and maintaining trail cameras around the site and along Bluff Creek. On our second day at Bluff Creek, BCP member Jamie Wayne retrieved memory chips from these cameras. That evening at Louse Camp, he scanned them with his laptop, showing us pictures of deer, martens, and bears. Unfortunately, there was no Bigfoot.

BIGFOOT: THE GREAT APE

Over the years, dedicated Bigfoot researchers have managed to convince a select few academics that the United States could be home to an undiscovered, ape-like creature. Physical anthropologists such as the late Grover Krantz of Washington State University and Jeffrey Meldrum of Idaho State University, wildlife biologist John Bindernagel, and primatologist Esteban Sarmiento of the Human Evolution Foundation have engaged with the subject. The former three have written a number of books that argue for the possibility of an undiscovered species and attempt to frame research into the phenomenon as a scientific endeavor, including *The Scientist Looks at Sasquatch* (Krantz), *Sasquatch: Legend Meets Science* (Meldrum), and *North America's Great Ape: The Sasquatch—A Wildlife Biologist Looks at the Continent's Most Misunderstood Large Mammal* (Bindernagel).[14]

Anyone with a conventional scientific reputation faces high costs for expressing a belief, or even an intense interest, in Bigfoot/Sasquatch.[15] When Jeff Meldrum held a Bigfoot symposium at Idaho State University in 2006, it provoked outrage. Thirty fellow ISU professors signed a petition criticizing the university for allowing the event. Martin Hackworth, then a senior lecturer in ISU's Physics Department, was especially critical of Meldrum's interest in Bigfoot and frequent TV appearances discussing the subject: "Do I cringe when I see the Discovery Channel and I see Idaho State University, Jeff Meldrum? Yes, I do."[16] Hackworth and others called for the university to revoke Meldrum's tenure. Another professor likened Meldrum's interests to researching Santa Claus.[17]

Meldrum has worked tirelessly to separate Bigfoot from unicorns, faeries, and Kris Kringle. He has even founded an online, peer-reviewed journal, *Relict Hominoid Inquiry* (*RHI*), with the stated mission to "promote research and provide a refereed venue for the dissemination of scholarly peer-reviewed papers exploring and evaluating the possible existence and nature of relict hominoid species around the world."[18] With the exception of its unusual subject matter, the content of *RHI* mimics the jargon-heavy style of mainstream academic journals. For example, one article utilizes multiple regression analyses of climatic, geographic, and socioeconomic data to predict the frequency of Bigfoot reports in an area. Assuredly to the chagrin of Insiders like Meldrum looking to separate Bigfoot from the wider world of the paranormal, the strongest predictor of sightings in an area was the number of UFO reports.[19]

Reiterating the importance of Patty to the Bigfoot subculture, two articles in *RHI* coauthored by Meldrum focus on the PG film. The first, "Analysis Integrity of the Patterson-Gimlin Film Image," dismisses claims that the film has been tampered with and concludes that its image quality is suitable for assessing the nature of its subject.[20] Similarly, the second analyzes various folds, creases and other characteristics apparent on the body of Patty in the film images and argues that these features would be too difficult to fake: "These observations support the conclusion that we are not observing a costume, but rather a real and novel hominid whose body has a modest natural hair coat."[21]

In varied works, Meldrum identifies this "novel hominid" as a relict population of Gigantopithecus, a ten-foot-tall ape that roamed China, Vietnam, and India until about one hundred thousand years ago.[22] The conclusion to *Sasquatch: Legend Meets Science*, argues that skeptics are too quick to dismiss the circumstantial evidence for Bigfoot's existence: "For me, it now seems more incredible to suggest this matter could all be dismissed as mere stories, misidentifications, and spurious hoaxes than it is to at least rationally entertain the well-founded suggestion that the legend of sasquatch possibly has its basis in a real animal and may eventually prove to be among the most astounding zoological discoveries ever."[23]

In the end, Meldrum kept his tenure and position. But his legacy ultimately depends upon his ability to convince skeptics that Bigfoot could be the next Bili Ape, Saola (a deer), or Sundaland clouded leopard; all large mammal species discovered in the last twenty years. Part of the problem is that Meldrum and others who share his views are not just fighting against dismissive academics and a skeptical public. They also face an intra-subcultural foe. Many enthusiasts believe that Bigfoot is *not* some sort of undiscovered hominid, but rather a mystical being that moves between dimensions.

SPIRIT OF THE FOREST

To get a better sense of the breadth of the Bigfoot subculture, I also attended the third annual *Sasquatch Summit* in Ocean Shores, Washington. The conference is geared to the general public and features a wide variety of Bigfoot researchers making presentations over two days. Many of these talks focused on the evidence for the existence of a heretofore undiscovered animal and what that evidence tells us about the habits, appearance, and characteristics of this mysterious creature.

For example, wildlife biologist John Bindernagel's talk largely focused upon the difficulties he has faced getting fellow academics to engage with the subject of Sasquatch, despite what he believes to be compelling physical evidence for the existence of an undiscovered great ape or human.[24] "There is strong scientific resistance to even exploring the issue," he complained.[25] The remainder of his talk contrasted dismissive quotes from skeptics with those of folklorists and anthropologists—such as Claude Lévi-Strauss—who have collected tales of hairy giants in indigenous folklore.[26]

Later that afternoon, the members of a Bigfoot research group known as the Olympic Project provided a series of lectures. Based in Washington State, the Olympic Project operates upon the working hypothesis that if Bigfoot exists, it is an undiscovered animal or human species. As such, they attempt to document the patterns, habits, and behaviors of that species with DNA analysis, motion-trigger cameras, and other such efforts to gather empirical evidence.[27]

The team's data analyst, Tom Baker, provided a statistical overview of sighting reports gathered by the group. He concluded that the best chance of sighting Bigfoot—most commonly described as about seven feet tall with dark brown hair according to Baker's data—would be to drive down an isolated road in the Olympic Peninsula of Washington state between the hours of 9 and 11 P.M., watching for the animal either crossing or walking near the road.[28] David Ellis, a "field researcher" for the group, played recordings of purported Bigfoot vocalizations and discussed how he failed to find a match for these recordings among known animal sounds cataloged by the Macaulay Library of Sound at Cornell. Cindy Dosen discussed hair samples collected by the group. A self-taught hair analyst, she describes herself as a "citizen scientist."[29] Comparing hairs found in an area believed to be a Sasquatch nesting site to those from cows, bears, and other known animals, she concluded that the samples represent an unknown species. Although the quality of the evidence presented by Bindernagel and the Olympic Project was hardly conclusive, an anthropologist or biologist who happened to wander into the event might have been intrigued by talk of an unknown species and its hypothetical habits.

But that same scientist would have fled in horror upon witnessing some of the conference's other presentations. For example, Thom Powell, author of several Bigfoot books and a middle school science teacher, followed up the Olympic Project with an impassioned, but good-humored call to give up on the quest to document an undocumented species, with a talk titled: "What is Bigfoot?" In the fifty years since the Patterson-Gimlin film, he argued, researchers have yet to prove conclusively the existence of Bigfoot. "I'm not holding out for scientific proof anymore," he said. Powell spent the remainder of his lecture focusing on cases that he says the "flesh and blood" Bigfoot researchers purposefully ignore.[30] Powell talked of a woman who claims to have seen Bigfoot reading a newspaper onboard a flying saucer and noted that UFOs and Bigfeet both tend to "emerge from underground hideouts" and have the ability to make observers forget their encounters.[31] He explained that the lack of clear photographs of Bigfoot, including the many blurry ones, were due to the creature's ability to "phase in and out" of physical reality and become invisible. In his summation slide, Powell noted that Bigfoot is likely a being of "superior intellect," with an advanced language and the ability to communicate telepathically. Most troubling for the "flesh and blood" camp, Powell said that Bigfoot is consciously contemptuous of "scientific documentation in general," and hence will actively avoid trail cameras.[32]

This ideological divide between the "flesh and blood" and "paranormal" camps was evident amongst the vendor tables too. John Bindernagel patiently autographed copies of his two books about an undiscovered species of ape. Meanwhile, a few tables to his left, Thom Powell autographed his aptly named *Edges of Science*, which forcefully argues for the futility of scientifically documenting Bigfoot.[33] And a few tables to Bindernagel's right sat psychically "sensitive" Samantha Ritchie, founder of the YouTube channel Planet Sasquatch.

Ritchie believes that Bigfeet are spiritual, benevolent entities that have the ability to become invisible. She displayed a picture of a deer in a wooded setting that was missing its head; not as if the deer had been decapitated, but rather as if its head had been photoshopped out of the picture.[34] A "cloaked" Sasquatch caused the anomaly when it approached the deer, she said. Ritchie is aware of the divide between naturalistic and paranormalist interpretations of Bigfoot, but does not let it concern her. Instead, she believes that she is operating at a higher level of understanding: "At level 1 are people who just don't believe in Bigfoot. Level 2 are people who believe they are just monkeys. The higher levels are for those who understand that Bigfoot is more than just an animal. I am at level 7."[35]

This fissure between naturalism and paranormalism has been present in the Bigfoot subculture for some time. The Bigfoot that readers will encounter depends entirely upon the author. Many Bigfoot sightings recorded by researchers over the years have included paranormal elements. For example, a series of events that occurred in Pennsylvania in the early 1970s featured Bigfoot sightings in the same time and place as UFOs. The creatures vanished into thin air when pursued or shot at. Many experiencers perceived telepathic communications with Bigfoot, and one witness was even possessed by a discarnate entity and spewed prophecies about the end of the world.[36] Similar events were reported from Rome, Ohio, in 1981, when a family told of an ongoing "siege" of their farm by Bigfoot, UFOs, and strange shadow-like entities.[37] Bigfoot books that are geared toward a general audience often include discussions of these "paranormal" Bigfoot reports. The books and websites of those who prefer a naturalistic explanation for Bigfoot simply ignore reports that involve telepathy, UFOs, or other phenomena, or omit the *parts* of a story that contain these more fantastical elements.[38]

For those trying to frame Bigfoot as a scientific endeavor, paranormalism is a terrible embarrassment. Their attempts to gain credibility in mainstream science are undermined by every report of telepathic communication with a forest spirit. In a textbook case of cultural boundary maintenance, Bigfooters with a naturalistic orientation openly and vigorously distinguish themselves from paranormalists. The Bluff Creek Project states on its website that: "It is our opinion that if Bigfoot exists it is a physical, biological animal and not paranormal in nature."[39] Anthropologist Grover Krantz, who faced extensive criticism for his involvement with Bigfoot research, openly warned about the perils of paranormalists: "The lunatic fringe has the sasquatch moving through space-time warps, riding in UFOs, making telepathic connections, showing superior intelligence, and the like. . . . Most of them will eagerly latch on to any scientist who shows an interest, and attempt to lead him/her down their own garden path. It is tantamount to academic suicide to become associated with any of these people."[40]

This long-standing divide within the Bigfoot community is becoming more pronounced, with the two camps now often holding their own conferences so that they do not have to mingle. Samantha Ritchie of Planet Sasquatch told me of a conference geared entirely toward paranormal interpretations of Bigfoot occurring later that year. Organized by Matthew Johnson, who believes that Bigfeet can arrive on Earth via dimensional portals, the "Team Squatchin' USA Bigfoot Habituation Research Conference," featured Ritchie, Thom Cantrall, and other paranormal luminaries within the Bigfoot community. Ritchie told me that while she was treated with respect at the Sasquatch Summit, she sometimes tired of having to explain her perspectives to the "flesh and blood" types. She was looking forward to the Habituation Conference where "everyone will be at level 7."

There are other organizations and gatherings dedicated to a paranormal view of Bigfoot. For instance, a "Psychic Sasquatch" group has begun holding an annual meeting for likeminded Bigfoot Paranormalists. The group's website provides a summary of what they believe Bigfeet to be. It is worth quoting at length:

> The Sasquatch are our Elder Brothers. We are more closely related to them than any other mammal. They were created by the Star Elders (ETs) before humans to care for Mother Earth and assist in spiritual evolution of Earth's collective consciousness. We used to live together with the Sasquatch when humans were more spiritually conscious and were connected with the Council of Elders.
>
> The Sasquatch are incarnate but they have advanced psychic abilities such as telepathy, mind reading, remote viewing, hypnosis, astral projection, dematerialization, teleportation, shape shifting and permeating consciousness.
>
> The ET allies of the Sasquatch People are unconcerned with science obtaining empirical proof since there will always be denial, no matter how much proof is provided. The global agenda now is a false doctrine and an ideology of domination. The rehabilitation of our collective consciousness is the ONLY thing that matters and it is the reason the Sasquatch People are here, giving this message.

The collective mission and real responsibility of humans is to find balance and heal karmas. The Sasquatch People are here to help us with this by speaking through our heart and souls. They can work with us and appear through dreams, images, apparitions, whirlwinds, whispers or physical sightings because that is their way of communicating.

There has been a very long evolution on Earth, several million years. The Earth has experienced 5 mass extinctions already which nearly eliminated all of the species that were here before us like the Fish People (mer-men), the Ant People (insectoids), the Bird-People, and the Lizard People (reptoids). The Sasquatch were the first of the Mammal People, such as humans are.

The purpose and process of co-creation and evolution of life is for our "spiritual consciousness" to awaken. The spiritual mission of our Elder Brothers, the Sasquatch and Almas, has been to be protectors and caretakers of all life forms and of the spiritual knowledge of our Star Elders, by saving these teachings. Of all hybrids created on Earth, only the Sasquatch People, some Bird-People as guardian angels, and the Elementals of Nature have remained faithful to the original cosmic spiritual mission. The Sasquatch People wish for the Human People to join with them and reintegrate the Council of our Star Elders, but need governmental help in achieving this as we all work together toward that goal.

These views of Bigfoot are obviously quite different from those in search of an undiscovered hominid. Understandably, there is a rancorous rift between those pursuing the discovery of a new species and those in search of enlightenment via spiritual communication with Sasquatch, special envoy of the Star Elders.[41]

CAGING THE BEAST: DEVIANCE MANAGEMENT STRATEGIES IN THE BIGFOOT SUBCULTURE

Jeff Meldrum once told a reporter that he was proud to have separated Bigfoot from other "paranormal" topics in the minds of at least some people: "It used to be you went to a bookstore and asked for a book on Bigfoot and you'd be directed to the occult section, right between the Bermuda Triangle and UFOs. Now you can find some in the natural science section."[42] Meldrum's statement succinctly demarcates the two major camps within the Bigfoot subculture.

Bigfoot naturalists believe that the subject of their inquiry is some form of undiscovered ape or human. The lack of conclusive evidence for the creature's existence is due to its rarity, elusiveness, and high intelligence. Nonetheless, it is a biological entity and will act accordingly. It eats and sleeps. It can be killed. It can be caught on camera, with luck and the right equipment. Given their belief that Bigfoot is "merely" an undiscovered animal, Bigfoot Naturalists argue that their enterprise is scientific in nature. They believe they will be vindicated one day, as were those who discovered the great apes of Africa. This quest for legitimacy is thwarted by the public's tendency to view Bigfoot as a myth or legend, part of the "occult," or akin to reports of unicorns and UFOs. As a result, Bigfoot naturalists often distance themselves from elements of the Bigfoot subculture that promote more exotic claims.

Bigfoot paranormalists believe that the subject of their inquiry is a "being" with extraordinary, supernatural powers. The lack of conclusive evidence for the creature's existence is due to its ability to become invisible, teleport to other dimensions, or escape in a flying saucer. Bigfoot has telepathic powers and may "mind-speak" with those who are open to this possibility. It will never be caught on camera, unless it wants to be. Since they do not face the constraint of seeking mainstream approval, Bigfoot paranormalists are relatively free to follow their own idiosyncratic interests and theories, wherever they may lead. Consequently, Bigfoot paranormalists tend to be open to multiple paranormal subjects, rather than focusing solely on undiscovered animals.

The motivations of the Bigfoot naturalists exemplify those of Insiders within a deviant subculture. Insiders message about their deviance by promoting affinity with respected societal institutions such as religion, family, science, or medicine (narrative fidelity) and by downplaying aspects of the subculture that threaten the public plausibility of that message of conventionality (narrative coherence).

In contrast, the motivations of Bigfoot paranormalists fit squarely with what we expect among Outsiders. While they are just as passionate about subcultural concerns as Insiders, Outsiders feel no pressure to sanitize their beliefs for a mainstream audience. They follow the muse, *wherever* it leads.

While our observations of the Bigfoot subculture over several years suggest an alignment between Bigfoot naturalists and paranormalists with our conceptions of Insiders and Outsiders, more systematic empirical analyses are needed to see if the patterns we observed in ethnographic research represent wider trends in the subculture. To see whether this was the case, we created and collected original surveys of attendees at a major Bigfoot conference, allowing us to categorize respondents as Insiders, Outsiders, Hiders, and Drifters. This allowed us to examine the extent to which deviance management styles are related to different orientations about the nature of Bigfoot.

TEXAS BIGFOOT RESEARCH CONFERENCE

It might be surprising to those who imagine Bigfoot as a creature that roams the Pacific Northwest to learn that Texas ranks seventh in the United States in reported encounters.[43] Most of these encounters arise from east Texas, much of which is heavily wooded, swampy, and sparsely inhabited. In 2009, a Bigfoot research organization then known as the Texas Bigfoot Research Conservancy (TBRC) held a public conference in Tyler, Texas, as a fundraiser for the group. At the time, we had been conducting ethnographic research with members of the TBRC for several years, attending group meetings, conducting informal interviews and join-ing them on field investigations.[44] As part of our ongoing research, they graciously agreed to let us conduct a survey of attendees at their annual conference.

We created a survey that asked a host of questions about the respondents, their involvement in the Bigfoot subculture and their beliefs about the nature of what they called "wood apes." We distributed the surveys to attendees when they regis-tered for the conference and provided reminders throughout the day to return them to a table outside the auditorium. The survey was voluntary, but we ulti-mately managed to get 191 completed questionnaires returned.

The data provide an unparalleled glimpse into the Bigfoot subculture, particu-larly Bigfoot naturalism, which was definitely the orientation of the TBRC. Speakers at the conference that year included the previously mentioned Esteban Sarmiento and John Bindernagel. Other speakers also were wildlife biologists, including TBRC member Alton Higgins and Olympic Project member John Mioncynzki. Talks focused entirely upon the presentation of evidence for the existence of an undiscovered biological species. There was not a hint of Bigfoot paranormalism to be found on the official schedule.

As we would expect from Bigfoot naturalists, the TBRC has both repeatedly distanced itself from the paranormal elements of the subculture and attempted to present its quest as purely scientific in nature. When asked during an interview what he would say to those researchers who believe Bigfoot has paranormal abili-ties, the group's "field operations coordinator," Daryl Colyer, responded: "Nothing, except that's all hocus-pocus. We think it's a flesh and blood animal."[45]

Ultimately, the group changed its name, from the Texas Bigfoot Research Con-servancy to the North American Wood Ape Conservancy (NAWAC). The press release for the new moniker explicitly outlines the goals of Bigfoot naturalists, describes the group's strategies for deviance management, and provides a stark contrast to the stated views of the Psychic Sasquatch group presented earlier. It, too, is worth quoting at length:

> In 1958, construction worker Jerry Crew discovered some large footprints in the dry, dusty Northern California soil and a legend was born. Crew's find was eventually related to the world via the Humboldt Times along with the name he and the rest of his work team had given to the maker of those tracks: Bigfoot.
>
> In the years that have followed, the name of this one individual (whoever or whatever it was) has come to stand for the entire phenomenon of large, hairy bipedal figures seen by people all over North America and the world, even though, in the minds of many, "Bigfoot" remains a solitary, presumably magical creature along the lines of the Tooth Fairy or Jack Frost. Eventually, the term "Bigfoot" was appropri-ated by the media as a proxy for the humorously improbable interests of simpletons and not the concern of serious, practical people.
>
> Our organization's mission is to help establish and conserve "Bigfoot"—through a partnership with governmental, academic and scientific interests—as what we

believe it is: an extant population of higher primates living in the forests and wild places of North America. In the course of our work we have found that using the popular vernacular often raises barriers when attempting to engage those outside our specific field of interest. "Bigfoot" is not something serious people, they feel, apply effort towards. It's a phenomenon that belongs to tabloids, late-night comedians and scoffing network news anchors.

In response, we have adopted the term "wood ape" as a name for the animal because that's what all our observations and experiences tell us it is. Neither a joke nor a myth, but a living, breathing primate species deserving of protection and study.

Jerry Crew's discovery may have created the legend, but the animal behind it has existed on this continent from a time far earlier than 1958. How much longer it's allowed to survive and thrive alongside man is very likely dependent on establishing it as real. Whatever helps us do that must be done, up to and including unmooring ourselves from a legendary, often ridiculed, name.

To that end, after long consideration by and following a unanimous vote of this organization's Board of Directors, we are pleased to announce that from this point forward, the Texas Bigfoot Research Conservancy (TBRC) shall be known as the North American Wood Ape Conservancy (NAWAC). While we recognize changing how language is used is a long and perhaps quixotic endeavor, we feel that the needs of this amazing species are poorly served by the silly patina that has accreted over the term "Bigfoot."

Hopefully, our efforts or the efforts of others will make the North American wood ape a serious topic. We believe changing the very words we use while getting there is an important part of that process.[46]

When members of the TBRC-turned-NAWAC were featured on the finale of the first season of the celebrity paranormal reality television show *The Lowe Files*—starring actor Rob Lowe and his two sons John Owen and Matthew—the group's appeal to conventionality through scientific rhetoric and mainstream credentialing paid dividends in how they were perceived by the Lowes and thus also the viewing audience. On the way to meet NAWAC members to venture into what the group calls "Area X" in search of Bigfoot,[47] the Lowes discussed the credibility of their guides:

John Owen Lowe: Who are we meeting right now?

Matthew Lowe: The Wood Ape Conservancy.

JOL: It's a society, right? And are they like legitimate scientists? Do they have degrees and are they . . . smart?

ML: They all have like PhDs and stuff.[48]

JOL: These people are learned scholars?

ML: Like literally from universities.

Sitting around a campfire in the dense forests of the Ouachita Mountains in eastern Oklahoma, John Owen Lowe talked with NAWAC members Brian Brown and Daryl Colyer about the organization's name change:

> JOL: I mean, here's my real question. So why wood ape? Why is it not Sasquatch or Bigfoot? Why wood ape?
>
> Brian Brown: Primarily we call them wood apes because we believe them to be apes and they live in the woods. We don't use Bigfoot because Bigfoot is a joke.
>
> Daryl Colyer: It's cartoonish.
>
> BB: It has a connotation to it.
>
> JOL: It has a stigma.
>
> BB: Right. It's a pejorative term.
>
> JOL: Wood apes sound more natural, more authentic.
>
> BB: We also want to, sort of release the stigma that these are somehow, mythical monsters, right? So a wood ape just sounds like an animal, right?
>
> DC: Which is what we think this is. It's not a myth for us.

The strongly naturalistic orientation of Bigfoot presented by the group on its website and its invited lineup of speakers to the annual conference works against our ability to find true Outsiders in the survey data from the TBRC (later NAWAC) conference. Someone with a strong Bigfoot paranormalist orientation would have found little of interest in the conference. A local newspaper writer was not shy in expressing his disappointment about the button-down nature and Insider proclivities of the event: "Bigfoot is boring. Correction. Bigfoot conferences are boring. Bigfoot could not be boring if the conference speakers weren't so dull. Heck, most of them were barely breathing. . . . And I guess that's what the conference was all about, attempts to prove that Bigfoot . . . does live someplace other than in legend. Actually what they're trying to do is get mainstream science to admit . . . that the creature lives in Texas and other states."[49]

But while the TBRC could control its content, anyone could attend. Thus, while the data skews toward Bigfoot naturalists, there was nonetheless enough variation in the sample of attendees to test whether and how differences in conventional and deviant identities affect strategies of deviance management for Bigfoot believers. The data we collected provide the necessary items to measure deviant identity via the depth of subcultural involvement, as well as a composite measure of stakes in conformity based on demographic indicators. Using these two measures, we can see whether Insiders, Outsiders, Hiders, and Drifters who attended this event do indeed express different ideas about the nature of Bigfoot.

Conventional Identity: Commitment to Normalcy

To measure conventionality, we use items that tap the extent to which the respondent has demonstrated a commitment to conforming goals and, therefore, faces higher costs for being labeled as deviant.[50] First, we asked if the respondent is currently married, which suggests alignment with conventional ideas about family, as well as the presence of a spouse who may or may not approve of involvement with a deviant subculture. Approximately 60 percent of respondents were married at the time of the survey. A college degree suggests a level of commitment to achievement by conventional standards, so we also asked if respondents had achieved a bachelor's degree or higher. Approximately one-fourth of respondents were college graduates. Another risk of participating in deviance is the loss of a high-paying job should the subculture member's beliefs be seen as discreditable or too embarrassing for the employer.[51] Responses indicated that the top one-fourth of our sample earned $100,000 or more per year. We coded this top quartile as high earners.

Combining these three items produces a conventional identity index that ranges from 0 to 3. Those who receive a 0 on this index have comparatively less to lose by openly pursuing deviance. They have not invested heavily in education, are not currently married, and do not have a high level of income. Those who score a 3 on this index have more to lose should their Bigfoot pursuits become a source of shaming; they risk a marriage, a high-income occupation, and the sunk costs they have invested in education. The average score for respondents on this measure was 1.5.

Deviant Identity: Involvement in the Bigfoot Subculture

Our survey of attendees at the TBRC conference included a number of questions gauging respondents' levels of engagement with the Bigfoot subculture. Several of these items were indicators of a casual interest in the subject. We asked respondents how often they had purchased Bigfoot books or magazines, watched Bigfoot documentaries on television, and visited blogs, websites, and/or forums related to the subject. From simple *consumption* of information produced by the subculture, we moved on to questions about direct involvement in cultural *production*. For example, we asked respondents how often they posted materials on Bigfoot-related blogs and forums.

Some enthusiasts progress from simply consuming or producing media to actively searching for Bigfoot. We also asked respondents how often they have "engaged in a field operation (i.e., entered the field to search for evidence of Bigfoot)," and how often they had attempted a practice known as "call blasting," where hunters try to solicit a response from a Sasquatch via shouts and recordings.[52] Finally, we asked respondents if they were official members of a Bigfoot research organization.

Engaging in any of these activities (and surely one's presence at the conference) is a sign of some level of involvement with the Bigfoot subculture. The greater the frequency of such activities, the more commitment there is to the subculture. But different activities also signal different *levels* of engagement. Reading books,

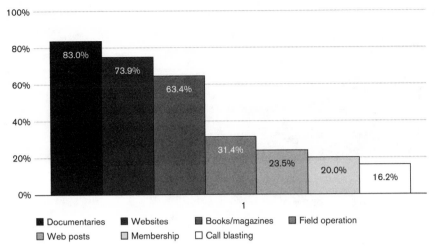

FIGURE 3. Participation in Bigfoot subculture activities. (Source: 2009 Texas Bigfoot Research Conservancy Conference Survey)

watching documentaries, and visiting websites are relatively low investments of time and money. Posting on Bigfoot blogs and forums signals a greater desire to interact with the Bigfoot community, but the ability to remain anonymous on some forums still limits the "outness" of such engagement. Once researchers join an organization and actively enter the field to search for and communicate with Bigfoot, they incur far greater costs in their time and resources, spending money on membership fees, travel, and equipment. Increasing subcultural investment also makes it more difficult to hide one's deviance from others, leading to a greater likelihood of incurring social costs.

Responses to the survey demonstrate the relative rarity of such higher-cost activities (see figure 3).[53] The vast majority of respondents engaged in lower levels of involvement in Bigfootry, such as watching documentaries (83 percent), reading books and magazines (74 percent) and visiting websites (63 percent). Far fewer respondents, however, engaged in comparatively higher-cost activities, such as field operations (31 percent), posting in Bigfoot forums (24 percent) and call blasting (16 percent). Only 20 percent of conference attendees were members of a Bigfoot organization.

We combined these items into a composite measure of deviant identity. To account for the higher cost associated with some activities, we standardized all items and assigned a higher weight to the comparatively rare forms of engagement (web postings, field operations, call blasting, and organizational membership). Once weighted and combined, our final deviant identity metric had high internal measurement reliability.[54] Someone who scores high on this measure is deeply

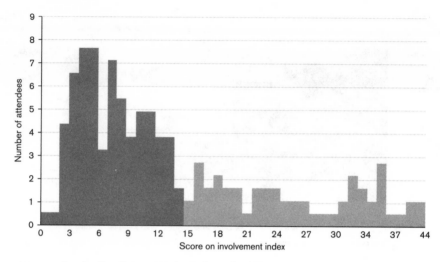

FIGURE 4. Levels of involvement in the Bigfoot subculture. (Source: 2009 Texas Bigfoot Research Conservancy Conference Survey)

involved in the Bigfoot subculture, combining frequent engagement in low-cost activities, such as watching Bigfoot documentaries, with more costly activities such as organizational membership and field operations (see figure 4). Those at the lower end of the measure are primarily participating in low-cost forms of subcultural engagement.

Deviance Management Strategies within the Bigfoot Subculture

We split the sample into Drifters, Hiders, Outsiders, and Insiders by determining who had higher and lower levels of investment in conventional and deviant identity. We characterized individuals as having a higher level of conventional identity if they had two or more of our markers of conventionality (currently married, four-year college degree and high income). We counted an individual as having a high level of deviant identity if they were above the mean on our measure of involvement in the Bigfoot subculture. This classification divided the sample into: 33 percent Drifters, 31 percent Hiders, 20 percent Outsiders, and 16 percent Insiders.

The Nature of the Beast

We asked respondents to the survey about their agreement with several statements regarding the nature of Bigfoot, some of which reflected a naturalistic orientation and some of which reflected a paranormal orientation:

1. Bigfoot is an unknown species of primate.
2. Bigfoot is a relic hominid, such as a Neanderthal.

3. Bigfoot has exceptional abilities that it uses to mask its existence (such as psychic powers, the ability to become invisible, or the ability to generate fear).
4. Bigfoot is somehow related to the UFO phenomenon.
5. Bigfoot has the ability to slip into another dimension or plane of existence.
6. Bigfoot is just one manifestation of a larger phenomenon. Bigfoot could appear as another creature if desired.
7. Most Bigfoot encounters are the result of hoaxes or misidentifications.

The first and second statements clearly reflect a Bigfoot naturalist orientation. Statements three through six capture some of the variety of ways that Bigfoot paranormalists connect the phenomenon to other paranormal topics. Given the possibility that some skeptics might be in attendance at the conference, we also included the last statement, which allowed respondents to attribute Bigfoot encounters to hoaxes and misidentifications.

Responses to these questions reflect the naturalistic orientation of this particular conference. Nearly three-fourths of respondents agreed or strongly agreed that Bigfoot is an undiscovered primate. Only a small minority of respondents were willing to endow Bigfoot with paranormal powers, with 12 percent believing that the creature has extraordinary powers and even fewer believing that Bigfoot is related to UFOs (7 percent), an interdimensional traveler (7 percent) or a shapeshifter (4 percent).

Despite these high levels of agreement about the nature of Bigfoot, we do find meaningful differences between deviance management strategies when we ask respondents to be more specific and choose what they believe to be the "single best explanation" for Bigfoot. Here we grouped respondents by whether they believe that hoaxes and misidentifications, a naturalistic explanation (an undiscovered primate or relic hominoid) or a paranormal explanation (UFOs, dimensional travel, or a shapeshifter) is the best explanation for Bigfoot reports. We also gave respondents the option to report "something else" as the best explanation for Bigfoot. *All* of the Insiders (100 percent) selected a naturalistic explanation to describe the nature of Bigfoot. In contrast, the *only* respondents who selected a paranormal version of Bigfoot as the best explanation were Outsiders.

Drifters and Hiders share a low commitment to a deviant subculture. That comparatively lower level of commitment is apparent in their selection of the best explanation for Bigfoot. No Outsiders or Insiders reported that hoaxes or misidentifications are the best explanation for Bigfoot, but nearly 15 percent of Hiders and 13 percent of Drifters reported that they actually find little merit in the idea of Bigfoot. Drifters and Hiders also displayed more idiosyncratic views than did Outsiders or Insiders. About 5 percent of Drifters and Hiders reported that the options provided did not capture their beliefs about Bigfoot and selected our "other" option.

The ideological differences seen between Insiders, Outsiders, Drifters, and Hiders would naturally have been much more pronounced if we had collected data at a conference that had material of interest to both the Bigfoot naturalist and Bigfoot paranormalist camps, such as the Sasquatch Summit. Yet despite this constraint, different deviance management styles are still evident in the distribution of varying ideas about the nature of Bigfoot.

Occultist or Bigfoot Hunter?

A meaningful distinction among paranormal believers is *how many* paranormal subjects they express belief in.[55] Skeptics discount all paranormal phenomena such as ghosts, Bigfoot, psychic powers, and UFOs. Others, paranormal particularists, express strong belief, but limit their interest to only one subject. We have met paranormalists who argue passionately for the reality of extraterrestrials, for example, but wonder how anyone could be gullible enough to believe in ghosts. At the other end of the spectrum are paranormal generalists, for whom the paranormal is akin to a cultural buffet. These believers combine beliefs about monsters, some ghostly phenomena, psychics, UFOs, and Atlantis all into an idiosyncratic, personalized mix.

Economist Laurence Iannaccone argues that the latter approach, believing in many different things at once, is a natural tendency of humans. We are risk averse; therefore, people should be inclined to invest themselves in multiple different belief systems simultaneously. By spreading their time, energy, and money over multiple interests, one minimizes the risk of betting everything on a single pursuit. Should one religious or paranormal phenomenon prove false, a diversifier still has "stock" in another. The concept is similar to what financial advisors recommend to their clients; putting all of one's resources in a single investment is too risky. Diversifying is the safest bet.[56]

However, Iannaccone notes that people face social constraints that limit this natural tendency toward diversification. For instance, strict, exclusivist religious groups demand high commitment from their members in terms of time, money, and other resources, and will be highly motivated to prevent members from sharing those resources with other groups. Strict religious groups actively discourage, and sometimes demonize, beliefs that fall outside of their purview. This keeps members from diversifying if they want to remain members in good stead. Indeed, there is a strong positive relationship between religious beliefs and experiences and paranormalism—but only outside of belonging to strict religious groups. People who belong to strict religious groups were much more likely to claim no paranormal beliefs, and if they did believe in paranormal subjects, they believed in significantly fewer of them than people belonging to less strict religions. Meanwhile, for those not strongly tethered to an exclusivist religious group, religious and paranormal beliefs and experiences had a strong, positive relationship to each other.[57]

Conventionality, writ large, can act as a similar constraint upon the diversity of deviant beliefs individuals will hold. A person who risks a high-paying career, investment in higher education, or important social attachments by being branded as deviant will be less likely to express *any* deviant beliefs, at least openly. But if a person *is* a committed member of a deviant subculture, conventionality will limit the breadth of that expression. In these cases, individuals will focus on those aspects of the subculture that demonstrate the greatest *narrative fidelity* with existing social systems and avoid investing in marginal aspects of a subculture or experimenting with other deviant subcultures in an effort to bolster the *narrative coherence* of deviance normalization efforts.

Regarding the Bigfoot subculture, we would expect members with highly salient conventional identities (Insiders and Hiders) to express lower levels of belief in other paranormal phenomena. To do so challenges the narrative of Insiders that they are interested in Bigfoot as a scientific discovery, and suggests instead that they are interested in the "occult" more generally.

To see if there were different profiles of paranormal belief depending on deviance management type, we created an index of belief in varied paranormal phenomena. On the survey we asked respondents whether they agreed or disagreed that the following phenomena were real: a coming "New Age," Atlantis, the ability to move objects with one's mind (telekinesis), psychics' ability to foretell the future, astrology, communicating with the dead, and having prophetic dreams. Respondents were coded as 1 if they believed in the reality of these phenomena and 0 if they did not believe. We then summed the items to create a paranormal belief index ranging from 0 to 7.

The results (see figure 4.3) support our hypotheses about the style of paranormalism most likely to be adopted by individuals with varying deviance management orientations. Outsiders had the highest number of average paranormal beliefs (3.3), followed by Drifters (3.0). In contrast, paranormal beliefs were significantly lower for Hiders (1.9) and Insiders (1.8). The fact that Insiders were the lowest overall speaks to the normalization strategy of specializing in beliefs in certain paranormal phenomena while rejecting others. Insiders passionately believe in Bigfoot but distance themselves from other paranormal subjects. Outsiders also believe passionately in Bigfoot, but simultaneously believe in a broader paranormal world, filled with all kinds of unexplained entities and phenomena. This pattern follows from differential stakes in conformity.

Killing Bigfoot

In recent years, one of the most heated debates within the Bigfoot world has been about whether a Sasquatch should be killed if the opportunity presents itself. The so-called pro-kill/no-kill debate.[58] The no-kill camp believes it would be immoral to kill what may be one of the last members of an exceedingly rare species. Further,

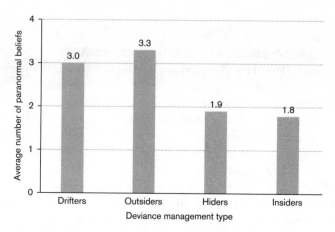

FIGURE 5. Average number of paranormal beliefs by deviance
management type. (Source: 2009 Texas Bigfoot Research Conservancy
Conference Survey; p <.01 for One-Way ANOVA)

shooting a Bigfoot may be tantamount to murder, should it prove to be a species
closely akin to humans. The pro-kill camp argues that the best way to protect an
endangered species is to prove conclusively, once-and-for-all, its existence. Photos
and footprint casts will never satisfy the skeptics.

The NAWAC appreciates the importance of a specimen to prove Bigfoot's existence to mainstream science. As stated on the group's online FAQ: "[T]here is an
established scientific method for the recognition of new animal species. There are
very few examples of an animal being listed through photographs or even DNA
evidence alone. A specimen is required. As such, the North American Wood Ape
Conservancy is actively proceeding with plans to obtain irrefutable definitive proof
to secure recognition of the existence of this large undocumented primate species."[59]

Similarly, The Gulf Coast Bigfoot Research Organization, a pro-kill group,
starred in a related television show called *Killing Bigfoot*.

Insiders are pulled in two directions—dedicated to a deviant subculture, but
constrained by conventionality. The optimal way to resolve this tension is to successfully legitimate one's deviant pursuit to the outside world. Therefore, we would
expect Insiders in the Bigfoot subculture to be the most motivated to resolve this
conflict quickly and definitively by killing a Bigfoot. Indeed, we find that compared to the other three deviance-management types, Insiders are much more
likely to believe that killing Bigfoot is necessary. When asked if "researchers are
going to have to kill a Bigfoot to prove its existence," nearly two-thirds (64 percent)
of Insiders agreed, compared to half or less of Outsiders, Drifters, and Hiders (see
figure 6).

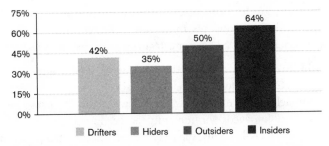

FIGURE 6. Support for killing Bigfoot by deviance management type. (Source: 2009 Texas Bigfoot Research Conservancy Conference Survey; p <.05 for chi-square value)

BIGFOOT AMONG THE ALIENS: THE INTERNATIONAL UFO CONGRESS

Considering conventional and deviant identities in conjunction provides insight into different types of subcultural participants, even within a sample of respondents who already lean toward a particular end of the broader subculture by virtue of attending a Bigfoot naturalist conference. Indeed, this represents a rather conservative test of our hypotheses. But beyond differences *within* a subculture, focusing on deviance management can also help explain differences *across* deviant subcultures. To explore this aspect of our framework, we compared attendees at the TBRC conference to Bigfoot believers who undoubtedly hew closer to paranormal views of the beast. To do this, we collected additional primary data from attendees at the 2010 International UFO Congress (IUFOC) convention in Laughlin, Nevada. The IUFOC is listed in the Guinness Book of World Records as "the world's largest UFO convention."[60]

While the conference is clearly geared toward UFOlogy rather cryptozoology, it nonetheless presented a general paranormal approach and IUFOC conferences have often included Bigfoot paranormalists as featured speakers, such as Kewaunee Lapseritis from the Psychic Sasquatch group.[61] As with the TBRC conference, we distributed questionnaires to attendees in their registration packets and collected the surveys just outside the main convention hall and vendor area. Although we did not have as much assistance from the IUFOC in encouraging participation in the survey as we did from the TBRC, we nevertheless managed to gather 156 completed surveys from attendees at the IUFOC conference. In order to make more meaningful comparisons to the TBRC attendees, we only use data from IUFOC conference attendees who reported believing in Bigfoot (n = 126).[62]

We posed some of the same questions about paranormal beliefs and experiences to the IUFOC attendees as we did to the TBRC attendees, providing unique primary data that allow for comparisons across a wide range of Bigfoot believers. Specifically, we asked respondents from both conferences about the following beliefs and experiences (coded answer categories are in parentheses):

- It is possible to communicate with the dead (agree, do not agree).
- Do ghosts exist? (absolutely, all other responses)
- We are approaching an entirely new age that will radically change our view of science, spiritual knowledge or humanity (agree, do not agree).
- Ancient advanced civilizations, such as Atlantis, once existed (agree, do not agree).
- It is possible to influence the physical world through the mind alone (agree, do not agree).
- Have you ever consulted a horoscope to get an idea about the course of your life? (yes, no)
- Have you ever called or consulted a medium, fortune teller, or psychic? (yes, no)
- Have you ever witnessed a UFO? (yes, no)
- I have seen a creature that I believe was Bigfoot (yes, no).

We began by comparing beliefs about paranormal phenomena other than Bigfoot or UFOs across attendees at the two conferences. Belief in ghosts and the possibility of communicating with the dead is much higher among Bigfoot believers at the IUFOC conference (62 percent and 78 percent, respectively) compared to those at the TBRC conference (33 percent and 28 percent, respectively). A similar pattern is evident for believing that we are living in a "New Age," that advanced ancient civilizations such as Atlantis existed, and that telekinesis is real. Nearly all of the Bigfoot believers at the IUFOC conference believed in a New Age (89 percent), Atlantis (98 percent), and telekinesis (90 percent). The percentages were much lower for TBRC attendees (56 percent, 59 percent, and 31 percent, respectively).

The same is true for paranormal practices such as consulting horoscopes or visiting psychics (see figure 7). Far fewer TBRC conference attendees reported consulting horoscopes (24 percent) compared to Bigfoot believers at the IUFOC conference (65 percent). An even greater disparity was evident for consulting psychics, with 70 percent of IUFOC Bigfoot believers having done so, compared to just 14 percent of those attending the TBRC conference.

A final way of comparing Bigfoot believers from these different conferences is to see how many at each claim the primary experience of the other. In other words, how many Sasquatch-believing attendees at the UFO conference claim to have encountered Bigfoot? Conversely, how many attendees at the TBRC conference who believe in aliens claim to have seen a UFO? The differences are striking (see figure 8). The percentage of Bigfoot-believing attenders at the IUFOC

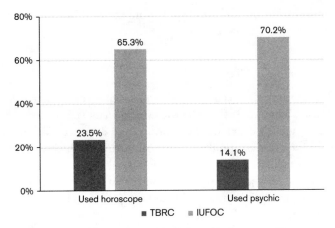

FIGURE 7. Use of horoscopes and psychics. (Sources: 2009 Texas Bigfoot Research Conservancy Conference Survey and 2010 International UFO Congress Conference Survey)

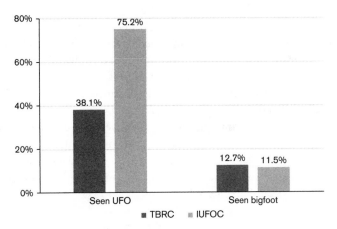

FIGURE 8. Seeing UFOs and Bigfoot. (Sources: 2009 Texas Bigfoot Research Conservancy Conference Survey and 2010 International UFO Congress Conference Survey)

conference who claim to have experienced a personal encounter with Sasquatch (12 percent) is essentially the same as the percentage of attendees at the TBRC conference who claimed to have had a visual encounter with Bigfoot (13 percent). In sharp contrast, 75 percent of attendees at the IUFOC conference claim to have seen a UFO in the sky, compared to only 38 percent of TBRC conference attendees who said they "absolutely" believe in extraterrestrials.[63] The disparities reported are even greater when comparing Insiders from the TBRC conference to Bigfoot believers at the IUFOC conference.

THE BEAST OF BURDEN

Many factors produce disagreements and factions within deviant subcultures. One primary cause of conflict is the extent to which members must simultaneously manage the competing demands of conformity and deviance. Within the Bigfoot subculture, this tension has resulted in two competing and highly distinctive subgroups: Bigfoot naturalists and Bigfoot paranormalists. Both groups are equally passionate about their quest and equally convinced about the reality of Bigfoot. Should you choose to join a group of Bigfoot researchers in the woods, you might be in the midst of a group of heavily armed men looking to shoot an undiscovered primate or in a contemplative circle of people holding hands in preparation to "mindspeak" with a nature spirit. Knowing in advance whether these hypothetical Bigfoot hunters are Insiders or Outsiders would undoubtedly provide advance warning about the experience to follow.

Applied to the case of the Bigfoot subculture in North America, our proposed framework for understanding deviance management shows predictive efficacy on a range of subjects, including messaging, ideological and behavioral strategies of deviance management, and explanation of subcultural conflicts. It also shows flexibility by providing insight into differences *within* as well as *across* subcultures. In this sense, our framework for understanding deviance management can be successfully applied at varying levels of analysis, whether narrowing or broadening in scope.[64] Likewise, both quantitative and qualitative research support our basic hypotheses. In many ways, our ethnographic fieldwork within and observations of the Bigfoot subculture were the original source of our broader ideas about deviance management. But to test the wider applicability of these ideas and refine their accuracy, we must examine other subcultures, such as LGBTQ communities.

5

Sexuality and Gender Identity

Assimilation vs. Liberation

Views of sexuality and gender have undergone a substantial transformation in American society, both in the extent to which the public condemns or accepts same-gender sexual relations and in the legalization of same-sex marriage. In 2013, fully 95 percent of LGBT Americans said that compared to ten years prior, social acceptance of sexual and gender minorities had increased and 94 percent believed acceptance would continue to increase. Of course, extensive homophobia and discrimination persist. The same survey showed that 30 percent of LGBT individuals in the United States had been threatened or physically attacked because of their sexuality and 60 percent had been subjected to verbal abuse.[1] Rates of victimization were even higher among gay men specifically. At the same time, there clearly have been some processes of relative normalization for sexual and gender minorities, as evidenced by the declining proportion of Americans who view same-gender sexual relations as moral damnation.

The combination of continued stigmatization and increasing acceptance poses a number of dilemmas for self-presentation among people with same-sex attraction, behavior, and identity—along with gender nonconformists. Which people, if any, should I be "out" to? Should I participate in movements for LGBT rights? Should I accentuate my differences or sameness to heteronormative culture, institutions, and people? While not all decision-making about sexuality, identity, and interpersonal relationships will or can be done this deliberately beforehand, individuals and groups must nevertheless find ways to provide answers to questions of personal identity and provide some guidance on strategies for integrating sexuality and gender identity into social relationships. Identity narratives are how organizations and individuals provide answers to these questions.[2]

In addition to wrestling with these issues of engaging conventional society, LGBTQ individuals also face framing conflicts within communities of sexual and gender minorities. Some argue that the best way to combat LGBTQ discrimination is to work within existing political structures to achieve rights afforded to other citizens, such as the right to marry or serve in the military. Commonly called *assimilationists*, this strategy seeks to demonstrate that gay, lesbian, bisexual and transgender individuals are valuable, moral citizens who positively contribute to mainstream society by raising families, holding high-status occupations, and giving back to their communities. Put another way, a true assimilation argument would claim that sexual minorities are just like everyone else, absent sexuality (and/or gender). *Assimilationists* use *narrative fidelity* in an attempt to convince others of their nondeviant status. *Liberationists*, on the other hand, believe it is futile to work within the same patriarchal, conservative, and oppressive systems that have caused so much suffering and discrimination for LGBTQ communities and people. Rather than trying to fit into those systems, liberationists argue that sexual and gender minorities should reject the status quo and demand to be accepted on their own terms.[3]

Sociologist Amin Ghaziani characterizes LGBT movements in the United States as oscillating between phases of emphasizing sameness and difference with mainstream society: "Numerous studies have shown that LGBT activists oscillate between collective identities that alternately celebrate and suppress their differences from the straight majority."[4] Further, Ghaziani's ethnographic fieldwork and cultural content analyses of LGBT movements shows that not only do the different strategies of Insiders and Outsiders cause subcultural conflict, such conflicts are extremely important in the formation, narrativizing, and maintenance of identities centered on gender and sexuality.[5] In this sense the heat from Insider vs. Outsider conflicts can produce some proverbial light. But such conflicts can also produce disintegration and subcultural fracture.

In the language of our framework, we would classify *assimilation* and *liberation* as two distinct deviance management styles used by Insiders and Outsiders, respectively. We test whether this is the case by examining patterns in the adoption of assimilation or liberation strategies among people who identify as LGBTQ. To do this we analyze two datasets that have measures for both conventionality and subcultural identity, while also containing relevant outcomes of interest, such as views about how to achieve LGBT rights and levels of participation in social activism. To illustrate themes in liberationist narratives, we also use interview excerpts from an Outsider: a self-described "radical queer."

Assimilationist and liberationist factions within sexual minority subcultures align with the messaging techniques we expect to be used by Insiders and Outsiders (see chapter 3). Individuals who are simultaneously committed to both conventionality and a deviant subculture (Insiders) will be under pressure to resolve the dissonance between these identities. Someone who is strongly attached to conventional people, highly dedicated to a conventional occupation, and committed to beliefs (religious or otherwise) that align with conventional morality systems has much to lose by being branded as deviant. Consequently, Insiders are more likely to be invested in convincing those beyond the subculture that the deviance in question is not as threatening or immoral as has been portrayed. The best way to achieve this goal is by claiming allegiance with existing normative systems ("gay is just another form of family") (narrative fidelity) and presenting a cohesive message that deemphasizes aspects of a subculture that threaten an image of "normalcy" (narrative coherence).

In this chapter, we explore five research questions related to deviance management:

1) How do strategies of stigma management vary depending on stakes in conformity and stakes in culturally stigmatized identities?

2) How do differing strategies of stigma management affect individuals' perceived goals for, framing of, and participation in social movements for LGBT rights?

3) How do differing deviance management styles produce subcultural conflict?

4) How do the patterns and prevalence of deviance management strategies change under varying levels of repression and punishment?

5) What are some of the most prominent themes in the narratives of Outsiders?

In addressing these questions, we want to highlight differences within particular sexual and gender *identities*, as well as within LGBTQ subcultures. In a modest sense, we hope this pushes against essentialist understandings of sexuality and gender, even if, unintentionally, we are essentializing about deviance management. There are clearly a number of critical dimensions of complex, intersectional sexuality and gender identities that we do not focus on—such as race and ethnicity, health and disability, and age and the life course, to name only a few—but we hope our analyses nonetheless provide insights into specific aspects of the diversity that exists within and among LGBTQ individuals and communities.

PORTRAIT OF AN OUTSIDER: MATTILDA

We've come to terms with our deviance, our defiance, our love for fucking and flowers.[6]

"Queer" theories and movements—which generally assume *liberationist* stances—frame issues and debates about sexuality in ways that raise poignant questions about deviance itself, particularly about normative assumptions, social change, and academic pursuits such as our own. For instance, can reform movements predicated on "queerness" (or an analogous label) truly be translated into new normative structures without becoming oppressive themselves? How can a movement aimed at undermining rigid identity categories articulate normative identities?[7] Or more philosophically, what happens when queer theory itself transitions from marginal to normative?[8]

The personal narrative of Mattilda (a.k.a. Matt) Bernstein Sycamore, a self-identified queer writer and activist, speaks to these questions in poignant ways. Mattilda describes herself "As an incest survivor who survived the abuse by retreating into my head and becoming the ultimate overachiever student." This is evident in her lucid, evocative writing style. But she self-consciously chose to reduce her investment in conventional society, leaving Brown University after only one year, because: "I realized I was just learning how to beat my parents on their own terms—instead, I wanted to reject the terms, and so at age nineteen I moved to San Francisco to find radical outsider queers, sluts, vegans, anarchists, direct action activists, incest survivors, runaways, drug addicts, freaks, and whores desperate to create alternatives to the status quo in the glorious ruins of our own lives."[9]

Mattilda's writings, such as her memoir *The End of San Francisco*, and editing, in provocative volumes such as *Nobody Passes, Why Are Faggots So Afraid of Faggots?* and *That's Revolting: Queer Strategies for Resisting Assimilation*, give voice to Outsider narratives and identities. The rhetorical framing of sexuality and politics offered within such texts illustrates some of the primary themes in liberationist messaging. In terms of activism, Mattilda's participation in ACT UP, Fed Up Queers (FUQ), and Gay Shame groups highlight some of the subcultural tensions and dynamics facing liberationists.

We would expect Outsiders to accentuate their differences from conventional society, stressing narrative *infidelity*, as it were. In doing so, Outsiders will be likely to adopt a "better than" stance toward conventional society. Such a stance puts Outsiders at odds not only with conventional society, but also with reform-minded assimilationists.

This is evident in Mattilda's experiences. When asked to describe her identity, Mattilda actively reclaims labels used to stigmatize LGBTQ individuals; a strategy of linguistic reappropriation.[10] "If I had to do it in one little statement it would be: 'A gender queer, faggot, and a queen, on the trans continuum, in a gender blur kind of place.' But the words I relate to the most are probably 'faggot' and 'Queen.' 'Queer' would be more of a broader political identity."[11] These labels are not just about sexuality, but identity: "When I identify as 'queer,' it is just not about being queer sexually, it is about being queer in every way: It is a way of creating alternatives to mainstream notions of love, who you fuck, what you look like, how you eat, and how you live."[12] In effect this means adopting a radically intersectional understanding of social inequality and integrating those concerns into personal identity and activism: "My politics as a queer person have always been centered on challenging racism, classism, colonialism and imperialism, misogyny, and homophobia—all of that. . . . I'm much more interested in an intersectional analysis that comes from a core; one that says, 'I'm queer *and that means* fighting racism, fighting classism, fighting homophobia; you can't take them apart.'"[13]

For liberationists, commitment to resistance identities is of the utmost importance. For the truly committed, deviant identity and the rejection of conventionality are one and the same. The condemning world of conventionality is fully rejected: "I realized first that *I was never going to belong*, and then that *I didn't want to belong* with these people who were enacting this kind of violence: The violence of social exclusion, of compulsive masculinity and of class attainment."[14] In practice, this means openly and brazenly rejecting conventionality in its myriad forms: "Flamboyance has always been important to me as a form of resistance to a world that wants us all to blend into blandness and conformity."[15]

Such a radical identity and political stance is enacted by challenging entire normative structures rather than narrow topics, such as sexuality, in isolation from other forms of oppression: "The possibility of engaging in a queer politic, or a queer life, is in challenging all hierarchies . . . all the dominant norms . . . rather than a, sort of, smiling, happy, 'we're just like you' kind of spoon-fed normalcy."[16] In essence: "I am not interested in becoming part of those structures in any form. I don't even want my own structure. I believe in building something on the margins, whatever that means, and I am interested in infiltrating the mainstream media. I am interested in creating our own media structures, I am interested in creating radical alternatives, but not in terms of a narrow policy or legal framework."[17]

Mattilda states that, if social identity means "conforming to either the violence of straight, normative lives, or of the smiling, happy, 'we're just like you,' hyper-patriotic gay normalcy, then I think that's not worthwhile. If it is about conforming, then I'm not interested in it."[18] This formation of a resistance identity—a sense of self built on what one is *not*—results in criticism becoming a central mode of thought and action: "I have to be critical in order to stay alive. And being critical is what gives me hope."[19]

Fighting Normal: Liberationist Activism

The way I see it, assimilation is violence.[20]

To fight the power, liberationists must engage in direct-action protests against the status quo. An illustrative example is the clandestine Fed Up Queers (FUQ), a group started in the late-90s. "Fed Up Queers started in New York [City] after a group of about twenty of us had come together initially to do a political funeral for Matthew Shepard. In the end, we tried to form a large radical queer group, but that didn't happen; it broke down over process issues. But one sort of affinity group that emerged from the political funeral was Fed Up Queers."[21]

The group was small, underground and exclusive: "you had to be voted in by the whole group."[22] As a result, "loyalty was definitely a shared value of FUQ."[23] Members of FUQ were "very clear about wanting to focus our energy on actions, and not trying to create an organizational structure," to the extent that "one of the shared values of FUQ [was] action over discussion."[24] Members of the group performed direct-action protests using civil disobedience and publicity to advance a wide range of social justice causes. For example, in February 1999, FUQ members were the first people arrested in protests over the killing of Amadou Diallo—an unarmed immigrant who NYC police fired upon forty-one times. In response, FUQ members "chained themselves together to block traffic on lower Broadway."[25] Their actions inspired other citizens to protest the killing and daily demonstrations soon swelled to enormous crowds, with "More than a thousand men and women [being] arrested for protesting police misconduct and brutality in the case of Amadou Diallo."[26] Mattilda was a founding member of FUQ and said it "was a turning point for me, where I transitioned from being an activist who got involved in various struggles, to an organizer who saw myself as an instigator, willing to create my own activism."[27]

In addition to fighting conventional society, Outsiders also are likely to clash with reform-oriented Insiders. Recalling the history of the group, a former FUQ leader said, "One thing we definitely valued was not assimilating into the mainstream of homogenous culture. We felt that most of the lesbian/gay community was headed in that direction."[28] Outsider orientation provided the identity and messaging of the group: "The name itself is edgy. There's something about saying FUQ loudly that feels powerful. One of our chants, I'd say our favorite was, 'Fuck, fuck, fuck with us, and we'll FUQ, FUQ, FUQ with you!'"[29] The group became somewhat legendary and widely influential, as word of their deeds spread, with local chapters springing up in different locations, including in much more conservative places, like Arkansas (see image 3).

Formalizing her opposition to assimilationists, Mattilda also started Gay Shame in 1998, which grew out of "a group called the Fuck the Mayor [Rudy Giuliani] Collective."[30] Gay Shame attempted "to create a radical alternative to the conformity of gay neighborhoods, bars and institutions—most clearly symbolized by Gay Pride."[31]

Gay Shame emerged in New York as a challenge to the assimilationist agendas of mainstream pride celebrations. . . . It was our goal to challenge the violence of the happy gay consumer that lies beneath all of those glamorous, sweatshop-produced rainbow flags, Tiffany wedding bands, Grey Goose Cosmo-tinis, and all of the rabid consumption. Beneath all of that is the policing of the borders, as if to say, "Oh no, we don't want any trannies; we don't want any of those people of color; we don't want any homeless people; we don't want any of those youth, unless of course it's late at night and you need somebody to warm your bed." . . . So that's why we started. From there it has become a direct-action group wanting to challenge all hypocrisies.[32]

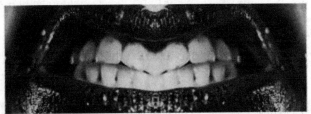

Darling... are you FED UP?!

Calling all Transfolk, Fags, Queers, Dykes, Gender Benders, Sex Workers, Trannies, Farries, Anarchists, Feminists, Queens, Sissies, Allies & Revolutionaries of all Shapes, Ages, Abilities, Colors & Genders (or lack of)

Tuesday June 30th @ 6:00

Main Library, Downtown

Fribourgh Room, 2nd floor

We are **FED UP** with the "gay mainstream", consumerism, capitalism, binaries, acronyms and state sanctioned institutions

E-mail us at FedUpQueers@RiseUp.net With any questions!

We aren't "just like you".
We are fabulous.
We are wonderful.
We are beautiful
We are **FED UP QUEERS**

Honey, won't you
Join us?

Visit:
FedUpQueers.WordPress.com
For more info!

IMAGE 3. Fed Up Queers (FUQ) in Arkansas Flyer.

For Mattilda, Gay Shame was "an opportunity to help build something transformative, deviant, and dangerous out of alienation and desperation."[33]

Like FUQ, Gay Shame eventually fractured due to internal conflict over a question "that had plagued us since the very beginning of Gay Shame: Who is 'our community?'"[34] Also like FUQ, Gay Shame spread beyond its origins, as similar performance groups arose in other places in the United States and other countries.[35] Reflecting on the origins of the movement, Mattilda said, "We were rejecting the worlds that rejected us."[36] This is the Outsider mantra. In practice this requires intense and sustained dedication to Outsider identity. Ironically this also often means subcultural exclusion as well:

Q: Can you talk about your "outsider" status within the gay community?
Mattilda: Well, first of all I don't believe that there is a gay community—or, to take the popular term of the moment, an "LGBT" community. I think this notion of a gay or LGBT community is so often used to oppress queers with the least access to power. . . . And when I was part of a protest outside of the LGBT Center, and Center staff called the cops because they didn't want queers protesting on their doorstep, then stood and watched as the cops beat us up—blood dripping down one person's face; I and several others were thrown into the middle of oncoming traffic—it's almost like my politics were proven too much. So, I don't have any illusions about gay community.[37]

The Conflict Within

This is the violence of assimilation—it robs people of their creativity, passion, critical engagement, analysis. I think the only way anyone can really exist in complex and liberatory ways is to basically ignore all the various ways our friends and enemies want us to silence ourselves in the service of a false consensus.[38]

In attempting to strike out against conventional society, as well as more reform-oriented minorities, radical liberationists fight for agency via creative destruction. They must do so in opposition to competing currents from both subcultures and conventional society. As Mattilda noted about LGBT rights movements: "One thing that is very different now than in the early 1990s is that back then there was a tension between the *gay* and *queer* cultures, between *assimilation* and a *liberationist perspective*, between a *narrow vision of gay identity* and a *broader vision* of fighting racism, militarism and homophobia, all intertwined. Since the 1990s the assimilationist agenda has become much more powerful."[39]

The framing and messaging in Mattilda's edited volumes articulate some of the central debates about assimilation and reform vs. resistance and defiance. Introducing some of these conflicts, Mattilda writes that recent gay rights movements, such as those aimed at same-sex marriage, are counterproductive:

A gay elite has hijacked queer struggle and positioned their desires as everyone's needs—the dominant signs of straight conformity have become the ultimate measures of gay success. Even when the gay rights agenda does include important issues, it does it in a way that consistently prioritizes the most privileged while fucking over everyone else. . . . For decades there has been strife within queer politics and cultures, between assimilationists and liberationists, conservatives and radicals. . . . Gay marriage advocates brush aside generations of queer efforts to create new ways of loving, lusting for, and caring for one another, in favor of a 1950s model of the white-picket-fence, "we're just like you" normalcy. . . . The radical potential of queer identity lies in remaining *outside*—in challenging and seeking to dismantle the sickening culture that surrounds us.[40]

For liberationists, resistance is called for against mainstream gay rights groups as much as against heteronormative society:

These days, lesbian soccer moms and gay military intelligence experts are all over the media, whether sermonizing in op-eds, befriending the liberal intelligentsia, or speaking softly to closeted cable news anchors: We. Are. Just. Like. You. Supposedly gay people have made lots of progress, and that's why the only issues we hear about involve marriage, gays in the military, gay cops, adoption, ordination into the priesthood, hate crimes legislation, and unquestioning gentrification and consumerism—please, stop me before I choke on my own vomit! . . . It's time to pull together a gang of queer troublemakers to tear this assimilationist agenda to shreds, okay?[41]

Responding to dual opposition from conventionality and normalizers, liberationist messaging often focuses on how stigmatized identities are actually better than a watered-down conventional identity. Hence, the Against Equality movement chose a "greater than" symbol as its logo, in direct contrast to the equals sign of the Human Rights Campaign.[42] Another example of directly countering the "we're just like you" messaging of normalizing movements is a viral blog post written by children raised by queer parents, which was included in an anthology of Outsider writings, aptly called *Against Equality*:

We're fed up with the way that the gay marriage movement has tried to assimilate us, to swallow up our families, our lives, and our lovers into its clean cut standards for what queer love, responsibility, and commitment should look like. . . . We refuse to feel indebted or grateful to those who have decided it's time for us to be pulled from the fringe and into the status quo. We know there are more of us on the outside than the inside, and we realize our power. We write this feeling as if we have to grab our community back from the clutches of the gay marriage movement. We're frightened by its path and its incessant desire to assimilate. . . . Having grown up in queer families and communities we strongly believe that queers are not like everyone else. Queers are sexy, resourceful, creative and brave enough to challenge an oppressive system with their lifestyle.[43]

Reflecting on how her personal identity is connected to collective communities situated in opposition to mainstream gay rights movements, Mattilda stated: "I exist in queer, genderqueer, trans and gender-defiant subcultures that are inspiring to me in their emphasis on truth-telling, fluidity, critical engagement, negotiation and developing mesmerizing alternatives to the dead-end emphasis on normalcy so intrinsic to gay *and* straight mainstream cultures."[44]

Outsiders do not face the same costs as Insiders for being branded deviant and are therefore freer to fully enact deviant identities with less concern for the perceptions of "normies." Consequently, Outsiders are more likely to express great pride in deviant identities and claim stigmatized statuses are actually superior to normalcy. Whereas Insiders' approach is defined by compromise, Outsiders view compromise as weakness. True Outsiders demand to be met on their own terms and will not change to become more "palatable."

MEASURING LGBT IDENTITIES
AND CONVENTIONALITY

While we would expect the messaging of Insiders to be more *assimilationist* and the messaging of Outsiders to be more *liberationist*, empirical tests are necessary to examine the extent to which this is the case. These tests expand what we know about how social identities and characteristics are related to strategies of deviance management, as well as how these patterns occur among LGBTQ communities. While scholars have recognized cycles of sameness and difference among LGBTQ movements, "research that finds a causal relationship between collective identity and a movement's tactics, organization, and outcomes has been largely qualitative and based on case studies of one cycle of activism."[45] We expand on insights from qualitative research by looking at quantitative patterns in deviance management styles across different historical contexts.

We can test our hypotheses about deviance management in the context of LGBTQ subcultures and individuals by analyzing datasets that contain relevant measures of stakes in conformity and minority sexuality/gender identity, along with outcomes of interest, such as the type of political issues prioritized and participation in LGBTQ social movements, levels of "outness" to others, and the presence of other types of deviance (such as drug use and suicidality). To do this we analyzed survey data from two national samples of sexual and gender minorities in the United States that contain the necessary measures: the National Lesbian Health Care Survey (NLHCS) and the Pew Survey of LGBT Americans.

The NLHCS was administered in the winter of 1985 to a sample of 1,925 self-identified lesbians using snowball and network sampling techniques. The survey specifically focused on reaching "a broad range of lesbians throughout the United States, including low-income lesbians, nonurban lesbians, lesbians of color, and lesbians with less formal education."[46] The sample included lesbians from all fifty states in the United States. The survey was designed to assess the health care needs of the lesbian population, both by examining the extent to which individuals received needed health care and mental health services, as well as determining the extent to which lesbians suffered from traumatic experiences such as incest or rape, abused alcohol or drugs, or considered or attempted suicide.[47] The survey included detailed batteries of questions on demographics; community and social life; current worries and concerns; depression, anxiety, and mental health; experiences of abuse and discrimination; the impact of AIDS upon respondents' lives; history of eating disorders; the use of counseling and other health services; and respondents' levels of outness to others.[48]

To the extent that a survey asks respondents how strongly they identify with a subculture or a particular named identity that is indicative of membership in the subculture, this can be used as a measure of identity salience. The NLHCS asks respondents the extent to which they self-identify as "lesbian only," on a scale ranging from 1 (heterosexual) to 7 (lesbian only) with 4 labeled as "bisexual." A majority of respondents (55 percent) identified as lesbian only. We used the highest value on the scale (7) as an indicator of strong identification with lesbian identity.[49]

We measured stakes in conformity for lesbian and bisexual women based on social and demographic characteristics. Socioeconomic measures such as income, employment status, occupation, and education again serve as measures of prior and current investment in conventional status systems. Attachment to conventional institutions also can be used to measure commitment to convention, so we also included affiliation with mainstream religious organizations as a measure of conventionality. Taken together, these measures provide a proxy of individuals' "stakes in conformity."

We created dichotomous variables for whether or not a respondent had achieved a college degree, was currently employed, was above the median in income ($20,000 per year and above in 1985) and whether she had a skilled occupation (professional, technical, managers, and administrators). Finally, we created a dichotomous measure of conventional religious identity. We coded affiliations with mainstream organized religions as 1 and non-affiliation or affiliation with religious organizations known to specifically cater to LGBT individuals—including "pagan/witch," and "gay church"—as 0. By summing these dichotomous variables, we created a measure of stakes in conformity for the NLHCS.

The Pew LGBT Survey was administered in 2013 to a nationally representative sample of nearly twelve hundred Americans who identified as lesbian, gay, bisexual, or transgender.[50] The sample was drawn from GfK's KnowledgePanel, a nationally representative pool of potential survey respondents. Among the basic questions given to the entire pool are items about sexual orientation and gender identity. Respondents in the pool who self-identified as gay, lesbian, bisexual, or transgender were randomly selected for inclusion in the survey.

For stakes in LGBT identity, we combined two self-assessment measures. The first asks how important LGBT status was to respondents' overall identity, with five answer choices ranging from "not at all important" to "extremely important." The second asks whether being LGBT has overall negative or positive effects on one's life, with answer choices of negative, neither positive nor negative, and positive. These indicators were mean standardized and combined into a composite measure of investment in subcultural identity.

To measure stakes in conformity in the Pew survey, we used a combination of employment status (not working, working part-time, working full-time), education attainment level, family income, intimate partner relationship status (not married or living with partner, living with partner, married), religious identity salience, and frequency of attendance at religious services.[51] Each indicator was standardized by its respective mean and standard deviation, then combined into an additive index of stakes in conformity.

EMPIRICAL TESTS

Conventional and Deviant Identities and Messaging about Deviance

The 2013 Pew LGBT survey included three questions that asked for a forced choice response between answer options that represent assimilation and liberation strategies. The question asked respondents: "Which statement comes closer to your own views—even if neither is exactly right?" The specific questions were about general distinctiveness, comfort being seen as different, and the maintenance of separate social spaces. After each item below, we list the percentage of respondents selecting each answer.

DISTINCTIVENESS

A. The best way to achieve equality is for LGBT people to be a part of mainstream culture and institutions like marriage (50 percent).

B. LGBT people should be able to achieve equality while still maintaining their own distinct culture and way of life (50 percent).*

COMFORTABLE BEING DIFFERENT

A. I don't want to be seen as different because of my [sexual orientation/identity] (75 percent).

B. My [sexual orientation/identity] makes me different from other people, and I am comfortable with that (25 percent).*

SEPARATE SPACES

A. It is important to maintain places like LGBT neighborhoods and gay and lesbian bars (58 percent).*

B. These types of places will not be important as LGBT people are more accepted into society (42 percent).

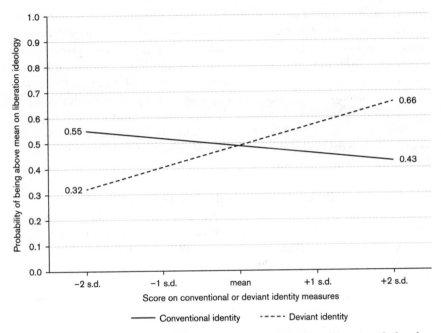

FIGURE 9. Predicted probabilities of scoring above the sample mean on liberation ideology by conventional and subcultural identity. (Source: 2013 Pew LGBT Survey)

For each of the questions above, we have marked with an asterisk (*) the response that we categorize as liberationist. We coded these measures such that the assimilation response = 0 and the liberation response = 1, then added the three items together to make a liberationist views index ranging from 0 to 3. According to our framework, those with greater stakes in conformity should tend to favor assimilation over liberation, while those with greater commitment to subcultural identity should be more likely to favor liberation over assimilation.

To test these hypotheses, we ran an ordinal logistic regression model predicting scores on the liberation index using the measures for conventionality and deviant identity salience as predictors. We controlled for demographic characteristics that were not part of our measure of conventionality, including age, identification as female, and race (black = 1). We also control for the sexual identity of the respondent, contrasting "lesbian," "bisexual" and "transgender" respondents with individuals who self-identified as "gay" (full model is available in appendix).

Figure 9 shows the relationship between stakes in conformity and liberationist views, as well as between commitment to subcultural identity and liberationist ideas, by showing the probability that respondents scored above the mean on the liberation index across different levels of stakes in deviant and conventional identity. In line with our expectations, higher levels of conventional identity are significantly related to a decrease in liberationist views. At two standard deviations below the mean on the stakes in conformity measure, respondents' probability of being above the mean on the liberation index was .55, while at two standard deviations above the mean it was .43. The strongest overall predictor in the model was subcultural identity, which was positively related to liberationist ideas. At two standard deviations below the mean on the subcultural identity measure, respondents' predicted probability of being above the mean on liberationist views was .32. At two standard deviations above the mean on subcultural identity, respondents' probability of being above the mean on liberationist responses was more than twice as high: .66.

Splitting the stakes in conformity and subcultural identity measures at their respective means in order to make categories for our four deviance management types shows that Hiders had the most assimilationist views (mean on liberation index = 1.0), followed by Drifters (mean = 1.2). We expected that Outsiders would have the highest scores on the liberation index and they do (mean = 1.43), but Insiders also expressed a similar level of liberationist views (mean = 1.38). So, to better understand differences between Outsiders and Insiders, we must dig deeper into the specific political issues that individuals prioritize.

Importance of Specific Issues

The Pew survey also included a battery of questions that asked respondents to rate the importance of seven specific issues: employment rights, same-sex marriage, same-sex adoption, AIDS prevention and treatment, civil union rights, support services for LGBT youth, and transgender health care services. Possible responses ranged from "not a priority at all" to "top priority."

Outsiders were the most likely to consider a wide range of movement goals to be "top priority" issues, including AIDS prevention and treatment, establishing civil unions, support for LGBT youth, and transgender health issues. Consistent with the idea of narrow messaging toward normative institutions, Insiders were the most likely to rate same-sex adoption as a top priority. Hiders were the least likely to prioritize all the issues addressed with one exception: equal employment rights. In contrast, Drifters were the least likely to be concerned about employment issues.

One way to get a better sense of the priorities of respondents is to see how highly they rank issues *relative to one another*. Since the survey itself did not ask the questions this way, we created relative rank scores by calculating an overall index score combining individuals' responses to all the items, then divided respondents' scores on specific items by their overall index score. This calculation provides an estimate of the importance of specific issues relative to overall concern about all the movement goals. It allows us to see, for instance, what Outsiders tend to prioritize most, taking into account their higher levels of support for all the issues, as well as what Hiders prioritize most, taking into account their lower overall levels of support for most movement goals (full results in the appendix). A simple way to think about these metrics is that they address this question: If people could support only one issue, what would it be?

When they supported anything, Hiders were most likely to support employment and civil union rights. Drifters prioritized civil unions, as well as AIDS treatment. Hiders showed lower levels of support for LGBT youth and transgender issues relative to other concerns. In direct contrast, and consistent with our expectations, Outsiders tended to weigh services for transgender health high relative to other issues, as well as support for LGBT youth. Consonant with appeals to family mores by normalizers, Insiders emphasized same-sex marriage and adoption. Relative to other issues, Insiders were less likely to prioritize AIDS prevention and treatment.[52] When we look at how each of the deviance management types rank the relative importance of specific issues, the results align with the expectations that Insiders will emphasize appeals to normative institutions and downplay more marginalized aspects of the subculture, while Outsiders will be more concerned with caring for the marginalized and relatively less concerned about appeals to normative institutions.

PROFILES IN STIGMATIZED IDENTITY

Throughout the book, we have argued that particular combinations of conventional and deviant identity will create distinctive deviance management orientations. Although Drifters, Hiders, Insiders, and Outsiders are necessarily ideal types—and many people will fall between or across the categories—we still expect these groupings to represent distinct factions within a deviant subculture. To look for meaningful distinctions between Hiders, Drifters, Insiders, and Outsiders with regard to issues such as openness about deviance, diversification of deviant activities, and participation in social movements, we analyzed the extent to which individuals in the deviance management categories varied in levels of outness to others, engaging in other forms of deviance (such as drug use and suicidality) and levels of participation in reform-oriented social movements.

For both datasets, we used our measures of conventionality and subcultural identity to create categories for the four deviance management types: Drifters are below the means for both stakes in conformity and stakes in sexuality/gender identity, Hiders are at or above the mean for stakes in conformity and below the mean for subcultural identity, Outsiders are below the mean for stakes in conformity and at or above the mean for sexuality/gender identity, and Insiders are at or above the mean for both stakes in conformity and subcultural identity.

Drifters

With a higher propensity to move in and out of subcultures and low concern with convention, Drifters should tend toward apathy and the diversification of deviance. Compared to the other deviance management types, Drifters were the most likely to say they were still not sure whether they even considered themselves LGBT in the Pew survey. Despite less definitiveness about sexual identity, and reflective of a general lack of communal engagement, non-transgender and non-bisexual Drifters were less likely than non-trans and non-bisexual Outsiders or Insiders to say they had "a lot" in common with transgender and bisexual people. This despite Drifters having the highest proportion of self-identified bisexuals (57 percent) in the Pew LGBT Survey. The higher concentration of a more fluid sexual identity among Drifters supports the hypothesis of less definitive specialization and identity investment.

In the Pew LGBT Survey, Drifters reported even lower levels of "outness" to their parents than Hiders—at least compared to Hiders out enough to take an anonymous survey. Reflecting lower social ties more generally, Drifters were the most likely to choose "not applicable" on questions about their mothers and fathers.[53] This absence of social ties can have dire consequences. Echoing sociologist Émile Durkheim's ideas about how lack of community and social solidarity produces higher rates of despair, Drifters had the highest levels of suicidal ideation in the NLHCS.[54] Also showing the potential effects of anomie (normlessness), both Drifters (18 percent) and Outsiders (17 percent) were more likely to report having problems with substance abuse in the past compared to Insiders and Hiders (both 7 percent); however, reiterating the potentially protective effects of subcultural belonging, Drifters were more likely than Outsiders to report having *current* problems with both alcohol and other drugs at the time of the survey.[55] Using a wider variety of drugs and a greater likelihood of ongoing drug use among Drifters in the NLHCS highlights their greater propensity for deviance diversification.

These patterns of suicidality and substance abuse also reflect differential exposure to victimization, trauma, and stress. Drifters were the most likely to have been sexually assaulted, both as children and as adults. Drifters also were the most likely to have been victims of incest as children. Indeed, differential exposure to victimization and subsequent negative affect help explain the differing paths of coping taken by individuals, which ultimately contribute to differential outcomes within the deviance management typology. Outcomes on the health survey are a case in point. As adults, Drifters were the most likely to report issues with body image and depression. Reflecting their higher levels of victimization as both children and adults, Drifters were also the most likely to attend support groups of various kinds, despite their general tendency toward social disengagement.[56]

Hiders

True Hiders would prefer that their involvement with a deviant subculture remain unknown to anyone in the outside world. Thus, to the extent that Hiders have an opinion on how a subculture should present itself, they should be more likely to express the belief that the subculture should remain apart from conventional society. To the extent that a Hider is asked for a general opinion of deviant subcultures, it is likely to be negative. Clearly, however, survey respondents who self-identify as LGBT are not "true" Hiders, at least in the full sense. As a result, the "Hiders" in our survey assessments must be understood to be Hiders *only in the sense of relative comparison to other people who self-identify as LGBT.*

These (relative) Hiders were much more likely to self-identify as bisexual (52 percent) compared Outsiders (28 percent) and Insiders (20 percent). Yet non-transgender and non-bisexual Hiders also were the least likely to say they had "a lot" in common with bisexual and transgender people. Consistent with expectations, Hiders were the most likely to say they "don't want to be seen as different," and the least likely to favor distinctive lifestyles and spaces for LGBT people. In the NLHCS, Hiders were the least out to all others, whether family members, straight friends, coworkers or LGBT friends. Hiders also understandably expressed the highest levels of fear that others would discover they were lesbian or bisexual. As we noted in the previous section, and detail further below, by the time of the Pew survey, Drifters had become the least likely to be out, showing a transformation to less extreme forms of hiding between 1985 and 2013.

A fascinating dynamic becomes apparent when comparing multiple questions about alcohol use and abuse that well illustrates the behavioral tendencies of Hiders. In the NLHCS, Hiders were the most likely to use alcohol daily and also the most likely to report that they worry about using alcohol too much. At the same time, Hiders were the *least* likely to actually admit that they currently had problems with alcohol. Thus, although Hiders *report* the lowest levels of ongoing issues with substance abuse, the differences between their actual alcohol use and self-admitted alcoholism provide reasonable suspicion about the accuracy of Hiders' self-diagnoses.

Reflecting their higher stakes in conformity, Hiders were the most likely to report a mainstream Christian affiliation, as well as a "born again" religious identity in the Pew survey. Hiders also were the most likely to be members of traditional religious organizations in the NLHCS, as well as to be members of professional groups and health clubs.

Looking at recent discrimination experiences in the Pew LGBT Survey, the management strategy of Hiders and Drifters shows some efficacy, as they are far less likely to have been victims of various forms of discrimination compared to both Outsiders or Insiders. So, while the deviance management strategies of Hiders and Drifters are not likely to advance social justice for sexual and gender minorities and undoubtedly have negative psychological consequences, they are reasonably effective strategies for avoiding discrimination and abuse.

Insiders

If assimilationists are making efforts to conform to conventional familial standards, which operate on a strict binary categorization of gender, they should be more likely to oppose violations of gender and sexuality as binaries.[57] Indeed, that is what we find. In the Pew LGBT Survey, Insiders had the lowest proportion claiming to be either transgender (3 percent) or bisexual (20 percent). Thought of the other way, lesbians (37 percent) and gay men (33 percent) were much more likely to be Insiders than transgender (12 percent) or bisexual individuals (13 percent).[58] Reflecting this tendency toward normalization, non-trans and non-bisexual Insiders were less likely than non-trans and non-bisexual Outsiders to say they had "a lot" in common with transgender or bisexual people.

In terms of "outness," Insiders in the Pew survey were the most likely to be out to "all or most" of the important people in their lives (75 percent), as well as to their mothers (78 percent), fathers (67 percent), brothers (76 percent) and coworkers (49 percent).[59] This suggests a higher level of familial and social integration among Insiders, at least in the less repressive cultural context of 2013. Accordingly, nearly 90 percent of Insiders said that knowing someone who is LGBT "helps a lot" for making the wider society more accepting of sexual and gender minorities. Politics is personal, after all.

Showing the importance of both affirmative sexual identity and stakes in conformity for mental health, Insiders reported significantly lower levels of suicidal ideation than the other three deviance management types in the NLHCS data. Similarly, Insiders reported substantially lower levels of struggles with fear and anxiety compared to all other categories and were the least likely to have problems with substance abuse. In terms of positive outcomes, in the Pew LGBT data, Insiders were the most likely to vote in elections and reported higher levels of general social trust than the other deviance management types.

In line with the hypothesis that they are more likely to adopt a generalist rather than specialist orientation to deviance management, Outsiders tended to participate in a wide variety of activities related to different topics in the NLHCS data. Reflecting greater specialization, Insiders were the most likely to attend groups focused specifically on lesbian rights. Overall, Insiders' higher levels of social integration tend to lead to a greater focus on reformatory rather than revolutionary or utopian social movement strategies.

Outsiders

A relatively high proportion of Outsiders in the Pew LGBT data were gay men (45 percent). Outsiders also have the highest proportion of individuals who identify as transgendered. Likewise, non-trans Outsiders reported the highest levels of affinity for transgender people, and non-bisexual Outsiders were the most likely to say they had "a lot" in common with bisexual people. Outsiders were the most likely to report that they were comfortable being different from other people and wanting to maintain distinctly LGBT spaces—such as public venues or neighborhoods—even if greater equality is achieved in conventional society.

There are interesting findings for Outsiders in terms of diversification of deviance. For instance, suicidal ideation is lessened by a sense of community, even if it is subcultural. Outsiders had the highest rates of *ever* attempting suicide in the NLHCS, but their levels of suicidality at the time of the survey were lower than both Drifters and Hiders. Mirroring the qualitative evidence from hardline liberationist rhetoric and groups, Outsiders were the most likely to attend women's rights groups, as well as groups advocating for other types of social minorities. Outsiders also had more subcultural social network closure, with a greater share of their peer networks being LGBT individuals. In the 2013 data, Outsiders were the most likely to identify as sexual minorities on social networking sites and to discuss LGBT issues online. There are obviously still heavy penalties to pay for openness, however, as Outsiders and Insiders were much more likely than Drifters and Hiders to report being victims of physical violence and epithets.

These profiles provide basic social and cognitive portraits of individuals using different deviance management strategies. Drifters are the most likely to have backgrounds of abuse, and correspondingly more likely to struggle with depression, substance abuse, and suicidality. Hiders do not want to be seen as different, often hold traditional religious views, and are more likely to struggle with alcoholism (while denying this is the case). Insiders are the most insulated from psychological and substance abuse problems, reflecting both lower rates of victimization as children and greater social integration as adults. Outsiders have higher rates of victimization, along with greater struggles with mental health and suicidality, but also mitigate these risk factors through subcultural community and belonging. Despite the fact that the best examples of Hiders and Drifters will be missing from survey data—and must therefore be studied using creative qualitative methods— these findings demonstrate how conventional and deviant identity are connected to patterns of social attachments, subcultural engagement, diversification of deviance, and messaging and narratives about stigmatized identity.

DIFFERENCES OVER TIME

Using datasets collected nearly thirty years apart provides an opportunity to analyze data from two periods with varying levels of the stigmatization of sexual minorities in American culture. We can restrict the 2013 Pew LGBT Survey data

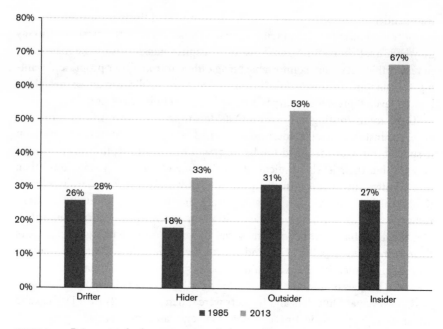

FIGURE 10. Being out to both parents among lesbian and bisexual women by deviance management type. (Sources: 1985 National Lesbian Healthcare Survey and 2013 Pew LGBT Survey)

only to lesbian and bisexual female respondents in order to compare across two national samples of lesbian and bisexual women taken at two very different points in American history. Although there are very few matching outcome measures between the NLHCS and the Pew LGBT Survey, there are some assessments of relative outness to others that allow us to make interesting comparisons. The NLHCS asked respondents how "out" they were to their family in general, while the Pew LGBT Survey asked whether respondents were out to their mothers and fathers (when applicable). Presuming high overlap between those who said they were out to "all" of their family and those out to both parents we can compare these outcomes.

Figure 10 shows a comparison of levels of outness by deviance management type for both surveys. In 1985, Outsiders were the most likely to report being out to all of their family. In 2013 there was greater outness among all respondents, but the growth among Insiders was by far the largest. Two-thirds of Insiders reported being out to both parents in 2013, compared to only one-fourth out to all of their family in 1985.

Similarly, the NLHCS and Pew survey both asked how many coworkers (if employed) respondents were out to (figure 11). In 1985, Outsiders (28 percent) were

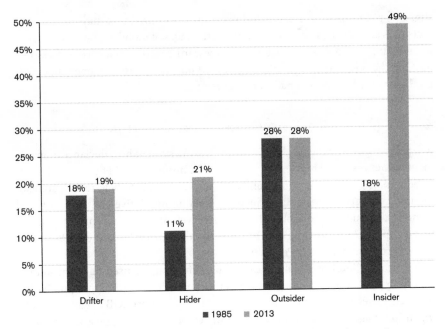

FIGURE 11. Being out to most or all coworkers among lesbian and bisexual women by deviance management type. (Sources: 1983 National Lesbian Healthcare Survey and 2013 Pew LGBT Survey)

more likely than the other management types, including Insiders (18 percent), to report being out to at least three-fourths of their coworkers. In 2013, the percentage of Outsiders who reported being out to "most or all" of their coworkers remained the same as the estimate from 1985. In sharp contrast, the percentage of Insiders out to most or all of their coworkers in 2013 increased substantially, up to 49 percent.

This provides evidence that Outsiders may clear the path for Insiders by facing the risks of public revelation and punishment during times of greater repression.[60] Conversely, when stigmatization has decreased, Insiders are the most likely to be publicly out. This lends credence to the idea of Outsiders often being the "leading edge" of social movements—those willing to sacrifice their bodies and potentially their freedom or lives to fight back. These findings also show how there can be differential distributions of behavioral strategies depending on thresholds of stigmatization and penalty.[61] As the stigma of deviance declines, more Hiders come out of the closet and become Insiders. Considering this dynamic over time, Outsiders are needed to forge subcultural communities in high-risk environments, with larger numbers of Insiders then coming out and supporting social change efforts as stigma is reduced. Thus, a successful normalization movement may require both Outsiders and Insiders, the former in the early stages of mobilization and the latter in later stages as a movement progresses toward practical reforms. Successfully pushing the boundaries of what is considered normative also can open more cultural space for Insiders to enact efforts at reform.

SOCIAL MOVEMENT PARTICIPATION

Related to movement goals, there is the critical question of how deviance management influences social movement participation. Insiders should be the most motivated to participate in reform-oriented social movements to help resolve some of the role conflicts between simultaneously holding normative and deviant social identities. Outsiders also should show higher levels of social movement participation compared to Hiders and Drifters, but should be lower than Insiders. We tested these hypotheses using the Pew LGBT Survey.

To measure level of social movement participation, we used questions on the survey that asked about being a member of an LGBT organization, purchasing products or services from companies because they support LGBT rights, boycotting the purchase of products or services from companies that oppose LGBT rights, attending an LGBT rally or march, attending an LGBT pride event, and donating money to politicians or political organizations that support LGBT rights. Each of the measures had response categories of never doing the activity (0), doing the activity in the past, but not in the last year (1), and engaging in the activity in the past year (2). We combined these measures into a composite measure for level of participation in LGBT social movement activities, ranging from 0 to 12. The category with the highest overall level of social movement participation was indeed Insiders (mean = 6.9), followed by Outsiders (5.3), Hiders (3.5) and then Drifters (2.6). Only 5.5 percent of Insiders reported never doing any of the activities in question, compared to 14 percent of Outsiders, 31 percent of Hiders, and 36 percent of Drifters. Further, Insiders were the most likely to have participated in each of the specific actions during the past year.

To explore these patterns with greater specificity, we examined levels of social movement participation at varying combinations of conventional and deviant identity, while also controlling for respondents' age, race, gender, and primary sexual identity (L, G, B, or T; full model in the appendix). Figure 12 is a graphical presentation of the results, showing that the highest levels of movement participation are found among Insiders, followed by Outsiders, then Hiders, and Drifters. At the opposite end of the spectrum from Insiders, "pure" Drifters have the lowest levels social movement participation.[62] While Outsiders may often be the leading edge, particularly in cultural and legal environments of repression, high participation from Insiders is necessary for successful mobilization for reform.

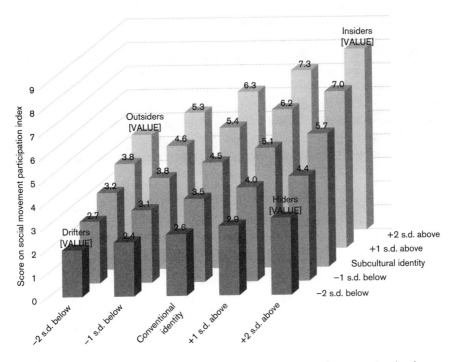

FIGURE 12. Social movement participation among LGBT Americans by conventional and subcultural identity. (Source: 2013 Pew LGBT Survey)

OUTSIDER PARADOXES

As we saw in the FUQ protests over the police killing of Amadou Diallo, Outsiders are often the first people willing to engage in direct-action protests that pose great personal risk. Outsiders are particularly important when activism requires using one's own body as a tool of resistance and protest.[63] An even more influential example than FUQ was the activism of one of its predecessors, ACT UP—which used confrontational and theatrical tactics, such as protesting at the Food and Drug Administration and the National Institutes of Health—to force governmental and societal recognition of the AIDS crisis during the late 1980s and 1990s.[64] ACT UP staged a number of successful protest actions in the first few years after its inception. But within the movement, divisions over gender, race, HIV status, and other identity boundaries, as well as divergence over the degree to which the organization should specialize only in AIDS activism or diversify into related issues of social justice, soon precipitated a rapid disintegration of the group from peak levels of membership, participation, and effectiveness. What began as a high-solidarity coalition focused on a common external enemy splintered as cohesion devolved into disputes over identity, recognition, and negative affect. Alliance begat animosity. Comradery became conflict.[65]

Ultimately, disputes between Outsider and Insider groups are about how issues should be framed and pursued, as well as the related internal emotional dynamics of group relations.[66] When Insiders become dominant, Outsiders are likely to challenge the dominant frames of reform and normalization. Outsiders will inevitably feel excluded from the in-crowd as Insiders attempt to promote *narrative coherence* with conventional society. They may react by highlighting narrative infidelity in the subculture. As usual, Mattilda says it succinctly and with a flourish: "It's time to show faggotry in all of its messiness, glamour, incendiary potential, movement, disastrousness and experimentation."[67]

This inclusion or rejection (or nonrecognition) of stigmatized statuses *other than* the primary one in question often becomes a central issue of contention in subcultures, with Outsiders stressing narrative infidelity with conventional society, as demonstrated by an open letter to LGBT leaders from queer activists:

> Looking into the community of people who base their lives on sexuality and gender, there's a lot of door-opening to do. Beyond L, G, B, and T, there's also Q for queer and Q for questioning. There's an S for sadomasochists, an I for intersex, an F for feminists, and another F for furries. Our community is additionally composed of sex educators, sex workers, adult entertainers, pornographers, men who have sex with men, women who have sex with women, and asexuals who have sex with no one but themselves. You want to create some real change? Make room for genderqueers, polyamorists, radical faeries, butches, femmes, drag queens, drag kings, and other dragfuck royalty too fabulous to describe in this short letter.[68]

Indeed, as this example shows, divisiveness within deviant subcultures can sometimes become a central goal of Outsider activism. As Mattilda quipped, "I know that anytime anyone talks against critiquing your own or makes an accusation of divisiveness it means that something is going right! I fully believe in not bridging the divide, but in making it wider."[69] Summarizing her dual opposition, she stated, "my politics is a politics of accountability for both the mainstream consumerist monoculture and for gay subcultures."[70] Again and again, Outsiders are antagonists to both the status quo and normalization movements.

Because of this dual conflict, there are immense challenges for building cohesive communities of Outsiders. Mattilda's experiences with activism and community building with groups such ACT UP and FUQ speak to this difficulty: "So it was us against them, but ultimately it was us against us. That's what I'm trying to examine, the ways in which we let each other down, the brutality of believing in something so strongly, something like community or chosen family, and then it ends up ripping you apart in ways that can end up feeling just as violent as the worlds you were fleeing."[71]

Mattilda openly confronts the challenges of building such communities. When asked what she thinks queer communities *should* look like, she tellingly demurs and appeals instead to Outsider *commitment*: "Oh, honey, I have no idea. Let's just say there would be a lot more emphasis on communal responsibility, on creating space for people on the margins, on exploration, on transformation, on negotiation, on intimacy that builds, on accountability—yes, accountability—, defiance, deviance, on coming together to challenge the violence of the world that wants us to die or disappear."[72] Additionally, there is the challenge of attempting to translate radical resistance identities and accompanying movements into new normative orders that are less oppressive than conventional society. As Mattilda observed, "I find over and over again that these queer worlds that we create often end up mimicking the violence of the worlds that we're trying to challenge."[73]

Reflecting on her participation in various Outsider movements, the in-fighting among queer groups and more mainstream gay groups, and the tendency for the once-excluded to become excluders, Mattilda said, "I think a lot of it ends up being queers or outsiders all their lives and then they get a taste of inside and then they act like the people who beat them up all their lives."[74] Seeing the inherent paradox in this process of change and the reproduction of inequality, she noted, "It is a cliché in a way to think that the margins determine the center, but it is true. If there are no margins, the center will never change. I guess the question is: 'How do you create space without becoming part of that same structure, like the gay establishment has become?'"[75] Mattilda's answer to this question is telling: narrative *infidelity*: "For me, the possibility of commonality emerges by expressing the absolute core of difference. . . . We actually have to explore the differences in order to find the commonalities, whatever the fuck they are."[76]

What alternative is there for a true believer? Idealism trumps pragmatism in the realm of morality. Outsiders fight back and fight on.[77]

6

Insiders and the Normalization
of Illegal Drugs

Having outlined some of the basic patterns and dynamics of deviance management and how they relate to participating in normalization movements, we now look at how and when normalization movements can succeed. To do this we explore changing public attitudes and policies regarding the ingestion of two illicit substances: alcohol and cannabis. Specifically, we look at the movement to repeal national alcohol Prohibition (1920–1933) and the reformation of cannabis laws at the state level during the early twenty-first century. While there is considerable work in the study of deviance on processes of drug criminalization, there is far less about the retraction of such boundaries of deviance.[1]

Insiders should be the most effective public advocates for normalization, as they alone can draw on conventional social capital to convince non-deviants that "we're just like you." Narrative coherence and fidelity are the rhetorical keys to changing public views about something defined as socially deviant. But in practice, how do Insiders successfully achieve narrative coherence and fidelity to alter public opinion about controversial issues? And when do changes to public opinion lead to changes in social policies? Is it necessary to win in the court of public opinion before policy normalization can succeed?

Examining instances of successful normalization movements helps answer these questions. Both the repeal of alcohol Prohibition and the increasing legalization of cannabis in the United States provide instructive case studies of successful normalization movements. In 1933, national alcohol Prohibition was repealed, decriminalizing a large percentage of the population. In recent years, states such as Colorado, Washington, California, and Vermont have legalized cannabis for recreational use and many other states have allowed medicinal cannabis use for the treatment of certain health conditions. Alcohol use—when not extreme—long ago moved from "deviant" to acceptable in American culture. Cannabis use appears to be on the same path.

Before we can analyze the respective normalization movements for alcohol and cannabis, we must consider how ingesting these substances came to be criminal in the first place. Throughout American history, there have been cycles of moral panics about drug use followed by punitive social policies about drugs. There are a number of discernible patterns to these cycles, including tying the use of the drug in question to a "dangerous class" of people, usually racial and ethnic minorities, and necessarily people of lower social class.[2] The disproportionate enforcement of drug laws along racial, ethnic and class lines belies the underlying exclusionary component of punitive social policies about drugs.[3] In the case of alcohol Prohibition, the demonized "dangerous class" was immigrants, particularly those from Catholic countries.[4]

Similarly, racialized framing of cannabis use was connected to Mexican immigrants during the first push for criminalization in the 1930s and then to minorities and the counterculture during the Nixon administration (1968–1974), which overtly used drug enforcement as an electoral and governing strategy.[5] In an interview while serving a prison sentence for crimes committed during the Watergate scandal, former Nixon lieutenant John Ehrlichman said:

> The Nixon campaign in 1968, and the Nixon White House after that, had two enemies: the antiwar left and black people. You understand what I'm saying? We knew we couldn't make it illegal to be either against the war or black, but by getting the public to associate the hippies with marijuana and blacks with heroin, and then criminalizing both heavily, we could disrupt those communities. We could arrest their leaders, raid their homes, break up their meetings, and vilify them night after night on the evening news. Did we know we were lying about the drugs? Of course we did.[6]

But politicians must sell their stories of demonization to the public. During panics about drugs, members of conservative religious groups have long been willing audiences. Conservative Christians, particularly Protestants, played a pivotal role in the criminalization of alcohol.[7] Likewise, high levels of religiosity and theological conservatism are the strongest predictors of opposition to cannabis use among the American public.[8] The demonization of both alcohol and cannabis combined racialized frames of substance use with a Puritanical righteousness about the morality of abstaining from drugs and "just desserts" harsh punishment for those who did not abstain. These are the grounds activists trying to normalize alcohol and cannabis had to fight on in order to convince the public that "upstanding" citizens support normalization. Having Insiders who can make convincing public arguments about their own conventionality and by extension the conventionality of supporting reform, are integral to achieving normalization.

INSIDER STRATEGIES

Successful normalization movements require: (1) the presence of advocacy groups with the ability to mobilize resources; (2) public officials willing to take electorally risky positions; and, perhaps most importantly, (3) the softening of public attitudes toward the deviance in question. In cases where the ingestion of a particular substance is punished with harsh penal enforcement and public condemnation, it will be difficult to achieve normalization. After all, there are not mobilized, coherent movements for the normalization of substances that remain widely condemned, such as methamphetamines.[9] In such cases, we can reasonably expect deviance management strategies to be limited to Hiders, Drifters, and Outsiders. But where public sentiment about the immorality of using particular substances does *not* match harsh enforcement policies, there are political opportunities for changes to social policy.

Insiders are not a *sufficient* condition for normalization to occur, of course, but they are a *necessary* condition. Insiders will be the most motivated to try and change public opinion about deviance. To be labeled deviant or immoral strains Insiders' attachments to conventional people, limits social advancement, and threatens identity. Consequently, Insiders must find a strategy for limiting the potential damage that deviance can do to their conventional social status. One way of engaging in this conflict is to convince conventional others that the deviance in question has been mislabeled. To achieve normalization, Insiders must articulate language, rhetoric, symbols, and narratives that will motivate enough and, especially, the *right kind* of individuals to enact legal reforms.

It is precisely these types of circumstances that we consider by examining movements in the United States to repeal the Prohibition of alcohol and contemporary efforts to legalize cannabis. In making comparisons between these movements, we are not implying that the substances themselves are equivalent or that the respective movements aimed at legalization are the same. Clearly the 1920s and the 2010s are vastly different cultural and legal contexts, even in the same country. Still, there is much to be gained from comparing how both movements attempted to alter public opinion and social policy about the consumption of illegal substances. In doing so we analyze Prohibition repeal and efforts at cannabis legalization as "natural social experiments," focusing on specific dimensions of these movements rather than attempting to provide comprehensive historical accounts of each.[10]

As we have outlined, Insiders possess a unique set of social attributes resulting from their dual allegiance to conventional society and deviant subcultures. As a result of these competing pressures, Insiders are highly interested in social reforms that will lessen the stigma of their deviance. As we saw in the case of sexual minorities, Insiders participate in such movements at high rates, particularly after public condemnation begins to decrease. How do Insiders successfully enact the changes necessary to create these reforms? Using our basic framework for understanding deviance management and the empirical patterns we have observed for Insiders, we can derive three important expectations about these processes.

First, Insiders will attempt to change public discourse about their deviance by appealing to conventional social institutions for the purposes of *narrative fidelity* and *coherence*. Bigfoot hunters appeal to science. LGBT rights activists to family, work, and law. While the institutions appealed to may differ depending on the deviance in question and cultural context, Insiders will use appeals to existing conventional social institutions as the primary rhetorical strategy when arguing for reform. For the sake of narrative fidelity, Insiders will advance narratives that "we're just like you." For narrative coherence to hold among conventional audiences, Insiders will emphasize the conventionality of people in their reform movement and simultaneously delegitimize or ignore elements of a deviant subculture that do not align with this narrative.

Second, if Insiders are able to successfully reframe their deviance as normative through public appeals—which is no small task—public opinion should follow and become increasingly more favorable. That is, to the extent that individuals and communities labeled deviant can convince members of the public that they really are "just like you," public opinion should shift in the direction of leniency and tolerance. In the case of LGBT Americans, appeals to family, the law, and to a lesser extent the military, have been successful. In contrast, Bigfoot hunters have not been able to convince mainstream scientists or the public that they are in fact engaging in science.

Third and finally, to the extent that the behaviors in question are regulated by law in democratic polities, changes to social policies about deviance will only follow *after* public opinion shifts toward normalization. So long as condemnation remains a majoritarian opinion in a democratic system, repressive laws will also remain. Changes to public opinion about homosexuality in the United States, followed soon thereafter by changes to the legal status of same-sex relations, are a case in point.

The path to normalization is changing public discourse about something labeled deviant by successfully appealing to conventional institutions, which results in a lessening of social stigma among the public and creates political opportunities for policy reforms. To evaluate these hypotheses empirically, we look at two parallel examples of the legalization of psychoactive substances that were previously deemed illegal: the repeal of alcohol Prohibition and the movement for cannabis normalization in the United States.

For the repeal of alcohol Prohibition, we focus on the efforts of the Women's Organization for National Prohibition Reform (WONPR), particularly its founder, leader, and primary spokesperson, Pauline Morton Sabin. As the most effective organization for Prohibition repeal, the WONPR in general and Sabin specifically serve as instructive case studies of Insider framing and tactics. We are especially interested in how Sabin and the WONPR were able to frame Prohibition repeal successfully in public discourse and what role Sabin's and the group's Insider characteristics played in this process.

PORTRAIT OF AN INSIDER: PAULINE SABIN

Pauline Sabin was born into immense wealth and privilege as the daughter of Paul Morton, a railroad executive and secretary of the Navy under President Theodore Roosevelt.[11] She extended this inherited prominence with her 1916 marriage to Charles H. Sabin, president and later chairman of the Board for Guaranty Trust, who, upon his death in 1933, was hailed as "one of the most prominent figures in American finance."[12]

Pauline Sabin was a lifelong Republican who was active in party politics. In the wake of women's suffrage, she founded the Women's National Republican Club in 1921, and two years later became the first woman elected as a member of the Republican National Committee.[13] She was well known in elite social circles for hosting galas at Bayberry Land, her sprawling manor overlooking Peconic Bay in the Shinnecock Hills of Southampton, on Long Island, New York.

Sabin was "ambivalent about Prohibition," but nonetheless remained committed to the Republican Party's nominee Calvin Coolidge in the 1924 presidential election.[14] By the summer of 1928, Sabin's ambivalence had transitioned into firm opposition, and she published an essay titled "I Change My Mind on Prohibition." Achieving narrative coherence for the idea that repeal was conventional was a particularly daunting challenge, as Prohibition activists had successfully framed repeal advocates as drunkards, degenerates, and people who profited from others' vices. To counter this narrative, Sabin framed her opposition as being about protecting children from the underground alcohol trade, as well as being in the spirit of teaching respect for the rule of law and the Constitution. To accomplish the latter, she emphasized that Prohibition was the "only Amendment which curtails personal liberty, the only one which attempts to control the habits of a human being."[15] Now that Prohibition had been the law of the land for nearly a decade, she was also able to point to the negative unintended consequences of the policy, such as increased levels of violent crime and political corruption.[16]

Sabin also began a long-term effort to counter the public perception that there were high levels of support for Prohibition among women, and in the process attempted to recover the moral high ground from the Temperance movement. To do so she claimed "true temperance" was legal regulation, which she argued was impossible under Prohibition. She said that representatives of the Women's Christian Temperance Union "appear before hearings of the various Legislatures and Congress and do not hesitate to state that 'they speak for the women of America.'

This, I know, is not the fact."[17] She further argued that women who voted for candidates solely on the basis of their support for Prohibition "without even taking enough interest to question his stand on other matters" had "what some of us call a 'one-plank mind.'"[18] She concluded by saying that she had "wholesome respect" for those who both lived and voted dry, "little respect" for those who opposed Prohibition but would not say so (Hiders) or those who were unconcerned because they could still obtain alcohol through various means (Outsiders) and "no respect for the person who votes one way and lives another" (breastplate of righteousness).[19]

Despite her now public stance against Prohibition, Sabin still vocally supported Republican presidential nominee Herbert Hoover in 1928.[20] She hoped the bark of Hoover's campaign rhetoric about enforcing the Volstead Act would not be matched by the bite of enforcement if he were elected. His inaugural address in 1929 convinced Sabin this would not be the case. Instead, he articulated a hardline stance on enforcement, claiming, among other things, that problems with Prohibition stemmed from the "failure of many State and local officials to accept the obligation under their oath of office zealously to enforce the laws."[21] The following day, Sabin resigned from the Republican National Committee and began assembling the WONPR, which would become the most effective organization ever mobilized to repeal Prohibition.[22] Sabin "emerged as the only repeal leader capable of harnessing the national discontent with Prohibition," and hence the "rise of the WONPR was the critical development in the campaign for the repeal of the Eighteenth Amendment."[23]

Sabin was the consummate Insider. She was deeply devoted to the cause of Prohibition repeal, but at the same time deeply bound by conventionality. As a person of wealth, privilege, and high social status, being viewed as deviant was anathema to Sabin. As an Insider, she fought to change public attitudes about alcohol and its regulation. Her success or failure in this regard could have led to being labeled a champion of freedom or a pariah. Sabin's success in changing public attitudes is ultimately attributable to her political connections, tactical savvy, and personal charisma. These, in turn, were all built on and reinforced by her high social status.

Between the founding of the WONPR in 1929 and the successful repeal of Prohibition in 1933, the *New York Times* ran more than 150 articles about Pauline Sabin—or "Mrs. Charles H. Sabin," as she was always called in print—and her efforts with the WONPR. In doing so, Sabin moved from society page reports about her soirées on Long Island to front-page news about the bitter social and political fight over Prohibition.[24] Content analysis of these articles provides an ideal method for identifying themes in the framing narratives and strategies used by Sabin and the WONPR, as well as successful Insiders more generally.

A month after Hoover's inauguration, Sabin used a dinner in honor of her retirement from the Women's National Republican Club to attack Prohibition as an "attempt to enthrone hypocrisy as the dominant force in this country." She characterized Prohibition as "the age-old effort of the fanatic," argued that it caused crime and corruption, and reiterated that her opposition was rooted in the Constitution. She called on women to work for "true temperance." This began her effort to achieve narrative coherence that Prohibition was a "grave menace in American life." Showing tactical acumen, she refused to say *how* she planned to fight Prohibition, so as not to telegraph her strategies to the well-organized dry movement. The *Times* ran the story on the front page, above the fold.[25]

On May 28, 1929, the WONPR held its first meeting, chaired by Sabin. The organization elected temporary leaders, until a nationwide convention could be held for an official vote. The group issued a statement of organizational goals and, in a telling bit of initial framing, promised an "aggressive effort for the protection of the American home." They decried the negative effects of Prohibition on the rule of law and children, vowing to "replace the present corruption and hypocrisy with sobriety and honesty."[26]

Employing another Insider strategy of appealing to credible experts, a delegate from Vermont emphasized the need, even and especially in rural states, for the organization to circulate "statements about local conditions under Prohibition made by college presidents, lawyers, local enforcement officers, district nurses, etc."[27] The Insider status of the group's leaders resulted in positive framing in national newspaper stories, which included lists of prominent members and lauded the "unimpeachable leadership" of the WONPR.[28]

One way of empirically assessing the relative conventionality of the WONPR leadership that is consistent with how we have measured stakes in conformity is to look at marital and social class characteristics. Analyzing membership rolls, only 3 percent (1 out of 33) of the WONPR national board members were unmarried. Likewise, only 3 percent of state-level board chairs (2 out of 66) were unmarried. Among all the leadership (all boards and other official positions) at both national and state levels, only 6 percent were unmarried (56 out of 863).[29] Marriage, especially to high status men, was a particularly useful tie to conventional power in a context where women's roles were limited by both convention and law. Likewise, the national board consisted of well-to-do society women, whose husbands were bank and railroad tycoons, politicians, and even the son of President Teddy Roosevelt. Further, those who were unmarried tended to otherwise be of social distinction, such as prolific psychiatrist and author Esther L. Richards, who served on the executive committee for the Maryland chapter of the WONPR. The WONPR purposefully selected its leadership from individuals with the greatest stakes in conventionality.

Not long after the initial meeting of the WONPR, Sabin made public statements about plans to survey the "wives of workers throughout the nation." Continuing the push to reclaim moral standing for women who supported repeal, Sabin said that the idea for forming the WONPR came from "the number of letters we received from mothers expressing their anxiety about the number of young people who are drinking and their belief that the Eighteenth Amendment is the principal cause."[30] Immediately below the news story about Sabin and the WONPR, a front-page story continued under the headline "2 Dry Agents Seized in Rum-Running Plot." The story told of a federal Prohibition agent charged with violent crimes in 1924 and 1925, who had then been dismissed in 1926 for "inefficiency and lack of initiative."[31] The deputy Prohibition administrator in charge of the eastern district of New York subsequently rehired him. Shortly thereafter, he was caught caravanning five trucks full of liquor through Long Island.[32] Serendipity for narrative coherence.

Behind the scenes, Sabin used member lists from organizations such as the Red Cross to recruit leaders for different states who were "outstanding in their respective communities as women of unimpeachable integrity, and known for their interest in public welfare and good citizenship."[33] Meanwhile, in the public eye, President Hoover's Wickersham Commission—tasked with assessing the criminal justice system under Prohibition—released its much-anticipated initial report in January 1930. Upping the ante on the rhetorical debate with the drys over who could rightfully claim to be protecting American families, Sabin quickly issued a public statement: "I can find nothing in [the Wickersham Report's] recommendations which promises to make the Volstead Act acceptable to the citizens of this country. I cannot be optimistic about its plan for expediting arrests, trials, and punishments and the expanding of Federal prisons. This plan places the government in the unfortunate position of a parent who has failed to win the respect of his children and now frantically tries to beat them into submission. It can only reach the bootlegger, the smuggler, and the racketeer."[34]

Two weeks later Sabin made front-page news, teaming with Republican James Wadsworth Jr.—a former senator and future long-serving congressman representing New York—to debate James Doran, federal Prohibition commissioner, and Mamie White Colvin of the New York Women's Christian Temperance Union.[35] Sabin argued that Prohibition "led to [the] largest organized criminal class in this or any other country." She also continued to reclaim the moral rhetoric of both family values and "true" temperance.[36]

In February 1930, women leaders of the repeal movement testified before the House Judiciary Committee. By all accounts, Pauline Sabin stole the show: "Applause interrupted the women more than once during their testimony. . . . Caustic remarks from Mrs. Sabin developed some of this applause, especially when she spoke of her organization's contempt for "drinking dry" members of Congress and State Legislatures. Mrs. Sabin spoke bluntly and her emerald ring glittered as she waved her hand when she referred to 'the heart-burnings and heart-achings' of mothers over prohibition, the 'co-educational speakeasies' and the 'political cabal of the Anti-Saloon League.'"[37]

Although she continued to frame Prohibition repeal as an issue of public safety and child welfare, Sabin also began adding new lines of rhetorical attack. In response to a question about whether Prohibition had diminished drinking, she cited data from nineteen million Metropolitan Life Insurance policyholders indicating a sixfold increase in deaths from alcoholism over the past decade.[38] Furthering her claim that Prohibition was unconstitutional, Sabin argued that the Eighteenth Amendment violated the Ninth and Tenth Amendments, which guaranteed individuals and states all freedoms not specifically designated to the federal government by the Constitution.

She also intensified her effort to wrestle the mantle of morality, femininity, and even sobriety away from Prohibition activists, arguing that women "have seen an alleged moral reform debauch public and private life." Appealing to a value strikingly similar to the *belief* element of stakes in conformity, Sabin told the committee: "I am here today to plead to this distinguished body to pass some remedial legislation which will replace the present era of lawlessness, corruption, hypocrisy and killings, with honesty, temperance and sobriety, and thereby will receive the support and obedience of the American people."[39]

As Sabin and other prominent leaders were advocating at the federal level, the WONPR organized and mobilized in state politics as well. The week following Sabin's testimony to Congress, Albany representatives of the WONPR attended an extended debate before the New York State Senate and Assembly Code Committee about a bill to increase state enforcement of Prohibition. Women had been prominent at such hearings for the dry side since 1920, but at this hearing "women were conspicuous on the anti-prohibition side" during debate, with "a larger representation of women than at any similar occasion in the past." This time, "women were constantly on the firing line" on behalf of repeal.[40] The bill failed due to lack of Republican support. Message delivered.

With the inaugural national convention of the WONPR set for late April of 1930, Sabin campaigned to increase recruitment. She targeted women in college.[41] Again making front-page news, she led the WONPR in staging "the first 'wet' mass meeting in New York City sponsored by women," which was "attended by men and women prominent in both major political parties and leaders in social work, civic affairs, the Church and the professions."[42] Two days before the national convention, Sabin again held a public debate with Mamie Colvin of the WCTU at a Harlem meeting of the New York Council of Women. In addition to her now standard lines of attack about the effects of Prohibition on children, crime, and the consumption of hard liquor, Sabin assailed hypocrisy, saying, "The Federal Government is saying—and is spending many millions trying to enforce its statement—'you can't have a drink,' and at the same time hundreds of thousands of people, many of them highly respected in their communities, are doing their very best to get one."[43] The appeal to conventionality could not have been more explicit.

Having done her best to increase initial public support for the WONPR, Sabin presided over the organization's inaugural convention, which began on April 23, 1930, in Cleveland, Ohio. Sabin reported one hundred thousand members were added in the previous year, with thirteen state chapters of the WONPR organized. Other states sent representatives to the convention, but had yet to formally organize. Convention representatives voted to work for repeal rather than modification of Prohibition, and to push for the control of alcohol by individual states. Although there was much discussion about changing the name of the organization from "Reform" to "Repeal," the WONPR decided "that 'Reform' was too valuable a word to abandon to the Drys, who had long claimed a monopoly on it, and that it truly represented the WONPR emphasis upon betterment of present conditions."[44]

The organization also proposed using a parliamentary procedure that had never been used before and that has not been used since: holding conventions in every state to vote on a constitutional amendment. This strategy laid out a viable, legal path for an amendment based on Article V of the Constitution; but it was also a risky tactic due to procedural disuse and lack of legal precedent. James Wadsworth Jr. called the procedure "something which not one person in ten thousand had ever heard of at the time Mrs. Sabin first advocated it."[45] This stroke of parliamentary genius would allow the repeal movement to sidestep voting on an Amendment in state legislatures, where the Anti-Saloon League wielded enormous influence. It also provided a mechanism of direct democracy that would allow citizens themselves, rather than their representatives, to vote on repeal.

Following the inaugural WONPR convention, Sabin set about trying to organize state chapters, of which there were thirty-three (plus Washington D.C.) by the summer of 1930. The WONPR began using a political strategy borrowed from the Anti-Saloon League, getting "every candidate for political office" to declare himself definitively for or against repeal of the Eighteenth Amendment. This included efforts in state politics to "include wards and precincts, so that even candidates for minor offices will know of the organized opposition to the prohibition law." Ultimately, however, due to the enshrinement of Prohibition as a Constitutional Amendment, Sabin believed that it was necessary to "campaign for a change in the personnel of Congress."[46] This focus bore fruit in the 1930 mid-term elections, when seventy seats in the House of Representatives and four in the Senate switched from dry to wet.[47] After special elections conducted before Congress reconvened, the Republican Party lost control of the House for the first time since 1919, and shared a fifty-fifty split with Democrats in the Senate.

Flush with mid-term momentum, the WONPR began framing the 1932 national election as a referendum on repealing the Eighteenth Amendment, at both the federal and state levels, arguing that: "'Repeal' or 'no repeal' has become the issue."[48] In the interim, Sabin continued to grow the WONPR using Insider appeals and connections, noting that "women educators, doctors, social workers and philanthropists" had joined. Attempting to broaden her constituency, Sabin stressed that the WONPR was "non-partisan" and "non-sectarian." Further, she said the group was determined "to rid this country of the domination of a well-organized fanatical minority and we will not be satisfied until we have cut this cancerous growth out of our body politic, whether it take five years, 10 years, or 50 years."[49] It would only take two.

In April 1931, the WONPR held its second annual convention, this time in Washington, D.C. By then, there were six states where membership was higher for the WONPR than the WCTU. In addition to continued growth, choosing Insiders as leaders and spokespersons was paying off. A delegate from the D.C. chapter of the organization opened the conference, reporting that, "several Senators and Congressman of the Wet Bloc had recently remarked that the WONPR's signal service had been that of *throwing the mantle of respectability* over the whole movement against Prohibition."[50] Going beyond the first conference, the organization resolved to back only candidates who supported outright repeal. Two days later, fronting a contingent of 534 delegates to the conference and using her extensive political connections in the Republican Party, Sabin brokered a face-to-face meeting with President Hoover. She presented him with a resolution from the WONPR asking for state control of alcohol because it would better represent the different views of populations from each state. She cited the findings of the President's own Wickersham Commission to support her request.[51]

Other connections began to pay off too. Two weeks after being a featured speaker at the conference, labor leader Matthew Woll began an effort "to align organized labor's full membership of more than 2,000,000 behind a campaign for dry law modification."[52] This connection to organized labor was the result of considerable effort on the part of the WONPR. The previous summer, while advocating for repeal in a variety of public forums, including radio, print and public debate, Sabin began laying the groundwork for a rhetorical defense against her greatest weakness for swaying popular sentiment: elitism.[53] She declared that, "prohibition is the grossest piece of class legislation ever passed in any country." Hyperbole aside, Sabin correctly noted that many a business owner supported Prohibition because he thought it was good for business, while simultaneously "reaching out his hand for another cocktail."[54]

This strategy distinguished Sabin and the WONPR from its most influential sister organization, the Association against the Prohibition Amendment. The AAPA was chaired by Pierre S. Du Pont II, who, as a captain of industry, had ideological and political—but mostly financial—reasons for supporting repeal, as part of a broader effort to reduce the size of the federal government and more importantly the tax burden on corporations and the wealthy.[55] In contrast, Sabin actively worked to ensure that, despite their high status leadership, elitism was *not* part of the WONPR's rhetoric or strategy. These efforts proved useful in the ongoing public debate over Prohibition and helped mobilize everyday citizens on behalf of repeal.

For instance, Woll and Sabin organized a mass protest of Prohibition by ten thousand blue-collar workers in Newark, Jew Jersey.[56] At the same time, the membership of the WONPR grew rapidly from seeking recruits "by working through head of departments and mangers in establishments employing women: hotels, clubs, factories, cleaning and dyeing works, department stores and the like."[57] Labor connections allowed Sabin to convincingly point to the economic benefits of repeal for workers, even as she continued to provide moral cover for the movement by also framing repeal as an issue of public safety and family values.[58]

While she was forming coalitions with the working class, Sabin also brokered coalitions with different types of women. Collaborating with the Junior League, she helped organize young women against Prohibition into a Service League.[59] Speaking at the initial meetings, Sabin emphasized outreach, such that, "By sending recruiting teams into schools and colleges, factories and stores, through theatre aisles at matinee and maintaining booths at conventions, the organizers . . . hope to enroll several thousand young women into the Service League."[60] With a diverse array of connections and a multifaceted but coherent reform narrative established, Sabin and the WONPR began preparing for the upcoming national elections.

On New Year's Day 1932, Pauline Sabin pressed for stronger political influence by going against her own original stance on Prohibition and "one-plank" voters. She sent a letter to local leaders of the WONPR, telling her organizers that the following year would be critical to the repeal effort. She instructed them to "put patriotism to our country ahead of any political loyalty, declare a moratorium on party affiliations and give our support to the party which represents the aims and purposes of the [WONPR]."[61]

On April 12, 1932, the third annual conference of the WONPR met in Washington D.C. Opening the convention, Sabin said that, "The influence which we of this Organization will be able to wield in the coming election, if our members are not led away from their cause to other issues, will be enormous." Further, "[We] will not be satisfied with apathetic acquiescence" by political parties. "We demand militant support."[62]

Howard McBain—a political scientist, constitutional scholar, and then dean of graduate studies at Columbia University—was a featured speaker at the conference. He had recently authored *Prohibition: Legal and Illegal*, a book about the constitutionality of altering the Eighteenth Amendment.[63] McBain rhetorically asked which tactics the group should use to fight for repeal. "My answer would be to take a leaf from the book of the Anti-Saloon League. Go into every congressional and senatorial campaign. Force the candidates into the open, absolutely.

IMAGE 4. Delegates to the convention of the Women's Organization for National Prohibition Reform gather in front of the Capitol Building for a group photo in Washington, D.C., April 13, 1932. The WONPR delegation is on hand to call on their representatives and senators to repeal the dry law. (Original caption. Source: AP Photo ID: 320413012)

Work for any candidate of any party who promises to vote for Repeal. Vote against any candidate of any party who refuses to promise. Fight the Devil with his own weapons."[64] The next day, hundreds of delegates from the conference gathered for news cameras in front of the Capitol steps (see image 4). The delegates then subdivided by states and called upon their respective Congressional representatives in person. The following day, Sabin spoke before the Senate Judiciary Subcommittee about "wet bills." Bringing a large contingent from the conference, "women . . . crowded so heavily into the first room in which the subcommittee met that the hearing had to be moved to a larger chamber."[65]

Following the convention, the WONPR began a "repeal week" drive for membership and donations in forty-one states. True to form, the "campaign [was] carried on by movies, the radio, street mailings, motorcades, mass meetings and booths."[66] All WONPR and Service League members were expected to participate, with a stated public goal of reaching a membership of one million. Opening the drive with a radio address, Sabin directly spoke to the necessity of reclaiming stig-matizing epithets.

> When I speak of changing attitudes toward prohibition, . . . I think about the word "wet," and how different its meaning is today from what was intended when first the term was hurled at the opponents of the eighteenth amendment. It was intended to be an insult, a sneer, or at best, a flippancy. Some of the women shrank from the characterization. We tried to think of ways to persuade public and press to give us a fairer, more accurate description. We failed. "Wet" was brief, "wet" would fit neatly into headlines. So we are fated to be "wets" to the end of the story—a story, by the way, whose end is in sight today. A term of contempt has been changed into one of honor. Today we wear our "wet" tags proudly. Today "wet" does not mean a person addicted to drink, any more than "dry" means a person who has forsworn alcoholic beverages.[67] To be a wet is to be one who reveres the Constitution as it was given to us by the Fathers of the Nation, and who resents making the Constitution a catch-all for police blue laws.[68]

This membership and donation drive resulted in the well-worn criticism that Sabin and the WONPR were out-of-touch elitists. Humorist Will Rogers used his "Daily Telegram," syndicated in more than five hundred newspapers across the country, to joke: "See a lot of pictures of Mrs. Vincent Astor and society women of New York taking up nickels on the street to aid the anti-prohibition campaign. Such antics as that are sure to win the small town and the farm women over. Yes sir, right over to the opposite side!"[69] Rogers argued that Prohibition would remain intact because "the wrong people want it repealed."[70]

For her part, Sabin used the opportunity to leverage the WONPR's conventional yet populist coalition, penning a letter to the editor of the *Times* that landed on the back page: "We are, of course, greatly disappointed that Mr. Rogers seems to have so little use for us as an organization, but we are wondering why he feels that the American Federation of Labor, the American Legion, the American Bar Association, the American Medical Association and innumerable Chambers of Commerce throughout the United States are 'the wrong people.'"[71] Successfully claiming allegiance with the AFL, veterans, the ABA, AMA, and business community was no small accomplishment. Sabin's counterpunch landed squarely.

Meanwhile, on the morality front, D. Leigh Colvin, chair of the Prohibition National Committee, used a radio debate with a representative of the WONPR to vituperate "women wets" as "Bacchantian maidens parching for wine." Despite a "storm of criticism," he doubled down the following day, adding that, "the wet women who, like the drunkards whom their program will produce, would take pennies off the eyes of the dead for the sake of legalizing booze" were "dominated either by appetite or avarice." His slander backfired. Provided another platform to tout the credibility of her leaders, Sabin publicly responded with an open letter demanding an apology, writing, "You state the wet women have been 'depriving the poor and unemployed of money which should have gone to them." May I call to your attention that, with the exception of one woman, every member of the executive committee of the unemployed for New York engaged in raising money for the unemployed this Winter is likewise a member of the Women's Organization for National Prohibition Reform? Where were your representatives on that committee?"[72] Other leaders of the repeal movement rallied to defend the WONPR, saying the attack was "entirely unwarranted, bigoted, and tyrannical—a gross insult to a splendid organization of women."[73]

As election season began to heat up in the summer of the 1932, the WONPR sent representatives to both major party conventions. WONPR representatives rejected the Republicans' mixed plank on repeal "because it would not cure the present prohibition evil" and was judged as merely "an attempt to befog the issue."[74] Even more directly, Sabin called the Republican position "a fraud and a deception" that "should be rejected."[75]

In contrast, the Democrats adopted a stance of outright repeal drafted by activist groups, including the WONPR. Sabin said the plank "incorporates every principle of our organization," and that as a result the Democrats' "chances of victory in November have been greatly strengthened, because the repeal action will swing millions of Republicans over to Democracy."[76] Following the conventions, the WONPR publicly endorsed Franklin D. Roosevelt for president.[77] Sixty-four Republicans in the WONPR openly dissented by petition, stating that they would still vote for Hoover. Issuing a public statement in response, Sabin said voting for Hoover was members' prerogative, but that they also should not delude themselves that Republicans supported repeal. She concluded, "I can find no comfort in this petition. But perhaps the Women's Christian Temperance Union, the Anti-Saloon League, the Methodist Board of Prohibition, Temperance and Public Morals, and Bishop [James] Cannon will."[78] In the end, only one of the public dissenters actually resigned from the organization.[79] By virtue of Sabin's deft management and active engagement with dissenting factions, the WONPR "received 150 resignations" in total from the national organization after endorsing Roosevelt. Meanwhile, they gained over one hundred thirty thousand new members.[80]

To clarify politicians' positions in the upcoming election, the WONPR conducted a poll of candidates for Congress across all states. They found overwhelming support for repeal among Democrats and even a considerable level of support among Republicans, 135 of whom broke rank from their party's platform and supported repeal.[81] When the election finally arrived, repeal candidates won victories all across America. "Wets" gained 49 seats in the House and six in the Senate. Roosevelt won 472 electoral votes to Hoover's 59. Democrats now controlled both chambers and the executive branch, with a clear mandate for repeal. As a foretaste of the final battle, "every referendum on the question of Repeal of the Eighteenth

Amendment or Repeal of state Prohibition laws and enforcement acts was won by an overwhelming popular vote."[82]

The WONPR now focused their efforts on getting a Constitutional Amendment through both chambers of Congress. Sabin immediately began urging Americans to pressure their political representatives to support repeal.[83] But getting politicians to support unqualified repeal, as opposed to compromises or modifications—such as only allowing beer and wine or other changes to the Volstead Act—would not be easy, especially because a repeal amendment required two-thirds support from both chambers. Likewise, successfully getting an amendment ratified by state conventions rather than state legislatures would be extremely challenging.[84] On the first day of the lame duck Congressional session, a repeal amendment bill was defeated in the House, despite getting 272 votes in favor and 144 against.[85] In response, the WONPR set up committees to study legislation.[86] They also established educational programs on "constitutional and legislative procedures" that could effectively enact repeal. The group's membership continued to grow as Sabin forecast 1933 as the year for a "return to temperance and tolerance" and "the end of the dark age of dry rule in this country."[87]

At the start of 1933 a repeal amendment bill was introduced in the Senate that included modifications from the Anti-Saloon League and a provision to ratify the amendment through state legislatures rather than conventions.[88] The WONPR vowed to have the provisions removed and opposed any bill other than an outright repeal amendment submitted to state conventions for ratification.[89] Sabin continued to use a variety of tactics to push a repeal amendment through Congress. During a radio address, she again called on all citizens to pressure their representatives, particularly senators, for full repeal and to oppose the provision giving the federal government the right to regulate liquor. Most of all, she implored people to stay in the fight.[90] As the legislative battle dragged on, Sabin managed to earn an (ever-elusive) endorsement for repeal from Jesus Christ himself. Well, at least some of his well-placed representatives. The rector of the New York City Episcopal Church of the Transfiguration sermonized to his congregants that, "I do not hesitate to name Mrs. Sabin as a great leader fighting heroically against a colossal evil," adding that, "such are the mighty souls Jesus Christ inspires."[91]

Apparently, Jesus swayed the Senate. Three days after her radio address, a bill for a repeal amendment—stripped of provisions—passed the Senate.[92] The next week, the bill passed the House 289 to 121. The WONPR called the bill's passage "an epoch-making event for the American people."[93] Never one to celebrate prematurely, Sabin's own official statement was far less triumphant: "We realize that only half the fight is won and will continue our efforts until the repeal resolution has been ratified by the necessary number of States."[94]

Leaders and delegates of the WONPR met in Washington, D.C., for their fourth annual conference in the first week of April 1933. They mobilized repeal drives in every state.[95] In the aftermath of legislative victory, Sabin opened the gathering by stressing the importance of "translating the emotional into the practical." The next month, the organization kicked off "Ratification Week" in New York at an event attended by theater, concert, and opera stars.[96] On the eve of the vote in New York later that month, Sabin used a radio address to call for a "twenty-to-one vote. It is the moral effect of a smashing victory in New York that we want."[97] The next day 96 percent of New Yorkers voted for repeal.[98] Pauline Sabin was elected as a delegate to the state convention to help cast the state's official vote for the repeal amendment.

Throughout the summer, the WONPR continued mobilizing at the state level, emphasizing that locations perceived as unlikely to support repeal, such as Alabama, Arkansas, Kentucky, Tennessee, and West Virginia were critical to ratification.[99] Sabin stressed that "much depends on the women voters in the South."[100] Showing the strength of the research arm of the organization, not only did repeal pass in all these states, Pauline Sabin correctly predicted the final tally of states that would ratify the Twenty-First Amendment: thirty-eight. As victory drew near, she urged lenient laws and quick action by the states to take control of liquor traffic, saying, "We must go back to where we left off 13 years ago when we abandoned our efforts toward liquor control and temperance and gave ourselves over to Dr. Fanatic to be bled. The liquor problem needs scientific diagnosis and treatment."[101]

On September 26, 1933, the leadership of the WONPR voted to dissolve the organization after the Twenty-First Amendment was ratified.[102] At the official disbanding, Sabin said, "I want to thank the 1,500,000 women who in every city, town and hamlet in the United States have made a gallant fight to restore good government."[103] The organization had accomplished what seemed impossible only five years prior.

Fortuitous aspects of political opportunity certainly played an important role in the repeal of Prohibition, such as the Great Depression and the subsequent increased need for revenue by state and federal governments, along with the creation of (legitimate) jobs for those in industries connected to alcohol production, distribution, and consumption. At the same time, opportunities do not translate into success without motivated, capable individuals who can effectively take advantage. The WONPR's political strategy rooted in elite Insider leadership combined with broad organizational inclusiveness and coalition building also deserves credit for repeal. Charismatic leadership also was undoubtedly important and Sabin's ability to argue for repeal in ways that achieved narrative coherence and fidelity was often the result of her charismatic yet articulate style. But charisma without Insiders' connections is merely the limited power to temporarily influence an audience.

A CONTEMPORARY EXAMPLE: THE NORMALIZATION
OF CANNABIS

While the parallels are by no means perfect, particularly given the difference in time and political environment, the successful repeal of alcohol Prohibition by Insiders such as Pauline Sabin does provide insight into contemporary efforts to legalize medical and recreational cannabis use in U.S. states. One difference is particularly important to consider in making this comparison. Because of the Eighteenth Amendment, the Prohibition repeal movement was necessarily a national movement that also fought on state grounds. Conversely, efforts at marijuana legalization have been state movements that also fight on federal grounds. The variation in laws about cannabis across American states in the early twenty-first century provides a natural laboratory for examining which attributes of states and their populations were most influential in the normalization of laws regarding cannabis use.

Having shown how *narrative fidelity* and *coherence* played into Prohibition repeal using content analysis, we now use state laws about cannabis as an empirical test of which social and political factors predict legislative changes involving the legalization of previously illegal drugs. As the example of Prohibition repeal shows, the first step to achieving normalization is demonstrating that conventional citizens support repealing drug criminalization (narrative fidelity). Here Insiders must successfully articulate narratives where reformers and users of the drug are convincingly portrayed as *not* deviant (narrative coherence). Appealing to conventional social institutions such as criminal justice, family, and medicine is necessary for achieving narrative coherence among public audiences. To the extent that movements achieve fidelity and coherence for their normalization narratives, they can more effectively influence public opinion about the il/legal status of the drug in question. As public condemnation of an issue softens, social and criminal penalties are likely to follow. Lower public condemnation and punitive thresholds also allow more Hiders to transition into Insiders, as we saw in the cases of both Prohibition repeal and LGBT rights movements.

Initial successful efforts at framing cannabis normalization primarily focused on creating compassion for users with life-threatening diseases such as cancer. Symbolically, the first medical marijuana state law was named the "Compassionate Use Act." As medical framing began to achieve some success at the state level, reform advocates started expanding the potential populations eligible by adding other chronic illnesses for inclusion in therapeutic use. This medical framing effectively provided a bridge between the predominantly criminal, "no medicinal use" claims of the federal government's "Schedule 1" classification of cannabis and the idea that the plant and its chemical compounds had a wide range of possible therapeutic uses.[104]

In conjunction with successful medical framing, beginning in the 1990s, mass media news stories began to normalize cannabis use among celebrities (e.g., Willie Nelson and Snoop Dog), even as standard news stories about drugs and crime continued to stigmatize lower-class users.[105] Recreational marijuana use also proliferated in popular media during this period, with movies such *Friday* (1995) and *Half Baked* (1998), to television series such as *That 70's Show* (1998–2006). The increase in recreational cannabis use in mass and popular media stories was followed closely by increases in adolescent rates of cannabis use between 1977 and 1999.[106]

These changes in cultural framing reflected the increasing acceptance of marijuana use among the American public. Since 1973, the General Social Surveys—nationally representative samples of American adults—have asked respondents: "Do you think the use of marijuana should be made legal or not?" Figure 13 shows the percentage of Americans who have favored the legalization and criminalization of cannabis between 1973 and 2016. In 1973, Americans favored cannabis being illegal rather than legal by a four-to-one margin. There was slight movement toward legalization at the end of the 1970s, but the "Just Say No" and "War on Drugs" rhetoric and policies of the 1980s pushed down support for legalization. The highest opposition to cannabis legalization was in 1990. Since then, support for legalization has steadily increased, such that in the 2016 wave of the survey, American adults supported legalization over criminalization by a ratio of three to two. These increasingly permissive views about marijuana across generations are also significantly connected to increases in levels of cannabis use among the public.[107]

The ascendance of the religious right as a political movement in the late 1970s and 1980s synchronizes perfectly with the nadir of support for the legalization of cannabis, just as increasing support for marijuana legalization synchronizes perfectly with the decline of Americans who are religiously affiliated.[108] While these changes to public opinion are important in their own right, how they connect to policy change is an open question, as the linkages between public opinion and policy outcomes are often contingent on other factors, such as political opportunities, the strength of opposition movements, and the availability of mechanisms of direct democracy.[109]

To test empirically and rigorously whether and how more permissive views of cannabis among the public led to more permissive legal policies, we created a dataset that uses American states as the organizing unit and includes measures for both public opinion and state-level social policies regarding cannabis. For public opinion about marijuana, we used the percentage of adolescents in each state who reported believing that occasional cannabis use was dangerous. We used adolescents' views as a gauge of whether ideologies of cannabis as a highly dangerous drug remain intact or have eroded. Views of youth are ideal for gauging this type

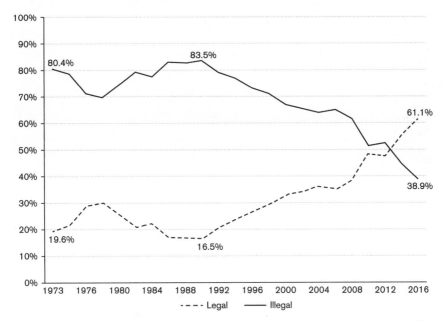

FIGURE 13. Americans' attitudes toward marijuana legalization. (Source: 1973–2016 General Social Surveys)

of change, as teenagers' views reflect the ideologies of both their parents and also of the most recent generation of adults. For outcomes, we coded whether each American state had cannabis prohibition (coded as 0), medical legalization (1), or recreational legalization (2) in the year 2018.

To account for other social and political factors likely to predict these policy outcomes, we aggregated information on the demographic, political, and religious characteristics of the citizens of all fifty American states. To account for political representation, we added measures for the percentage of state legislatures that were Democrats. To account for structural political mechanisms, we created measures for two aspects of direct democracy that provide for greater influence of public opinion over social policy: the ability of citizens to initiate referenda on legal statutes and the ability of state legislatures to initiate referenda for citizen votes. To account for a political constituency likely to oppose legalization—and the population most connected to the demonization of illicit substances throughout American history—we included measures for the percentage of each state that identify as conservative Protestants.[110] We also controlled for the racial composition, region, urbanicity, education level and political ideology of the citizens of each state.

The most important predictors of state-level policies about marijuana, in order of strength, were: (1) adolescents' views of whether cannabis is dangerous; (2) the

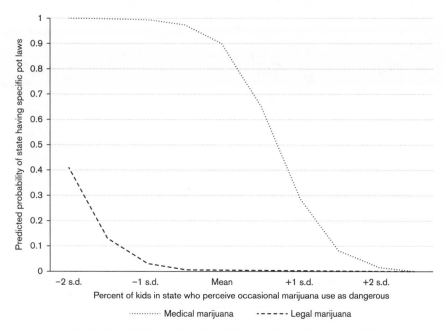

FIGURE 14. Predicted probabilities of medical and recreational marijuana by adolescents' views of whether occasional marijuana use is dangerous.

percentage of a state that is evangelical Protestant; and (3) whether citizens can initiate referenda on statutes. Figure 14 shows the predicted probability that a state has legalized either medical or recreational marijuana use across the range of adolescents' views about the danger of cannabis use. In states where public opinion is more favorable (two standard deviations below the mean of adolescents' views of whether pot use is "always dangerous"), the likelihood of having medical marijuana is nearly 100 percent and the likelihood of having recreational cannabis is 40 percent. For states where greater shares of young people continue to believe that cannabis use, even in moderate amounts, is dangerous (two standard deviations above the mean of adolescents' views of whether pot use is "always dangerous"), the likelihood of having legalized medical cannabis is reduced to only 2 percent and the probability of having recreational cannabis is effectively zero. In essence, the range of the variable about adolescents' views of the dangerousness of cannabis predicts the entire range of probability for whether states have legalized medical or recreational marijuana.

Noticeably, however, having low levels of positive public opinion about cannabis only makes recreational cannabis possible, not highly probable. Rather, it takes a *combination* of factors for states to pass legislation legalizing recreational can-

TABLE 2. Attributes of States That Had Recreational Marijuana in 2018

State	Public Initiated Statute	% Teens Think Cannabis Use Is Dangerous	Percent Evangelical Protestant
Alaska	✓	17	26
California	✓	20	18
Colorado	✓	17	23
Maine	✓	20	15
Massachusetts	✓	19	11
Nevada	✓	20	13
Oregon	✓	20	30
Vermont		21	08
Washington	✓	16	25

SOURCES: Ballotpedia for public initiated statutes; 2012 National Survey on Drug Use and Health for percent of teens who think occasional cannabis use is dangerous; 2007 Pew Religious Landscape Survey for percent Evangelical Protestant.

nabis use. Table 2 shows the attributes for the significant predictors of cannabis policy outcomes in the nine states that had recreational cannabis in 2018 (Alaska, California, Colorado, Maine, Massachusetts, Nevada, Oregon, Vermont, and Washington). Importantly, all states other than Vermont have mechanisms for citizens to initiate and vote on state-wide referenda. To get recreational cannabis in a state typically required a combination of having favorable public opinion, publicly initiated referenda and less than 30 percent of a state's citizens being evangelical Protestants. Vermont was the first state to pass standard legislation legalizing recreational marijuana rather than using a state-wide referendum. Notably, in Vermont there was considerably less opposition from evangelical Protestants, who constitute only 8 percent of the populace.

Our empirical model explains 85 percent of the overall variance in cannabis policy outcomes (results from the full model are available in the appendix). As social science and public policy analyses go, the model is extremely efficient. Using measures for public opinion, religious characteristics, citizen-initiated referenda, and political representation accounts for nearly all the variation in cannabis policy outcomes. If public opinion toward the normalization of cannabis continues to become more favorable, as it has in the past twenty-five years, many more states will legalize medical and recreational marijuana in the near future.[111] Based on the criteria outlined by the model, we predict that the next states to legalize recreational cannabis will be Michigan and Montana.[112] Inevitably, Midwestern and Bible Belt states with high levels of condemnation about marijuana use, high concentrations of conservative Protestants and without direct democracy initiatives will be the last states to legalize cannabis use, if they do so at all.

PROHIBITION REPEAL AND CANNABIS
LEGALIZATION IN COMPARATIVE CONTEXT

The repeal of Prohibition and the contemporary legalization of marijuana in American states highlight some implications of deviance management strategies for normalization movements. First, vocal Insiders who effectively argue for narrative fidelity and coherence about normalization are needed to shift public debate and perception from stigmatization to tolerance, if not acceptance. Without Pauline Sabin, the repeal of Prohibition would not have happened as quickly as it did. Her Insider credentials, savvy political acumen and high-status connections made her an ideal leader for normalization.

Second, Insiders are likely to have the most success leading efforts at normalization when they can effectively appeal to existing normative social institutions. Although cannabis reform has yet to produce a singular figurehead like Pauline Sabin, the movement has nonetheless made substantial inroads to normalization by appealing to the therapeutic uses of cannabinoids. The success of the medical marijuana movement opened the door to wider legalization efforts by destigmatizing some forms of cannabis use. Once the door to decriminalization was open, normalization advocates were able to appeal to two issues that also proved vital to the repeal of Prohibition: the potential for government revenue from taxation and populist appeal to let the constituents of states decide for themselves how best to regulate the drug.

Finally, both cases point toward the dual importance of organized religion and public opinion in both the stigmatization and normalization of drugs. Conservative Protestants were the driving force behind the temperance and Prohibition movements. Similarly, the religious right was a strong supporter of the harsh enforcement policies of the War on Drugs in the 1980s, helping drive down support for cannabis legalization from its higher levels at the end of the 1970s. Ultimately, however, this alliance of conservative religion and politics backfired in two related ways. First, the alignment of conservative Protestantism and the Republican Party led to generational decline in organized religion among the American public. Concurrently, the Puritan approach to substance use in general, and marijuana use specifically, contributed to a backlash among younger generations of Americans, a majority of whom now support legalizing cannabis. Both Prohibition repeal and empirical analyses of policy outcomes demonstrate the power of public opinion to sway laws about the regulation of leisurely vices, at least in representative democracies.

Insiders are the most effective reform advocates. The best rhetorical strategies for normalization are appeals to conventional social institutions and the conventionality of Insiders. Population characteristics also are inflection points for the cultural and political stigmatization/normalization of "lifestyle" deviance. Here public opinion about deviance is key. The examples of both the repeal of alcohol Prohibition and the reform of cannabis laws at the state level demonstrate that changes in public discourse, opinion, and policy do follow discernable patterns. When Insiders can turn public discourse and therefore opinion in the direction of normalization, social policy reforms follow. Winning in the court of public opinion is indeed necessary for winning in the court of law.

Conclusion

Studying Deviance Management

In *Obergefell v. Hodges* (2015), The United States Supreme Court issued a ruling that consolidated six lower-court cases related to the legal status of same-sex marriage from Michigan, Ohio, Kentucky and Tennessee. By a vote of 5–4, the Court ruled that all U.S. states, possessions, and territories must issue marriage licenses to same-sex couples and recognize same-sex marriages enacted in other states and territories.

While a signature moment for gay and lesbian civil rights, *Obergefell v. Hodges* represented the culmination of a major social change, rather than its beginning. Prior to the ruling, courts in twenty-six states already had legalized same-sex unions.[1] In eight other states, legislatures already had voted in favor of same-sex marriage prior to the Supreme Court ruling.[2] Also prior to the ruling, same-sex marriage had been legalized via popular vote in Maine, Maryland, and Washington. How did this normalization occur?

The General Social Survey has been asking nationally representative samples of American adults about the morality of "sexual relations between two adults of the same sex" since 1973 (see figure 7.1), with the possible responses of "always wrong," "almost always wrong," "sometimes wrong" and "not wrong at all."

In 1973, most Americans (73 percent) strongly believed in the immorality of homosexuality, an attitude that reached its zenith in 1986 (79 percent). From there, however, attitudes began to change. The belief that same-sex relations are "always wrong" had dropped to 61 percent by 1996 and then to 56 percent by 2006. The sea change occurred in 2010, the first time the belief that homosexual relations are "always wrong" was held by less than half of Americans. By 2018, this number dropped to approximately 32 percent. Put simply, until the 2000s, you were devi-

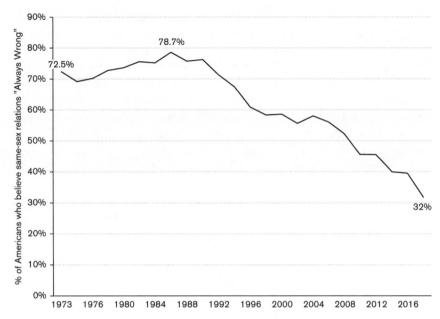

FIGURE 15. Percentage of Americans who believe that "sexual relations between two adults of the same sex" are "always wrong." (Source: 1973–2018 General Social Surveys)

ant as an American—in the sense of normative evaluations—if you were gay or lesbian (or supportive of gay rights). By 2008 and later, people who viewed homosexuality as inherently immoral had become the deviants, at least statistically speaking.

This book has told an important part of the story about how such change happens—how an entire category of people can transition from deviant to "normal." Much existing research has focused upon the role of organized social movements in fostering change, emphasizing the important roles played by resource mobilization, organizational structures, political opportunity, and coalition building.[3] But outside of studies of social movements explicitly examining issue framing, how individuals message about their own deviance has been a tangential concern at best.[4] Further, how and why individuals choose particular strategies for managing stigma is generally obscured by a focus on whether social movements succeed or fail.

Our approach differs by focusing on patterns of deviance management from the perspective of those labeled, and how these patterns are rooted in the relative salience of both deviant and normative social identities. Put another way, while much existing research on reform-oriented social movements has focused on *how* such movements can change their social status over time, our book has tried to explain *why* members of a deviant subculture might be motivated to seek normalization in the first place; as a proactive strategy for managing stigma.

Deviance researchers have long noted the conflicts that can occur within deviant subcultures, as different factions use varying messaging, signaling, and goals. As we have shown, some subcultural conflicts have predictable origins. Depending on the relative salience of stakes in conformity and subcultural deviance, members of deviant subcultures use different deviance management strategies to reconcile role conflict between simultaneously holding deviant and conforming identities.

Those who are only tangentially affiliated with a deviant subculture and only loosely bound by concerns of maintaining a conventional lifestyle, *Drifters*, typically have little influence upon a subculture. Should Drifters become disenchanted by changes in the subculture or find their needs met elsewhere, they will simply move on. Drifters are archetypal "free riders." *Hiders*, those who are highly motivated to maintain a conventional identity but who are only loosely connected to a deviant subculture that is fulfilling some desire or need, will not want to be publicly identified with a deviant subculture. Hence, they will play little role in the subculture (except anonymously), and some may actively and publicly demonize the very deviance in which they partake.

With regard to how a deviant subculture messages about itself, the real "action," so to speak, originates with *Outsiders* and *Insiders*, as well as the potential conflict between these two strategies. Outsiders and Insiders share deep devotion to deviant subcultures. Where they differ is in the extent to which they are devoted to maintaining a conventional identity, and therefore, by extension, concerned about integrating a deviant subculture into conventional society.

Insiders face great costs for being stigmatized, such as loss of a career or job advancements and the breaking off of valued conventional relationships or simply being viewed as "immoral," "dangerous," or "sick" by the wider community. When representatives of a deviant subculture express a desire to be viewed as normal and acceptable, that messaging will come from Insiders. They will seek to mollify the public by convincing mainstream society that members of the subculture bear great affinity to "normal people" (*narrative fidelity*) and will attempt to downplay elements of the subculture that threaten that message (*narrative coherence*). Outsiders, on the other hand, are comparatively free from the concern of maintaining a conventional lifestyle because they have either not achieved related statuses or made the choice to remain apart. Indeed, given their lack of conventional concerns, Outsiders might actually lose status if their subculture were "taken over" by those who wish to compromise its principles of difference, defiance, and resistance.

Across a wide variety of case studies, our basic framework for understanding deviance management helps explain the behaviors of individuals in deviant subcultures, interpersonal dynamics within such subcultures, and how a subculture chooses to present itself to the outside world. It is our hope that future scholars will carefully consider the extent to which individuals are attached to conventional and deviant identities when studying topics related to deviant subcultures. In doing so, it is vitally important for researchers to utilize mixed-methods approaches when studying these issues. In particular, hardline Hiders and Drifters only can be studied using qualitative methods, because they will not show up in standard survey data. Likewise, while we appreciate survey research and quantitative methods, and have used them throughout this book, some groups will be difficult to understand by such methods because a deeper appreciation of their values and orientations can only come through fieldwork and observation. Because most quantitative analyses are "frequentist" in orientation, they necessarily obscure examples that deviate from patterns that are easy to quantify.

As a final illustration, as well as an example of how qualitative inquiry can be used to understand complicated cases, we end where we began, with the Westboro Baptist Church.

GOD HATES THE WORLD, BUT NOT ITS RESOURCES

Why do members of WBC spend countless hours preaching at people in public spaces if they believe me, you, America and the entire world—save themselves—won't hear the message and are therefore predestined to go to hell? And what's the point of protesting social policy about sexuality, not to mention free speech, if you believe that legislators "don't have the power to stop the Destroyer who draws nigh?"[5] In one sense, these questions are rooted in the inherent contradictions of Calvinist theology, a subject of considerable obsession among preeminent professionals in our line of work.[6] But unlike Max Weber, we don't see these paradoxes as inherently rooted in conflicting ideas, at least for the members of Westboro.

As we have noted throughout this book, one important marker of an Insider is holding commitments to conformity. Insiders are constrained by conventional, high-status occupations, marriage to a conventional spouse, normative belief systems, and investments they have made in their futures through pursuits such as education. Fearing the loss of these commitments pressures Insiders into presenting their deviance in a way that is more palatable to those outside the subculture. Creating or finding measures of such commitments is comparatively easy and can be done in survey form via standard sociodemographic measures that are readily available on many existing surveys. And we have shown the utility of this measurement strategy throughout the book.

But such simple indicators are insufficient for fully assessing the relative strength of conventional versus deviant identities for some groups. Such is the case with the Westboro Baptists. Using basic survey measures, the members of Westboro appear to hold high stakes in conformity. Nearly all members have regular jobs and college degrees, are married, and would score at the maximum on measures of Christian religiosity.[7] Given their obvious and quite public devotion to their deviant group, we would classify the WBC as *Insiders* if we were to be limited to standard quantitative data about the group's stakes in conformity.

And there are some aspects of WBC's activities that bear the mark of Insider activism. For instance, patriarch and self-proclaimed prophet Fred W. Phelps, Sr. regularly ran for public office: three times for governor of Kansas, twice for U.S. Senate and once for mayor of Topeka. WBC also uses some movement strategies common to Insiders, such as nonviolent, legal protests, going on mainstream media programs, and petitioning local and state governments. Classifying WBC as Insiders also would lead to the expectation that the group would attempt to present a sanitized image of their beliefs to the public.

But the WBC are far from sanitized. They are more like shock jocks of street preaching. They are brash and offensive, flamboyant and obnoxious. The content of their message is that of an archetypal Outsider. They continually present a message of superiority. They are the Elect, and you, and everyone else are the Damned. They know the public will not receive their message, but still they preach: "When people say that my attitude is that, 'they're not going to hear, well then why preach?' Because the Lord says to. He says to preach even though your preaching is going to stop up their ears and harden their hearts and blind their eyes. That's what we still got to do."[8]

The actions of the WBC become much clearer and their status as Outsiders certain once one understands how they *feel* about their work. Surprised that WBC members had such high levels of education and maintained conventional careers outside the group, we asked them many questions about this during in-depth interviews. What immediately became clear is that WBC members do not go to college and enter career paths in order to fit into conventional society. Rather, they do so for two major reasons.

First, some members learn occupational skills that directly help the group in its operations. Some members of the group have technology careers and maintain the group's extensive collection of websites and videos. Several other members of the WBC are lawyers. This provides them with valuable knowledge about how to understand local regulations so that the group can safely protest. Having a team of lawyers also helps the group respond to the lawsuits against them, as well as restrictive new legislation targeting their activities.[9] Shirley Phelps-Roper, Fred Phelps Sr.'s daughter and longtime organizer of the group's protests, told us that winning lawsuits is a key source of income for the WBC.

Second, the members of the WBC are not required to find a job that provides skills of immediate benefit to the group; people can follow whatever path they choose. However, no matter what job members hold, they view those occupations as a means to an end—a way to provide financial resources to the group. As a younger member of the group, told us: "Well, um . . . everybody, you know, works so that you can earn income, and then you use that income to help the ministry whether it be plane tickets, hotels, or being able to actively get out and preach. So any job that produces any sort of income is directly related."

Another young member told us about her occupational goals:

> I just started the nursing program which is going to take two years, and then I can go on to be a nurse practitioner, which is a master's, and it will take two more years, or I can go to work, which is probably, I'm thinking, I don't know the answer. But probably that would be the best because, the only way that we can keep this ministry up is if we have money, because we have to have it to go travel all these places to tell all these people, we have to get this word throughout the entire earth. Paul was a tentmaker. You have to have an occupation because you have to have money. It's not because you love money or anything, it's just because that's what it takes.

You might assume that engaging in outside occupations and earning an education could lead members of the WBC to develop attachments to coworkers or fellow students, potentially watering down their devotion to the group. Our interviews with the WBC were clear in this regard, too. Members do not have real friends outside the group. Those who do make friends outside the group often leave.[10] Group members' primary social contacts are to other members who all strongly believe in the group's ideology, namely a righteously wrathful and incomprehensibly omniscient God who also happens to be virulently homophobic. Group members keep relations with those outside the group distant and utilitarian, and do not believe anyone outside the group can be a true friend. We asked a male member in the tech industry if he had friends at work:

> The people I work with, I don't ever bring up religion in the workplace. It's not an appropriate thing to do. But the people I work with, all know I am different than they are. . . . Yeah, I get along with them but, when it comes down to who are my friends, who are the people I count on? It is none of them. They are a resource for me to make the money to get along through this life. I have been very blessed in that respect. They are the means by which God provides. It's a great thing.

Likewise, two teenagers told us that, while they are respectful of their teachers and generally have no problems at school, they do not have close friends there:

WBC1:   They're more like acquaintances.
WBC2:   There's no people that actually . . . If you don't believe what we believe, if you don't believe what the Bible says, then there's no way that you can have any kind of a real friendship or fellowship with those people. So, there's people that are friendly, but you know . . .

Of course, protesting your own school during lunch breaks is not a great way to make friends.

Chris B: In your high school did you picket or preach publicly? How did you handle that kind of stuff?

WBC 1: We uh, every Thursday we picket right outside the high school, so they all knew.

WBC 2: We were there, so they all know, and if they don't yet then they're sure to find out soon.

Chris B: So you guys, as a family, every Thursday, before school y'all go out there?

WBC 1: No it's like a during lunch deal. Open lunch, so we go out there with some of the other people that don't have school or anything.

We have argued that conventional identities are composed of attachments to conventional people, commitments to conventional goals and beliefs that align with conventionality. Deviant identities, on the other hand, are composed of attachments to members of a deviant subculture, commitments to the goals of that subculture, and beliefs that align with subcultural ideals. Were we to be limited to only the most cursory, easily quantifiable measures of commitment, we might have mistakenly classified the WBC as Insiders. But a fuller accounting tells us that they are only using those commitments *to further deviant goals.* Their attachments to conventional others are superficial. And certainly, they are as committed to a deviant ideology as any group we have ever encountered. God does indeed hate us, according to the WBC, but that does not stop the group from using our resources. In the end, WBC members are Outsiders due the salience of their deviant collective and individual identities.

At the same time, WBC's stakes in conformity do necessarily influence their activities and result in a number of interesting behavioral patterns. As was clear in the interviews, the members of WBC must walk a fine line between publicly protesting and remaining quiet about their views during regular work or school time. And the combination of maximal commitment to deviant identity combined with still having stakes in conformity helps explain the highly unusual protest strategy of WBC. Their strategy is to be as deviant as possible but without breaking any laws. In this sense they are an exemplar of being deviant but not criminal. This strategy ultimately resulted in the passage of new laws about funeral protests in forty-seven states, as well as two federal statutes and a Supreme Court case.[11] These changes to social policy and law were the result of consensus opposition to the group, which itself resulted from WBC being deviant for both the political right, by virtue of protesting military funerals, and for the political left, by virtue of their aggressive homophobia. In effect, the WBC's strategy of using maximally deviant but not criminal methods combined with the political profitability of opposing the group resulted in mainstream society attempting to outlaw their behavior.

Another interesting aspect of WBC's deviance is the fact they are *resisting* societal changes—specifically the change in public opinion about homosexuality that we document above—rather than advocating for them. This makes WBC similar to other reactive, far-right movements seeking to maintain or reinstate discriminatory practices that are being phased out, such as white-power groups. In this sense, Westboro is a regressive movement, stigmatized for attempting to re-stigmatize something else that has recently been normalized. They are quite literally shouting obscenities and attempting to shame conventional society as it changes. Thus, changes to what is considered socially deviant ironically inspire new forms of deviance. Overall, the unique identity and protest strategy of WBC, as well as the legal response to their actions, can be explained by applying our ideas about deviance management to the group; but a full understanding of WBC's shocking antics requires applying a mixed-methods research approach.

As the examples of WBC and other empirical applications throughout the book show, there is much to learn about the dynamics of deviant groups by considering the struggle between dual identities, but a full appreciation of these dynamics requires a pluralistic methodological approach that incorporates quantitative data, ethnographic fieldwork, interviews, content analysis, and examination of changes to social policies.

RESURRECTING THE SOCIOLOGY OF DEVIANCE

Some scholars have proclaimed the sociology of deviance moribund, or at the very least in a perpetual coma, pointing to the rise of criminology and specialized areas such as social movement studies, sexology, and gender studies, as well as the declining use of deviance as a concept in sociology.[12] We believe reports of this death are greatly exaggerated, but this will be true only if other people see the value in and undertake studies of deviance. Our contribution to the project of resurrection has been in providing a conceptually parsimonious yet widely applicable approach that can be used as a framework for studying deviance management sociologically. We have made the case for its usefulness to studies of identity, religion, sexuality, social movements, and public policy, as well as to other areas of substantive inquiry.

While no theory is perfect or explains everything, our framework has many virtues. It is conceptually parsimonious, testable using a variety of methods, and empirically supported. It provides a systematic framework for exploring an aspect of deviance and social control that has, until this point, not received enough attention from theorists.[13] And not least of all, it is flexible enough to be applied in a variety of contexts and at different levels of analytic resolution.

Just as deviance is required for creating communal boundaries, those so labeled will be required to manage the stigma (or potential stigma) of being socially deviant. There is no shortage of movements, groups, and individuals for whom deviance management is a central concern. We have provided an extensive consideration of the patterns and implications of these processes in the hope that others will examine deviance management in different subcultures and movements, actively assess the adequacies and oversights of our basic framework, and build on the ideas we have outlined.

By their very nature, deviants are always pushing boundaries. The study of deviance can do the same for the social sciences. By studying rule breakers, we can better understand those same rules—and why, how, and under what circumstances rules change. Put another way, an understanding of deviance is foundational to an accurate understanding of social groups and societies more broadly. As long as there are social groups, there will be deviance. And where there is deviance, there will be people hiding, drifting, rebelling, and fighting to change what is considered "deviant."

On Applying the Theory Deviance Management

We have attempted to provide a useful research agenda for future studies of deviant subcultures. While we cannot detail all the extensions and connections that can be derived from both the conceptual framework and the empirical findings outlined in this book, we can provide guidance on what we believe to be additional testable hypotheses that can be derived from our theory, as well as advice on how researchers can measure key concepts.

HYPOTHESES

Below is a selection of additional empirical hypotheses, subdivided into four areas: self-labeling, "outness," framing, and subcultural conflict.

Self-Labeling

- **Hiders** will be the least likely to label themselves as members of a deviant subculture and the most likely to deny affiliation.

- **Hiders** will be the most likely to report shame about their deviant status.

- **Outsiders** and **Insiders** will be the most likely to label themselves as members of a deviant subculture.

- **Outsiders** will be the most likely to reappropriate pejorative terms used for a subculture and to use those terms to label themselves.

- **Insiders** will prefer mundane descriptors of their deviance and will tend to select labels that are palatable to those outside a deviant subculture.

Outness

- **Hiders** will be the least likely to tell others about their deviant status.
- **Outsiders** will be the most likely to tell others about their deviant status.
- To the extent that a deviant subculture involves visual markers of identity (clothing, tattoos, hairstyles, etc.), **Outsiders** will be the most likely to use visual signifiers that are difficult to hide.
- **Insiders** will prefer markers of commitment to a deviant subculture that can be hidden or masked when in conventional company and situations.

Framing

- **Hiders** will prefer to avoid discussion of their deviant activities.
- When forced to discuss their deviance, **Hiders** will be more likely describe that identity/activity as immoral and/or shameful.
- **Outsiders** will prefer messaging that demands that conventional society accept deviants on their own terms, without compromise.
- **Insiders** will prefer messaging that attempts to normalize the deviance in question. Often that messaging will attempt to convince others that the deviance has been mislabeled and bears much in common with existing, accepted societal institutions (narrative fidelity).

Subcultural Conflict

- **Drifters** often will be viewed with disdain by both **Outsiders** and **Insiders**; considered tagalongs who drain subcultural resources without contributing.
- **Hiders** often will be viewed with disdain by both **Outsiders** and **Insiders**; particularly to the extent that **Hiders** have publicly expressed antipathy for the subculture.
- **Outsiders** often will have negative views of **Insiders**, whom they view as "sellouts" who are more concerned with conventional approval than the needs of members of the subculture.
- **Insiders** often will have negative views of **Outsiders**, whose extremism threatens messaging that the subculture should be considered normal.

QUANTITATIVE MEASURES OF CONVENTIONAL AND DEVIANT IDENTITIES

Of course, to test any hypotheses, quality data containing relevant measures of central concepts are necessary. The fundamental concepts that underlie our framework are the relative salience of *deviant identity* and *conventional identity*. As noted in chapter 2, our measures of the strength of deviant and conventional identities utilize the concepts of social bonds and stakes in conformity and nonconformity. Individuals vary in the strength of their bonds to both deviant subcultures and social conformity. These social bonds consist of interpersonal attachments, the accrual and expectation of future social status, participation in group activities, and one's beliefs related to deviance and conformity.

Researchers who utilize secondary data, as we often do, will of course be limited by the items asked on the survey in question. Luckily, most social surveys have measures that can be used to gauge stakes in conformity. The simplest and most commonly available measures will be demographic in nature. To the extent that individuals have achieved a high level of education and social class, or have a professional occupation with chances for advancement, they face significantly elevated risks for loss if a master status of "deviant" is successfully applied. Marital status also can be used as an indicator of maintaining conventional relationships and status. If a survey also includes information on mainstream religiosity, these also are useful measures of commitment to conventionality. An individual who affiliates with a conventional religious group may face censure should other group members discover participation in discrediting deviance. Although demographic characteristics are not ideal measures of conformity, they are serviceable proxies. Deviance measures are harder to come by, but as we have shown, there is still much that can be done with extant data.

For researchers collecting primary quantitative data, there are some important considerations for measurement. The interpersonal relationships that individuals maintain should play a pivotal role in determining where their loyalty lies. If a person's closest relationships are within a deviant subculture, then we should expect that person to assign precedence to the subculture's demands. Those whose closest relationships are conventional are at risk of losing valued relationships if they are branded as deviant or immoral. Thus, life becomes more complicated to the extent that balancing the demands of those inside and outside a deviant subculture is required.[1]

For survey researchers, we recommend gauging the level of deviant attachment by asking a similar question. The way such questions are worded will depend upon the type of deviance under examination, but the focus should be on demarcations between those inside and outside of a subculture. One such marker is official membership(s), assuming the deviant subculture under observation involves at least semi-formal organizations. Another marker is a status or characteristic that is sufficiently distinctive that an alternative can be provided in order to measure how many friends and family are outside the subculture. For example, in studies of sexual minorities, researchers can ask how many of the respondents' best friends and family are LGBT and how many identify as heterosexual. Finally, if the deviance in question involves core beliefs that are stigmatized, such as believing in the existence of Bigfoot, researchers can inquire about the number of friends and family who are believers.

Questions about social networks will tend to mirror one another, regardless of whether they are about conventionality or deviance, as they necessarily involve gathering data on relationships inside and outside of subcultures. But other measures of commitment, such as the accrual and expectation of social status, depend upon whether one is measuring deviant or conforming identity. With regard to commitment to a deviant subculture, good measures evaluate the extent to which individuals have significantly invested effort and money in that subculture. Should the subculture in question include membership status, the simplest measure of commitment is whether the individual is, in fact, a member. If the subculture involves leadership positions or ranks, then holding, or wishing to hold, these positions and ranks is another indicator. Making donations to a subcultural organization also is a clear sign of commitment. Amount of time spent engaged in subcultural activities can be measured with participation questions, such as the number of Bigfoot hunts one has been on, the number of rallies one has attended, or questions about volunteering for subcultural projects.

As our example of the Bigfoot subculture shows, forms of commitment and involvement vary widely in the amount of effort required to participate. If available measures include comparatively low effort items (such as consuming media content) and comparatively higher effort items (participating in rallies, attending gatherings), these items should be weighted to account for the relative costs involved. Someone who actively hunts Bigfoot and spends considerable money on "call blasters," plaster casting equipment, camouflage gear, and night-vision goggles is clearly more committed than a passive enthusiast who primarily watches videos and reads online forums about Sasquatch.

Finally, there is the ideological component of identities. To the extent that people hold beliefs that are consistent with the ideology of a deviant subculture or that are consistent with conventionality, such beliefs will strongly reinforce the related identity. Different deviance management styles correspond to different ideas about how the subculture should interact with "normal society," and also what the goals of the subculture should be. One of the more difficult aspects of measuring ideological components of a deviant identity is keeping measures conceptually distinct from outcomes of interest. Social relationships and statuses operate in a feedback loop of cognitive processing that overlays ideological frameworks on past experiences. Accordingly, ideological elements of subcultural commitment should be used cautiously as measures of identity.

But there also are clearly instances in which ideological components can rightly be considered as predicting behavior. When a deviant subculture centers on a controversial belief, such as Bigfoot or conspiracy theories, it is possible to gauge the certainty and salience of respondents' beliefs about that topic. Those with more certain and salient beliefs about the existence of Bigfoot would clearly be expected to have a stronger deviant identity than those who are skeptical, uncertain, or simply not willing to significantly structure their social and cognitive lives around thoughts of undiscovered primates. To the extent that a subculture involves a deviant status or label, such as sexual identity, an individual's willingness to self-identify with specific labels (e.g., LGBTQ+) can serve as a useful measure of the ideological component of deviant identity.

Ideological aspects of conventionality are easier to measure. If an individual is wedded to conservative, conventional beliefs, they are placed under greater strain by a deviant identity. Therefore, political affiliation and relative conservatism can serve as a measure of conventional ideology and identity. For religious beliefs, questions about issues of orthodoxy are also useful indicators of conventional ideology. Notably, however, religious beliefs can pass through conventionality and into deviance if they are radically different from the surrounding sociocultural environment.[2] Likewise, political beliefs that push beyond conservatism into deviant designations such as "far right" transition from socially conventional to deviant. Because deviance is relative, it is necessarily a moving target across space, time, and culture. Today's Outsiders can be tomorrow's trend setters if enough people follow their message. Likewise, yesterday's paragons of virtue and tradition can become today's bigots if they stand pat while others become more tolerant of differences.

After obtaining and properly coding measures of conventionality and deviant identity, the next step, at least for reporting and summary purposes, is classifying individuals as Drifters, Hiders, Insiders, and Outsiders based on the salience of each identity. The simplest means of coding the four types (and the method we have frequently used) is by categorizing someone as "high" in identity salience if they are above the mean in a sample and "low" if they are at or below the mean on a summative identity measure.[3] An individual's deviance management strategy is then predicted by comparing the low/high scores for each identity.

To reiterate, we are not claiming that all deviant subcultures will have people of each deviance management type. To the extent that a subculture, or faction within, requires extensive time, expense, or effort to participate, Drifters may be excluded. Should an Outsider group be focused upon public displays or require visible markers of commitment, hiding may not be possible. Some forms of deviance may be viewed by near consensus to be repugnant and/or harmful, such as pedophilia, and as a result, subcultural members will find it impossible to normalize their actions, rendering being an Insider impossible, and effectively forcing all participants to be Hiders or Drifters.[4] Depending on the case, researchers may wish to develop absolute, rather than relative, measures of deviant identity, such as requiring official membership to be considered as a highly salient deviant identity. This method allows for the absence of particular management styles in some deviant subcultures.

REFINING THE THEORY WITH QUALITATIVE METHODS

Of course, what quantitative assessments contribute by virtue of their breadth and information about wider patterns of behavior, they necessarily lack in depth. There's simply no substitute for talking to people about their own lives and observing their social interactions. While we clearly place a premium on systematically testing hypotheses to evaluate the adequacy of any social theory, many of the foundational ideas and concepts for our theory were created and refined using observations from qualitative fieldwork. Likewise, many aspects of the theory can be best evaluated and improved using qualitative methods, particularly ethnography.

Interviews are also clearly well suited to assessing self-conceptions of identity, although this method necessarily omits true Hiders. Interviews allow researchers to query the relative salience of conventional and deviant identities, and to probe how this relates to strategies of deviance management. If done longitudinally or in life history format, interviews can provide valuable information on how individuals change deviance management strategies and social identities over time. Content analysis is another useful method, particularly for assessing identity messaging, both inside and outside of deviant subcultures. Internal messaging is an informative data source on collective identity, and also sometimes on the official rhetoric of subcultural conflict. For external messaging, content analyses can point to the key components of framing, as we demonstrated with the case of Pauline Sabin and the Women's National Organization for Prohibition Reform.

Regardless of the methods used, studying deviance management can lend insight into a wide range of substantive topics of political, academic, and social import. In the end, we are methodological pluralists, and have endeavored to create a framework for studying and understanding deviance management that is informed by both qualitative and quantitative research. It is up to others apply these ideas to new case studies, and in doing so expand our collective understanding of how deviance management affects individuals, subcultural communities, and society more broadly.

Supplemental Data Analyses

Below are data analyses supporting some of the findings presented in chapters 5 and 6. Table A.1 presents the results of an ordinal logistic regression model predicting levels of liberationist LGBT ideology by levels of conventional and deviant identity, controlling for gender, age, race, and specific sexual/gender identity (L, G, B, or T). The first column shows unstandardized coefficients, and the second column shows coefficients standardized by the independent variables' respective standard deviations and divided by an estimate of the standard deviation of the logit-transformed dependent variable.[1] Figure 9 in chapter 5 is based on results from this model.

Table A.2 shows the results from One-Way ANOVA means tests for differences in the relative weight given to specific LGBT rights issues by Insiders, Outsiders, Hiders, and Drifters. Relative weights were created by dividing scores for the importance of specific issues by scores on the overall index that includes respondents' answers about the importance of all the issues asked about on the survey. These relative weights were then standardized, such that positive scores indicate an above-average relative weight for the specific issue, while negative scores indicate below-average weight given to a specific issue. These results are discussed in chapter 5.

Table A.3 shows results from an ordinary least squares regression model predicting levels of participation in LGBT social movement activities by conventional and deviant identity, controlling for age, gender, race, and sexual/gender identity (L, G, B, or T). The first column shows unstandardized coefficients and the second column shows standardized coefficients. Model 2 includes an interaction effect between the measures of conventional and deviant identity, which is significant and positive, indicating that levels of social movement participation are the highest among respondents who have high levels of *both* deviant and conventional identity. Figure 12 in chapter 5 is based on results from this model.

TABLE A.1. Ordinal Logistic Regression Model Predicting Liberationist
Ideology by Conventional and LGBT Subcultural Identities

Variables	b	β
Demographics		
Age	−.085*	−.140
Female	.009	.005
Black	.165	.042
Sexual Identity[a]		
Lesbian	−.458*	−.193
Bisexual	−.383*	−.188
Transgender	.344	.064
Conventional/Deviant Identity		
Conventionality	−.039*	−.121
Subcultural identity	.213***	.350
Model stats		
Cut 1	−1.973	
Cut 2	−.054	
Cut 3	1.770	
N	1158	
Adjusted R^2	.067	

SOURCE: 2013 Pew LGBT Survey.

[a]Gay men are reference category.

*p <.05; **p<.01; ***p <.001 (two-tailed tests).

NOTE: (β) indicates standardized coefficients.

TABLE A.2. Means for Weighted Relative Importance of Specific LGBT Rights Issues by Deviance
Management Type

Issues	Drifters	Hiders	Outsiders	Insiders
Equal Employment***	−.08	.25	−.13	−.01
Gay Marriage***	−.08	−.09	.01	.18
Gay Adoption**	−.02	−.04	−.01	.09
AIDS Treatment	.04	−.02	.01	−.07
Civil Unions***	.11	.16	−.12	−.17
LGBT Youth*	−.03	−.17	.09	.09
Transgender Health**	.01	−.13	.16	−.03

SOURCE: 2013 Pew LGBT Survey.

***p <.001; **p <.01; *p <.05 (One-Way ANOVA).

NOTE: Relative importance measures were mean standardized, so positive values indicate above-average weighting
for an issue and negative values indicate below-average weighting.

TABLE A.3. Ordinary Least Squares Regression Model Predicting Social Movement Participation Index by Conventional and LGBT Subcultural Identities

Variables	Model 1		Model 2	
	b	β	b	β
Demographics				
Age	.156**	.127	.153*	.069
Female	.914**	.070	.907**	.126
Black	−1.185***	−.081	−1.150**	−.078
Sexual Identity[a]				
Lesbian	−.904*	−.104	−.907*	−.105
Bisexual	−2.178***	−.291	−2.177***	−.291
Transgender	−2.902***	−.144	−2.835***	−.141
Conventional/Deviant Identity				
Conventionality	.171***	.144	.170***	.143
Subcultural identity	.858***	.384	.858***	.384
Interaction				
Conventional*Subcultural	---		.043*	.060
Model stats				
Constant	3.840		3.838	
N	1143		1143	
Adjusted R²	.307		.310	

SOURCE: 2013 Pew LGBT Survey.

[a]Gay men are reference category.

*p <05; **p<.01; ***p <.001 (two-tailed tests).

TABLE A.4. Ordinal Logistic Regression Predicting State Laws about Cannabis

Variables	Standardized Coefficients
Percent adolescents say occasional pot use dangerous	−1.679**
Percent Evangelical	−1.556*
Initiated statute	1.512*
Percent Democrats in state legislature	.935
Midwest[a]	−.881*
West[a]	−.652
Northeast[a]	−.434
Percent college degree	−.282
Percent white	−.173
Citizen political ideology	.044
Percent urban	.039
Legislatively referred statute	.033

(continued)

TABLE A.4. *(continued)*

Variables	Standardized Coefficients
Model stats	
Constant 1	−2.153
Constant 2	6.471
N	50
Nagelkerke R²	.836

**p <.01 *p <.05.

ªSouth is reference category.

NOTE: All measures are standardized by their respective standard deviations, allowing for comparisons of magnitude.

GENERAL SOURCE: Aggregated dataset of American states.

SPECIFIC DATA SOURCES: 2017 *Governing* magazine summary of cannabis laws; 2012–2013 National Survey on Drug Use and Health; 2007 Pew Religious Landscape Survey (percent Evangelical); Ballotpedia (direct democracy mechanisms); 2010 National Conference of State Legislatures (percent Democrats); 2010 Measure of America (demographics); Berry et al. (1998) (citizen political ideology).

Table A.4 presents the results of an ordinal logistic regression model predicting the legal status of cannabis (illegal, medical marijuana, legal recreational cannabis) in American states in 2018 using states' characteristics such as public opinion about cannabis, percent evangelical Protestant in the state, and the presence of direct democracy mechanisms. The coefficients were standardized so they can be compared for relative magnitude based on absolute value. The variables are rank-ordered by magnitude of effect in the table. Figure 13 in chapter 6 is based on results from this model. Likewise, in chapter 6, the attributes listed for states that had legal recreational cannabis in 2018 in table 2 are for the three strongest predictors from table A.4.

NOTES

INTRODUCTION: INSIDERS, OUTSIDERS, HIDERS, AND DRIFTERS

1. It deserves note that disdain for homosexuality alone does not make Westboro distinct among conservative Protestant churches, although as we detail, it does put them at odds with trends in views of sexuality among the American public more generally. Rather, it is Westboro's protest tactics and the crudeness with which they present their hatred of homosexuality, along with the general intensity of that hatred, that make the group distinct from other conservative Protestant groups.

2. A transcript of the sermon delivered by Fred Phelps Sr. on November 3, 2008, is available here: http://www.godhatesfags.com/sermons/outlines/Sermon_20081123.pdf. In addition to an outline of the sermon, all congregants received a copy of an encyclopedia page about Komodo dragons in an effort to demonstrate the literal existence of dragons and thus the literalness with which members were to understand the Bible.

3. The text of the "Homosexual Manifesto" was taken from a satirical piece in the now defunct Leftist *Gay Community News* in 1987. It satirized the fears behind prejudice and discrimination directed toward sexual minorities. The piece originally began with the statement: "This essay is an outré, madness, a tragic, cruel fantasy, an eruption of inner rage, on how the oppressed desperately dream of being the oppressor." The text was entered into the Congressional Record when notoriously homophobic Representative William Dannemeyer (R–California) asked for its entrance into the record under the heading and title: "MILITANT WOLVES IN SHEEPISH DRAG, NO LONGER! AMERICA: IS THIS THE GAY DECLARATION OF WAR?" Dannemeyer (1987:21194; also see Dannemeyer 1989) vowed to combat "normaphobes" advocating for gay rights, saying, "I commend the following article to the American public so they can read for themselves the extent of homosexual militancy." The text was used as evidence of "the homosexual agenda" purportedly influencing all aspects of life and society. WBC is not alone in their use of the

text for the purposes of propaganda, as it periodically surfaces in fear-mongering about homosexuality.

4. Special thanks (and apologies) to Michael Boling, Adria McLaughlin, Erin Mauck, and Lindsay Toman for assistance coding Fred Phelps's sermons.

5. The differences in the level and intensity of social reactions to WBC's protests between LGBT individuals and soldiers shows the relative stigma and sanctity, respectively, directed toward these status groups (Baker, Bader, and Hirsch 2015).

6. The Supreme Court ruling is available here: https://www.supremecourt.gov/opinions/10pdf/09-751.pdf.

7. http://cjonline.com/stories/100406/bre_phelps.shtml#.WgYLjGhSyM8.

8. "Letter to Earth-Dwellers," 2006. http://downloads.godhatesfags.com/wpfb-file/2006 0704_letter-to-earthdwellers-pdf/.

9. Here we borrow ideas from role theory, which itself draws upon a dramaturgical theory of interaction (Goffman 1959).

10. Biddle (1986:82).

11. Bianchi and Milkie (2010); Skinner (1980).

12. Hochschild and Machung (1989).

13. See Palepu and Herbert (2002). While researchers have noted similar feelings of role conflict among men attempting to balance careers with home life, gender role expectations clearly place a greater burden upon working women (see Becker and Moen 1999).

14. Indeed, sexism and gender discrimination can be fruitfully understood as the stigmatization of women and the feminine (Schur 1984).

15. See Simon and Gagnon (1967a, 1967b).

16. Goode (2005:5).

17. Sampson and Laub (1993).

18. Schiemann, McBrier, and Van Gundy (2003); Pomaki, Supeli, and Verhoeven (2007); Stryker and Macke (1978).

19. Peiro et al. (2001).

20. Pomaki, Supeli, and Verhoeven (2007).

21. See Emslie, Hunt, and MacIntyre (2004); Hochschild and Machung (1989).

22. See for example: Stryker (1968, 1980, 1981, 1987); Stryker and Burke (2000); Stryker and Macke (1978).

23. Stets and Burke (2003).

24. Stryker and Burke (2000:286).

25. Following the lead of other researchers, we do not utilize the *involvement* element of the social bond (see chapter 2).

26. Hirschi (1969).

27. Lofland and Stark (1965).

28. As we outline in chapter 2, we are effectively synthesizing expectations derived from social control and differential association theories.

29. For a reconstructed version of Weber's (1949) original concept of ideal types and its importance to theories and empirical studies of identity and motivation, see Aronovitch (2012). Our typology closely matches the "peacocks," "chameleons," and "centaurs" posited by Brekhus (2003) in his study of suburban gay men.

30. Goffman (1963:137–38).

31. Stryker and Burke (2000:290).

32. Central here is the ethnographic turn toward studying deviants and deviance with an "appreciative attitude," as exemplified by Becker ([1963] 1991). Notably, however, whether condemnatory or appreciative, nearly all research focuses on Outsiders, with the exception of studies of "positive" deviance (Ben-Yehuda 1990; Heckert and Heckert 2002; cf. Goode 1991; Sagarin 1985).

33. Humphreys (1970).

34. See Goffman (1963) on the differences between being discredited and discreditable and how this affects strategies of action and resulting interactions.

35. As Stryker and Burke (2000:290) note: "If multiple competing or conflicting identities involve high and roughly equivalent commitments and salience, considerable stress is likely to be generated."

36. As Du Bois (1897) noted in his original formulation of double consciousness, it simultaneously carries the possibilities of both alienation and liberation.

37. Allport (1954).

38. Burke et al. (2015); Herek and Capitanio (1996); Pettigrew et al. (2011).

39. Twenge, Carter, and Campbell (2015:382).

40. Kozloski (2010); Ohlander, Batalovab, and Treas (2005).

41. Altemeyer (2002:68).

42. Discussing the process of normalization among the visibly handicapped, Davis (1964:128) notes that normalization is a "redefinitional process in which the handicapped person projects images, attitudes and concepts of self which encourage the normal to identify with him (i.e., 'take his role') in terms other than those associated with imputations of deviance." Notably, identification does not necessitate equality and can lead to further issues of stigmatization through "marking" (Goffman 1963).

1. THE COMPLEMENTARITY OF DEVIANCE AND CONFORMITY

1. Durkheim ([1895] 1982:100).

2. This tradition typically runs through Durkheim ([1893] 1997).

3. On the persecution of "Puritan" groups in England, see Cragg ([1957] 2011).

4. On the background of the Salem trials and their importance as an instance of the wider phenomena of witch hunts, see Jensen (2006).

5. Notably, however, these conflicts for control played out along preexisting political, socioeconomic and gendered fault lines in the community. On role of political and economic factionalism see Boyer and Nissenbaum (1974); on the gendered nature of these conflicts, Reed (2007).

6. See Ben-Yehuda (1985) for a similar discussion of European witch trials. For criticisms of functional approaches to deviance, see Taylor, Walton, and Young (1973).

7. As Erikson (1966:11) summarized, "The deviant is a person whose activities have moved outside the margins of the group, and when the community calls him to account for that vagrancy it is making a statement about the nature and placement of its boundaries."

8. Erikson (1966:9).

9. Altheide (2004, 2006) examines the production and consumption of culture surrounding terrorism in post-9/11 America as it relates to collective identity.

10. See Jenkins (1998); Simon (2007); Travis (2002).

11. Merton (1938).

12. Cohen (1955:133). This is not to be confused with "reaction formation" as a psychological defense mechanism, which "involves converting a socially unacceptable impulse into its opposite" (Baumeister, Dale, and Sommer 1998: 1085). Such reactions are an integral part of the "breastplate of righteousness" strategy of deviance management.

13. This observation is echoed in the work of Anderson (1999).

14. As all children know, defiance of norms results in situational, temporary empowerment; however, it typically results in long-term disempowerment, assuming punishment follows. Thus, young men who are criminalized may ironically act in criminal ways as a form of defiance to their being labeled criminal. See Rios (2011).

15. See Kraybill and Olshan (1994) for a collection of essays detailing how the Amish encounter "modernity."

16. However, like many strict religious groups, the high birth and retention rates among the Amish have led to increases in number. This population expansion has actually driven many of the conflicts resulting in accommodations by Amish communities toward mainstream society, such as micro-entrepreneurship and allowing work in external factories (Kraybill 2001:242). Not everyone can farm if there is no more land.

17. Merton (1968).

18. Berger (1963).

19. Iannaccone (1992, 1994); Kelley (1972).

20. Iannaccone (1995:287).

21. On Rumspringa, see Shachtman (2006); Stevick (2014).

22. See Loftus (2001) on the liberalization of attitudes toward homosexuality among the American public from the 1970s to the 1990s.

23. For example, the Yearning for Zion ranch just outside of Eldorado, Texas, continually faced interactions and conflict with local authorities. Warren Jeffs, the prophet of YFZ, who was incarcerated for child sexual assault, has been accused of encouraging members to commit food stamp fraud in order to bring money into the group (Wright and Richardson 2011).

24. Pfuhl (1980:69–70).

25. Cf. Gagnon and Simon ([1973] 2005:115–19); Simon and Gagnon (1967b:181).

26. Gagnon and Simon ([1973] 2005:116).

27. Gagnon and Simon ([1973] 2005:118).

28. McQueeney (2009:152).

29. Rodriquez and Ouellette (2000).

30. Rodriquez and Ouellette (2000:334–35); also see Sumerau, Cragun, and Mathers (2016).

31. Simon and Gagnon (1967a:213).

32. Goffman (1959).

33. Often reproduced in work using a dramaturgical perspective is a line from Shakespeare's *As You Like It* (act 2, scene 7), "All the world's a stage, And all the men and women merely players."

34. Turner (2003).

35. See Goffman (1967, 1969, 1971).

36. See Biddle (1986) for an in-depth discussion of the many different ways sociologists have conceptualized roles.

37. Stryker and Burke (2000:284).

38. Stryker and Burke (2000:286).

39. See Stryker (1989) for an in-depth explication of the simultaneous singularity and multiplicity of the self.

40. Athens (1994, 1995).

41. Hitlin (2008:36).

42. Cf. Fisher and Gitelson (1983); Stryker and Macke (1978). On role conflict among gay and bisexual men, see Szymanski and Carr (2008).

43. Stryker (2007:1091).

44. On how commitment to deviance is compelled through punishments and stigma over time, see Stebbins (1971). Indeed, "Deviance, like marriage, is almost always far easier to get into than out of" (Simmons 1969:65).

45. Goffman (1963:2).

46. Parsons (1951:282).

47. This is a foundational premise of general strain theory (Agnew 1992).

48. Stryker and Serpe (1982); Stryker (2007).

49. Simi and Futrell (2009); also see Futrell and Simi (2004).

50. Simi and Futrell (2009:92).

51. Simi and Futrell (2009:92).

52. Simi and Futrell (2009:99).

53. Simi and Futrell (2009:98).

54. Simi and Futrell (2009:100).

55. Stryker and Burke (2000:285–86).

56. Stryker (2008). See, for example, Stryker and Serpe (1982), who found that the salience of a religious identity is significantly related to time spent in religious activities; and Callero (1985), who found that the frequency of blood donations was significantly related to the salience of identity as a blood donor.

57. Stryker and Burke (2000:286). On the relationship between commitment and status, see Becker (1960).

58. Stryker (2007).

59. On the intricacies of role distance for interactions, see Goffman (1961).

60. For an overview of how identity economics advances economics theory and modeling, see Akerlof and Kranton (2000). On how identity economics solves puzzles in macroeconomics created by an inadequate conception of motivations based on identities and norms, see Akerlof (2007).

61. Akerlof and Kranton (2010).

62. There are some extremes of situation, condition, and identity where there may be very little commitment to conventional identity, such as solitary confinement. Yet even here there are severe punishments for not following role expectations and protocols such that even the most recalcitrant and (more) fully deviant individuals must still abide by social expectations at least some of the time. Perhaps the most ideal typical circumstances of an individual without social expectations for conventionality would be hermits and social isolates. Here the limitations of behavioral potentials based on conventional expectations is

self-evident. A hermit is hardly free to do anything he chooses, but rather is confined only to that which will not result in encountering the outside world.

2. DEVIANCE AND CONFORMITY: THE PRESSURE OF DUAL IDENTITIES

1. See Adams (2009); Irwin (2003); Kosut (2006); Vail (1999).

2. Kornhouser (1978).

3. Hirschi (1969). Forerunners of Hirschi's control theory include Matza (1964); Nye (1958); Reckless (1961, 1967); Reiss (1951); Sykes and Matza (1956); Toby (1957). The roots of control theory also extend through the work of Émile Durkheim ([1897] 1979) and formulations of "classical" criminological theory such as Beccaria ([1974] 2008). See Melossi (2008) for an insightful discussion of the overlap and divergence of control theories relative to other theories of crime and control.

4. Hirschi (1969:84) does acknowledge the importance of whether "delinquent behavior is valued" among peers, but overall, social control theory downplays the influence of peers on deviance.

5. See Foshee and Bauman (1992); Jensen and Brownfield (1983).

6. Sutherland and Cressey (1974). For an empirical test of differential association with Hirschi's (1969) Richmond Youth data, see Matsueda (1982); Matsueda and Heimer (1987); cf. Costello and Vowell (1999).

7. Humphreys (1970).

8. One of the most thorough and compelling assessments of the sociological dimensions of normality/deviance, identity and their intersection remains Lofland (1969; also see Horwitz 2004).

9. Matsueda (1997).

10. To be sure, deviance and crime can and do occur as solitary activities. A youth might shoplift cold medicine from a drug store in order to get high alone at home. A rapist or serial killer may stalk a neighborhood searching for easy victims when sadistic impulses strike. Yet, criminological theorists have long noted the importance of a criminal or deviant subculture for facilitating individual acts of deviance, even in the case of highly personal behaviors such as self-harm (see Adler and Adler 2011). The type of deviance a person manifests will depend upon the presence of an *illegitimate* opportunity structure. To the extent that an area is characterized by a stable, well-organized deviant subculture, an individual will be more able to find the goods or people required to engage in deviance and learn the skills necessary to participate. In many cases it is not simply enough to *want* to deviate, there must be an opportunity to do so.

11. Here we draw on the insights of Ulmer (1994, 2000), who posits that individual commitment can be usefully conceptualized as having social structural, personal, and moral dimensions. Further, this commitment may be conceived as being tied to conventional *or* deviant identities.

12. The weight of the evidence from empirical tests of social control theory indicates that theorists should take into account the beliefs held by the people to whom someone is attached. For example, mere attachment to parents does not prevent drug use by youth. What is important in predicting such behavior is the *attitudes* of the parents. Children who

are strongly attached to parents who do not use drugs are less likely to use drugs themselves. As might be expected, attachment to drug-using parents does not prevent drug use in children (see Bahr, Hoffman, and Yang 2005; Miller-Day et al. 2000). In general, a long line of research demonstrates that people who are strongly attached to deviant others are more likely to engage in deviance themselves.

13. For a background on the concept of "deviant careers" see Adler and Adler (1983); Becker ([1963] 1991); Best and Luckenbill (1980, 1982); Lofland (1969); Steffensmeier and Ulmer (2005).

14. Simi et al. (2017).

15. Sykes and Matza (1957) first posited the idea of techniques of neutralization, along with first five techniques listed. The additional techniques were added by Klockars (1974), Minor (1981), and Coleman (1994).

16. Notably, those who perceive themselves as righteous will use rationalizations but not excuses, as the latter implicitly uphold the rightness of the norm in question.

17. See Lofland (1969).

18. See, for example, the typologies of Becker (1991:20), Lofland (1969) and Best and Luckenbill (1982:25). We draw heavily on all of these theorists to build our conceptualization of the relationships between conventional identity, deviant identity, and the management of deviance. Becker's idea of the "secret deviant" closely resembles our "Hider" type. Lofland's work provides much of the framework for our understanding of deviance and identity, and Best and Luckenbill's analysis informs our understanding of how deviant outgroups organize toward to the goal of normalization.

19. Link (1987); Link and Phelan (2001, 2014).

20. Link et al. (1989)

21. On modified labeling theory, also see: Kroska and Harkness (2006); Smith and Hipper (2010); Mingus and Burchfield (2012); Ray and Dollar (2014).

22. Kaufman and Miles ([2009] 2014:82).

23. Miller (1958). Similarly, and more recently, see Rios (2011:97–123).

24. Anderson (1999); Cohen (1955).

25. Merton (1938).

26. Lofland and Stark (1965).

27. Burke (1991); Vaisey and Lizardo (2010).

28. Haenfler (2010).

29. Lamy (1996); Peterson (1984). See also Linder (1982), which Peterson draws upon.

30. Fox (1987).

31. Fox (1987:355).

32. Fox (1987:361–62).

33. For example, Daschuk (2010) argues that punks utilize the image of the "emo kid" on message-boards as a symbol of an inauthentic punk. Also see Grossman (1996–1997) for a discussion of the struggle within the punk subculture to excise those perceived as lacking in commitment.

34. On the problems of mainstream acceptance and promotion of "diversity" in LGBT activist groups, see Ward (2008).

35. The quote in the heading is Bishop Eddie Long's response to allegations that he coerced sex from three young men.

36. Lincoln and Mamiya (1990).

37. Data from the Baylor Religion Surveys show that Black Protestant denominations are significantly more likely than Evangelicals to agree that the government should distribute wealth more evenly and fund faith-based initiatives. However, Black Protestants are not statistically different from Evangelicals in their beliefs about abortion and homosexuality. Both Evangelicals and Black Protestants, for example are more likely than other religious traditions to believe that gay marriage is "always wrong" (Froese and Bader 2010).

38. Eddie Long, "God Is After Himself" DVD (New Birth).

39. Masculine God imagery was a common feature of Long's rhetoric.

40. Long, "God Is After Himself."

41. Mock (2007).

42. Anthony Flagg vs. Eddie L. Long. September 21, 2010. Civil Action Number 10A32029-4. State Court of Dekalb County, Georgia.

43. *Flagg vs. Long*, p. 3.

44. Chipumuro (2014:8). In this quote we have corrected the two-word spelling of "Long Fellows" in the original quote to be one word, as the official name of the program was "LongFellows."

45. *Flagg v. Long* 2010, p. 4.

46. *Flagg v. Long* 2010, p. 4.

47. Chipumuro (2014).

48. *Flagg v. Long* 2010, p. 8

49. *Flagg v. Long* 2010, p. 8.

50. Edecio Martinez, "Bishop Eddie Long Settled so He Didn't Have to Go on Record, Says Lawyer," *CBS News*, May 27, 2011. http://www.cbsnews.com/news/bishop-eddie-long -settled-so-he-didnt-have-to-go-on-record-says-lawyer/.

51. For full text of Georgia Senate Resolution 43 honoring Long, see: http://www.legis .ga.gov/Legislation/20172018/163041.pdf.

52. Christian Boone, "Men Who Sued Eddie Long for Sexual Misconduct Address Bishop's Death," *Atlanta Journal Constitution*, January 15, 2017. http://www.ajc.com/news/local /men-who-sued-eddie-long-for-sexual-misconduct-address-bishop-death/A1E6CzW4 Ehd1RkJsVsKGsM/.

53. On Larry Craig's voting record, see www.ontheissues.org/Domestic/Larry_Craig _Civil_Rights.htm.

54. Humphreys (1970).

55. On whether Humphreys himself may (or may not) have played other roles in the subculture, see Galliher, Brekhus and Keys (2004).

56. Humphreys's dissertation and book are an interesting example of symbolic boundaries in the field of sociology, as his methodology breached professional rules concerning the ethical limitations of research. Reactions to this deviation from group norms follow the processes outlined by researchers and theorists in the field of deviance (for example, Ben-Yehuda 1985:167–207). In this sense, *Tearoom Trade* is both research on deviance and deviant research.

57. Goffman (1959).

58. Goffman (1963).

59. Humphreys (1970:135, 145).

60. See Goffman (1963:73–91) on "passing." Renfrow (2004) provides a refinement of the concept based on the degree of stigma attached to the deviance that is being hidden and the different strategies that individuals may employ in order to pass.

61. Fox (1987:361).

62. Shaw (1930:93).

63. Canter and Hodge (1996); Jenkins (1994).

64. See for example: Blumstein et al. (1988); Brame, Mulvey and Piquero (2001); Cohen (1986); DeLisi (2005); Piquero (2000); Wright, Pratt and DeLisi (2008).

65. Cohen and Felson (1979); Felson (1994); Gottfredson and Hirschi (1989); Miller (1958).

66. Conklin (1972:70).

67. On the place of *The Jack-Roller* in historical and contemporary criminology, see Maruna and Matravers (2007).

68. For theoretical critiques of *The Jack-Roller*, see Denzin (1995); Gelsthorpe (2007); Shaw (2009).

69. Snodgrass and "Jack-Roller" (1982).

70. Snodgrass (1983:454, 457).

71. On the image of Drifters implicitly built into labeling theories of deviance, see Broadhead (1974). On the "New Drifters" as chronic patients in hospitals and with psychological disorders, see Lamb (1982).

72. Vaughn, Salas-Wright, and DeLisi (2016:564). These researchers further identified three sub-types within this general category based on rates of crimes against persons and property, mental health disorders, and substance abuse. They labeled these types "Normative" (elevated substance abuse and antisocial behavior), "Psychologically Distressed" (abused women with extremely elevated rates of psychiatric disorders) and "Comorbid Antisocial" (highest levels of all types of crime).

73. Ferrell (2018).

74. Ferrell (2018:46–47).

75. Humphreys (1970:129).

76. See Hensley and Tewksbury (2002); Hensley, Tewksbury and Wright (2001); Kirkham (2000); Sagarin (1976). For a comprehensive historical study of sexualities inside prisons in relation to societal understandings of sexuality more broadly, see Kunzel (2008).

77. See Adler and Adler (2005, 2007); Hodgson (2004).

78. Gottfredson and Hirshi's (1990) descriptions of individuals with "low self-control," who are essentially unable to maintain social bonds with anyone and who engage in deviance based on impulse and opportunity, closely align with our conceptualization of Drifters.

79. Fox (1987:363).

80. Presidential hopeful Mitt Romney, discussing Mormonism in his "Faith in America" speech. A transcript of the speech is available at: http://www.npr.org/templates/story/story.php?storyId=16969460.

81. In the lead-up to Romney's 2008 bid for the Republican nomination, Hewitt wrote the book *A Mormon in the White House?* It included the chapter "Mitt Romney's Got a Mormon Problem (and So Does a Lot of the Country)," which outlined the concerns of many conservative Protestants about Mormonism. Hewitt argued that Romney's Mormonism should *not* disqualify him from the presidency.

82. When asked "How much does the Mormon religion have in common with your own beliefs?" respondents could select from the options: "A great deal," "a lot," "a moderate amount," "a little," or "nothing at all." Thirty-four percent of Evangelical Protestant respondents chose "nothing at all." Only 1.5 percent selected "A great deal." When asked "Do you think the Mormon religion is Christian, or is it not Christian?," 59.4 percent of Evangelical Protestant respondents selected "not Christian." Source: 2012 ANES.

83. The ANES (2012) asked respondents if Mitt Romney's Mormonism was a factor that influenced their voting decision and if so, who they voted for as a result. Some 13.7 percent of respondents said this factor led them to vote for Barack Obama. For a detailed overview of American ambivalence toward Mormons, see chapter 7 of Campbell, Green, and Monson (2014). Also see Medhurst (2009:196).

84. Are Mormons Christian? (n.d.). Retrieved April 12, 2017, from https://www.lds.org /topics/christians?lang=eng&old=true.

85. https://www.mormonnewsroom.org/style-guide.

86. A complete set of LDS holy books would include the Christian Bible, the Book of Mormon, the Pearl of Great Price, and Doctrine and Covenants.

87. For an overview of Mormon beliefs and practices in relation to politics and voting, see *Could I Vote for a Mormon for President?* (Cragun and Phillips 2012).

88. Cragun and Phillips (2012:16).

89. For example, the musical *The Book of Mormon*, which mocks Mormon beliefs, was first staged in 2011 and became extremely popular, winning a Tony Award for Best Musical.

90. Hewitt (2007:209). Wards and branches are the equivalent of congregations in non-LDS churches. Stakes consist of multiple wards and branches. Sometimes wards will share the same church building but hold services at different times.

91. Romney (2007).

92. Campbell, Green and Monson (2014:198).

93. Campbell, Green and Monson (2014:216) also argue that Romney deployed the tactic of *deflection*—side-stepping queries about religion when possible. Consequently, they argue that Romney's tactics also occasionally slipped into *avoidance*.

94. Medhurst (2009:207).

95. Romney (2007).

96. Romney (2007).

97. Romney (2007).

98. Medhurst (2009:196).

99. Romney's Health Care Overhaul (2006).

100. Reilly (2006).

3. FIGHTING FOR NORMAL?

1. Best and Luckenbill (1994:12–13) use four criteria to differentiate forms of deviant social organization: mutual association, mutual participation (engage in deviance together), elaborate division of labor, and extended organization. Loners possess none of these criteria—engaging in deviant behavior without interacting with others. Colleagues are those deviants who associate with one another on occasion. Peers associate with one

another and mutually participate in deviant acts. Teams couple association and participation with an elaborate division of labor. Finally, formal organizations possess all five characteristics.

2. Best and Luckenbill (1980:15–16).

3. See Bader, Baker and Mencken (2017).

4. We can only roughly estimate the number of individuals who claim a Bigfoot sighting. The Bigfoot Field Researchers Organization (BFRO) gathers Bigfoot reports through its website (www.bfro.net). As of this writing, the site lists 4,990 different reports from across the United States. Not all of these are reported sightings. Some are reports of finding Bigfoot tracks, hearing something believed to be a Bigfoot without seeing it, or of otherwise believing one has been in the presence of a Bigfoot or finding evidence of its passing. Given the number of reports gathered by the BFRO, the fact that it is only one of many organizations that collects Bigfoot sightings, that many such sightings likely go unreported, and that some Bigfoot reports involve multiple witnesses, we are comfortable positing that, at minimum, five thousand individuals in the United States claim a Bigfoot sighting. The Chapman University Survey of American Fears, Wave 3 (2016) asked a random sample of adult Americans their level of agreement with the following statement: "Bigfoot is a real creature." Nearly 14 percent (13.5 percent) agree or strongly agree with this statement.

5. Bader, Baker, and Mencken (2017).

6. Becker ([1963] 1991:39).

7. See Benford (1993); Zald and Ash (1966); Zald and McCarthy (1980).

8. E.g., Grattet (2011).

9. Becker ([1963] 1991:39).

10. Goffman (1963:3).

11. Goffman (1963:102, 116).

12. Goffman (1963:74).

13. McQueeney (2009:157). To be clear, not all of the members of the congregations that McQueeney interviewed were gay or lesbian. Some were straight but accepting/affirming of LGBTQ individuals; however, we focus on the openly gay and lesbian members of the churches McQueeney studied.

14. McQueeney (2009:157).

15. McQueeney (2009:159).

16. McQueeney (2003).

17. McQueeney (2009:166).

18. McQueeney (2009:167).

19. McQueeney (2009:167).

20. Sykes and Matza (1957).

21. Galinsky et al. (2013).

22. See Martin (2000) for a discussion of the management of the stigma and shame of obesity through various methods and ideological frames. Of course, obesity presents an outwardly visible form of deviance and is therefore difficult to hide. Accordingly, the strategies employed tend to be those of the Outsider or Insider, or efforts to remove the stigmatizing condition through various means. The isolation of Drifters can also be strategy in the case of obesity.

23. On code switching as a general process in relation to norms and deviance from a sociolinguistic perspective, see Myers-Scotton (1988, 1993, 2000).

24. Anderson (1999).

25. Hathaway (2004).

26. On the original conception of cognitive dissonance, see Festinger (1957). For elaborations and refinements of the social psychological components of cognitive dissonance and how it motivates individuals, see Cooper (2007); Elliot and Devine (1994); Matz and Wood (2005); Stone and Cooper (2000).

27. Normalization has also been used to refer to a form of groupthink, in which members of a group or organization become so used to the occurrence of a particular form of deviance that it is no longer viewed as deviant. Vaughn (1996) provides an excellent example of this form of normalization in her study of the *Challenger* shuttle disaster. Ultimately the decision was made to launch the shuttle despite the fact that the joints on its rocket boosters were not meeting expected performance parameters. The team assessing the joints continually reinterpreted data suggesting that they were not operating properly in order to find acceptable performance. Put another way, the deviance in question was only defined as normal in a particular context of in-group pressures. We use the term normalization in a broader sense.

28. Of course, it is always possible that a major shift in societal attitudes and beliefs could move a "normalized" group back into deviant status. This could occur, for example, if there were a dramatic change in attitudes about homosexuality that recast gays and lesbians as immoral/deviant.

29. Fisher (1987).

30. Becker (1967). For a discussion of how the hierarchy of credibility relates to research and theory in criminology—one that is consonant with our own perspective—see Liebling (2001).

31. On the social processes of moral entrepreneurs and claims making, see (Becker [1963] 1991; Gusfield 1966, 1986; Schur 1980; Reasons 1974; Reinarman 1988; Spector and Kituse 1987; Troyer and Markle 1982).

32. Stark (2003:261).

33. This is not to say that Scientology is actively hostile toward Christianity, as the church publicly claims that it honors all faiths and that one can be both a Christian and a Scientologist. Rather, we mean Scientology does not make active use of Christian culture in its teachings and does not claim to be a Christian religion. This does not mean that new religious movements cannot succeed without cultural continuity; however, it does necessarily alter the numerical upside of the group and result in an appeal to a different type of religious consumer, namely those interested in novel cultural experiences and perspectives.

34. Williams (2002:247).

35. Broad, Crawley, and Foley (2004); Lehr (1999). On religion's relationship to normative and deviant designations of "the family," see Perry and Whitehead (2016).

36. Bernstein (1997, 2002:101), see also Moon (2004, 2005).

37. See Cragun, Nielson, and Clingenpeel (2011).

38. Zald and McCarthy (1994).

39. Epstein (1999:75).

40. Cory (1951).

41. Duberman (2002:66).

42. Duberman (2002:67, 69).

43. Humphreys (1970). For an experimental and empirical confirmation of the breast-plate-of-righteousness process of prejudice and discrimination see Weinstein et al. (2012).

44. On the possibilities of mobilization among communities of Drifters, see Ferrell (2018:52–69)

45. Liazos (1972).

46. Sagarin (1969:17).

47. Schur (1980:191).

48. See Murray (2008).

49. See, for instance, Ellis's (1963, 1965) views on "curing" homosexuality.

50. Duberman (2002). Ellis then wrote a "strikingly ambivalent" introduction to subsequent editions of *The Homosexual in America* (Murray 2008:335).

51. Kameny (2014:89–90).

52. Kameny (2014:90)

53. Sagarin (1973:10).

54. Sagarin (1973:11–12).

55. Sagarin (1973:5).

56. Duberman: (2002:94) Also see Goodwin, Horowitz, and Nardi (1991); Sears (2006:529–30).

57. Murray (2004:138).

58. Murray (2008:342).

59. Lemert (1972).

60. Gamson (1968:169–70) argues that "alienated groups" will favor coercion since they are already resented and have nothing to lose. However, a deviant group that desires to be socially accepted and does not simply want short-term benefits will likely avoid coercion.

61. Stewart, Smith, and Denton (1984:11–12); see also Gamson (1968:75).

62. Plummer (1999:144).

4. BIGFOOT: UNDISCOVERED PRIMATE OR INTERDIMENSIONAL SPIRIT?

1. On cross-cultural accounts of "wildman" myths as folklore, see Dendle (2006); Forth (2007). For cultural histories of Bigfoot/Sasquatch, see Buhs (2009); Regal (2011).

2. Here we mirror the title of a chapter in John Green's (1978) influential Bigfoot book *Sasquatch: The Apes Among Us*.

3. Genzoli (1958). Within the subculture, Bigfoot is believed to be an undiscovered species, not a singular creature that roams the woods. Witnesses have claimed sightings of adult male, adult female and younger "Bigfeet." However, some Bigfoot paranormalists claim that all sightings are of a singular entity that manifests in different times and places.

4. Patterson (1966).

5. Patterson and Murphy (2005).

6. We base this conclusion on our participant observations at Bigfoot conferences where speakers have generally taken as a given that the PG film depicts a "Bigfoot." Indeed, many of the presentations we have observed assess the credibility of new sightings based on their similarity to what is depicted in this film. Further, we asked attendees at a major

Bigfoot conference (to be discussed in more detail later in this chapter) how credible they find the PG film. The vast majority (80 percent) find the film to be either "somewhat" (23.7 percent) or "very" (56.5 percent) credible.

7. For example, Patterson and Murphy (2005) combine a reprint of Patterson's earlier, self-published book with an in-depth discussion of the film events by Christopher Murphy. Munns (2014) and Long (2004) also focus on the film (the latter a skeptical overview). Krantz (1992), Meldrum (2006) and Murphy (2004) all devote extensive space to the film and argue for its authenticity.

8. From shortly after the PG film was shot until nearly 2005, Bob Gimlin, with only a few exceptions, refused to talk about the events. He has recently reengaged with the Bigfoot subculture and regularly appears at related conferences, where he is lauded as a hero. I met Gimlin twice at such events. It also is worth noting that, were this book concerned with assessing the validity and truthfulness of Patterson and Gimlin's claims, we could have devoted considerable space to questions raised about Patterson's personal character, problems with the timeline presented, allegations of fraud by a purported accomplice, and so on. We are only interested in the *social* reality of the PG film. Whatever else it may be, it is undeniably the wellspring of a devoted Bigfoot subculture.

9. Streufert (2011).

10. See Munns and Meldrum (2013).

11. I was joined on this trip by L. Edward Day, chair of the Department of Sociology at Chapman University, Mark Hopkins, a photographer from Washington State, Ernie Alonzo, founder of a paranormal tour group called Haunted Orange, and Ben Hansen, star of a paranormal television show called *Fact or Faked*.

12. Bluff Creek Project (n.d.).

13. Bluff Creek Project (n.d.).

14. Krantz and Sprague (1977); Bindernagel (1998); Meldrum (2006).

15. Of course, the costs of researching Bigfoot are much less for those who write books and articles that utilize Bigfoot as an example of pseudoscience.

16. Alderman (2006).

17. Alderman (2006).

18. Meldrum (n.d.).

19. Chibnall (2017).

20. Munns and Meldrum (2013b).

21. Munns and Meldrum (2013a).

22. Munns and Meldrum (2013a).

23. Meldrum (2006:276).

24. Bindernagel noted during this talk that, while he used to be convinced that Bigfoot was an undiscovered great ape, he has become more open to the possibility that it may be more human-like than ape-like.

25. All quotes from the 2015 Sasquatch Summit are from field notes taken at the event.

26. Lévi-Strauss ([1975] 1982:65).

27. Olympic Project (n.d.).

28. Baker's talk and conclusions are discussed at greater length in Bader, Baker and Mencken (2017:170–71).

29. See https://www.facebook.com/cindy.dosen/ for more information about Dosen.

30. In his talk, Powell divided the Bigfoot subculture into two camps; "flesh and blood" (Bigfoot is merely an undiscovered species of ape or human) and "paranormal" (Bigfoot is a paranormal entity or spirit with extraordinary powers).

31. In the UFO subculture this phenomenon is called "missing time."

32. Quotes are from Powell's presentation at the 2015 Sasquatch Summit.

33. Powell (2015).

34. PlanetSasquatch (2015).

35. Notes from interview with Samantha Ritchie at 2015 Sasquatch Summit. Ritchie did not describe levels 3–6 and I did not press for more details on her classification scheme.

36. See Gordon (2010) and Bord and Bord (2006:chap. 7).

37. Pilichis (1982).

38. For example, many Bigfoot books include the "Ape Canyon Incident," a 1924 report of a group of Bigfeet attacking a cabin near Mount Saint Helens in Washington State. Frequently omitted from the tale is the claim by one of the witnesses, Fred Beck, that the creatures had psychic powers and the ability to become invisible. See Beck (1967) for his recounting of the events. See Green (1978:88–92) for an example of a retelling with the paranormal elements omitted.

39. Bluff Creek Project (n.d.).

40. Krantz (1992:123).

41. This rift aligns with more general distinctions in the paranormal between pursuits of *discovery* and *enlightenment* (see Bader, Baker and Mencken 2017:45–47).

42. Alderman (2006).

43. The Bigfoot Field Researchers Organization maintains a database of Bigfoot encounters reported to the group. As of August 2017, the BFRO website had 222 reports from Texas. Washington (631), California (436), Florida (310), Illinois (284), Ohio (270) and Oregon (245) have a higher number of reported Bigfoot encounters. See http://www.bfro.net/gdb/.

44. See Bader, Baker, and Mencken (2017:155–60).

45. Kummer (2017).

46. "New Name, Same Mission." (2013). Retrieved August 31, 2017, from http://woodape.org/index.php/news/news/227-nawacannounce.

47. The organization has produced a lengthy scientific-style monograph compiling their assortment of evidence from "Area X." See Colyer et al. (2015)

48. To the best of our knowledge, none of the members of the NAWAC has a PhD, although there are members with master's and professional degrees (e.g., MD).

49. Leggett (2009).

50. We asked respondents several questions about their religious beliefs, including their religious tradition, frequency of attendance at religious services, level of personal religiosity, and view of the Bible. Unfortunately, the religion items had more missing data than other variables and could not be used.

51. During our fieldwork, members of the Bigfoot subculture frequently raised concerns about employment. A Bigfoot hunter who is a physician told us of his concerns about embarrassing himself among coworkers. Another told us that he worried that clients might be concerned about the competency of a financial professional who "chased Bigfoot on the weekends."

52. Hunters attempt to communicate with Bigfoot by playing recordings of wounded animals or purported Bigfoot screams. More often, Bigfoot researchers attempt to mimic

Bigfoot yells themselves by loudly shouting. Bigfoot hunters hope that a Sasquatch will either respond with its own vocalization or appear to investigate the sounds.

53. With the exception of "membership," possible responses included "never," "rarely," "once in a while," "somewhat often," and "very often." Figure 3 combines responses for the top three categories for these items. The bar for membership provides the percentage of respondents (20 percent) who were members of a Bigfoot organization.

54. The deviant identity measure's Cronbach's α = .81. For the weighted index of deviant identity, we recoded the individual measures such that the low-cost items (watching documentaries, reading books and magazines, and visiting websites) ranged from 0 to 4, and the high-cost items (web postings, organizational membership, field operations, and call blasting) ranged from 0 to 8. Therefore, each step in the high-cost measure is equivalent to two steps in the low-cost items (0, 2, 4, 6, 8 instead of 0, 1, 2, 3, 4). We coded the organizational membership item as a dichotomous measure with 0 for "no" and 8 for "yes." Once combined, the final measure has a mean of 13.5 and ranges from 0 to 44.

55. Bader, Baker, and Mencken (2017:163–91).

56. Iannaccone (1995).

57. Bader, Baker and Mencken (2017:107–28); Baker, Bader and Mencken (2016).

58. Krulos (2015:158–60).

59. North American Wood Ape Conservancy (n.d.). The organization has evolved over time, from prioritizing the conservation of an endangered species to prioritizing proving the existence of the species to mainstream science and society.

60. Lee Spiegel "Big Honors for UFO Congress," *Huffington Post*, September 18, 2014. http://www.huffingtonpost.com/2014/09/18/guinness-worlds-largest-ufo-convention_n _5813890.html.

61. Lasperitis's talk at the 2014 IUFOC was entitled: "Interdimensionalism: The Secret to the Bigfoot/UFO Connection." See http://ufocongress.com/kewaunee-lapseritis/.

62. The higher percentage of IUFOC attendees who said they "absolutely" believe in Bigfoot (42 percent) compared to the percentage of TBRC attendees who said they "absolutely" believed in extraterrestrials (24 percent) speaks to the paranormal particularist and generalist orientations of these conferences, respectively.

63. All differences shown across the conferences are significant at p <.001 in chi square tests, except for encountering Bigfoot, where there were *not* statistically significant differences across the conferences.

64. On fractalization as a basic dynamic in social scientific research and theory, see Abbott (2001). Applying the idea to our theory, it is dynamic enough to generate insights when applied to different levels of analytical scope, using different methodologies, and across subcultural contexts.

5. SEXUALITY AND GENDER IDENTITY: ASSIMILATION VS. LIBERATION

1. Percentages are from 2013 Pew LGBT Survey.

2. For an empirical assessment of how framing has shaped the change in public opinion concerning homosexuality, see Brewer (2008).

3. For more detailed historical overviews of the movements for gay assimilation and liberation in the United States, see Rimmerman (2001) and Cruikshank (1992).

4. Ghaziani, Taylor, and Stone (2016:166). Bernstein's (1997) ethnographic research with LGBT movements in the United States outlines the strategic uses of both conventional and subcultural identity under varying political contexts.

5. Ghaziani (2008, 2014).

6. Weiss (2012:1).

7. Gamson (1995).

8. Cf. Seidman (1996); Halpern (2003); Green (2007).

9. Weiss (2012:835).

10. Galinsky et al. (2013).

11. Motta (2011).

12. Motta (2011).

13. Ruiz (2008:238–39, emphasis in original).

14. Motta (2011), emphasis in original.

15. Motta (2011).

16. LeMaster (2013)

17. Motta (2011).

18. LeMaster (2013).

19. Ruiz (2008:242). A similar dynamic is evident in other resistance identities, such as active atheism in highly religious social contexts (Baker and Smith 2015).

20. Shapiro (2013).

21. Ruiz (2008:240–41).

22. Flynn and Smith (2008:250).

23. Flynn and Smith (2008:261).

24. Flynn and Smith (2008:254, 252).

25. Flynn (1999).

26. Lewis (1999). Also see Finkelstein (1999) Swarns (1999). On media coverage of the Diallo murder, see Lindsey (2004).

27. Flynn and Smith (2008:258–61).

28. Flynn and Smith (2008:254).

29. Flynn and Smith (2008:261).

30. Ruiz (2008:242).

31. (Sycamore 2008b:269). On the beginnings and strategies of the Gay Shame movement see Taylor (2014); Weiss (2008). For academic perspectives on gay shame more generally, see Halpern and Traub (2009). On the interplay between academic queer studies and queer movements in relation to gay shame, as well as Mattilda's involvement, see Rand (2014:139–47).

32. Ruiz (2008:241).

33. Sycamore (2008b:270).

34. Sycamore (2008b:291)

35. See Winn-Lenetsky (2015).

36. Iftikhar (2013).

37. Lewis (2008).

38. Rooney (2014).

39. Motta (2011), emphasis in original.

40. Sycamore (2008a:2–6, emphasis in original).

41. Sycamore (2014:87).

42. http://www.againstequality.org/.

43. Kaufman and Miles (2014:82–83).

44. Gipson (2012). Emphasis added.

45. Ghaziani, Taylor, and Stone (2016:178).

46. Ryan and Bradford (1999:91).

47. Bradford and Ryan (1984–1985, 1988).

48. Bradford, Ryan, and Rothblum (1994).

49. This measurement strategy is clearly different from the one used for the Pew LGBT Survey in that it asks for identification with a specific sexual identity rather than allowing respondents to claim an identity and *then* measure the level of investment in that identity; however, this does still allow for an assessment of commitment to identity, albeit toward a more specific target. The largest drawback is that self-identified bisexuals cannot be Insiders or Outsiders using this measurement. But as the analyses of the Pew LGBT Survey show, this largely conforms to the general patterns that occur even when there is an available measure of commitment to bisexuality.

50. Full details on the sampling and measures for the Pew LGBT Survey are available here: http://www.pewsocialtrends.org/2013/06/13/a-survey-of-lgbt-americans/.

51. Notably, marital status was not available as a measure of conventionality in the NLHCS due to the illegality of same-sex marriage in the United States in 1985.

52. Outsiders and Insiders both showed lower levels of concerns about same-sex civil unions, likely because, at the time of the survey, same-sex marriage reform actions were achieving success and civil unions represented a lesser form of partnership rights.

53. The "not applicable" responses were not included in the comparisons for levels of outness, but do make for an informative outcome category.

54. Durkheim ([1897] 1979). For a review of empirical studies of integration and suicide, see Stack (2000). For a recent theoretical elaboration of Durkheim's theory using an empirical case study, see Mueller and Abrutyn (2016).

55. One substance with higher usage rates among Outsiders was habitual cannabis use (at least once a week), which was the same among Drifters and Outsiders (16 percent), with lower rates of marijuana use among Hiders (12 percent) and Insiders (8 percent).

56. Drifters were also the most likely to attend a "spirituality" group, reflecting a tendency toward unconventional religion.

57. Butler (1990).

58. This percentage was taken from all transgender respondents to the Pew LGBT survey, not just those who listed being transgendered as their most important identity marker, among whom the percentage who were Insiders was slightly higher (19 percent).

59. Percentages for outness to mother, father, and siblings are given only for those for whom these relationships are applicable.

60. It is possible that differences in sample composition and/or measurement are at least partially responsible for some of the changes across the surveys; however, if methodo-

logical differences were driving the results, we would expect to see more uniform changes, such as a similar increase among all deviance management categories. Given that the changes over time are not uniform across the categories and conform to the expectations that Outsiders play path-breaking roles for Insiders (and Hiders), the weight of evidence is against methodological sources as being the cause of differences across surveys.

61. Granovetter (1978); Macy (1990, 1991).

62. It is worth noting that this represents participation that is relatively low cost and is occurring in a less repressive environment than would have been the case even twenty years prior. In cases of participation that entail higher personal risks, we would expect Outsiders' participation to be greater than Insiders. In support of this, "pure" Outsiders—those at the highest level of subcultural identity and lowest level of conventional identity—reported the highest levels of participation in lesbian rights groups in the 1983 NLHCS.

63. DeLuca (1999) provides a comparative analysis of how three different Outsider-oriented protest groups—including ACT UP and Queer Nation—strategically deployed their bodies in direct action protests.

64. On the early organization and tactics of ACT UP in relation to studies of social movements, see Gamson (1989).

65. The definitive account of the rise and fall of ACT UP is Gould (2009). Also see Rand (2014).

66. Gould (2009).

67. Gipson (2012).

68. Bornstein (2014:25–26).

69. Ruiz (2008:243).

70. Ruiz (2008:242).

71. Rooney (2014).

72. Mattos (2012).

73. LeMaster (2013).

74. Shepard (2010:248).

75. Motta (2011).

76. Ruiz (2008:240).

77. We have used Mattilda's life stories, activism, and writing to provide an insightful example of Outsider identity, narratives, and communities. In doing so, we necessarily are guilty of appropriation, a fact Mattilda has highlighted as her work has gained visibility among academics: "I use the phrase trickle-down academia to describe the process by which academics often appropriate anything they can get their hands on—especially people's lived struggles, identities, methods of activism, and other challenges to the status quo—and then, claim to have invented the whole package. Historically, this is perhaps most obvious in disciplines like anthropology or sociology. . . . But more often than not I think it becomes a quest for ownership—string together some cool new vocabulary words (or rework some old ones), and the territory is yours, you own it" (Weiss 2012:833–34). While we certainly do not intend to claim ownership over particular narratives or communities, we have little defense for our appropriations. Like so much of Mattilda's work, it is a critique well made.

6. INSIDERS AND THE NORMALIZATION OF ILLEGAL DRUGS

1. For an introduction, see Goode (2015).

2. Musto (1991), Reinarman (1994).

3. Provine (2007).

4. Clark (1976); Gusfield (1986).

5. Musto and Korsmeyer (2002); Provine (2007).

6. Baum (2016:22).

7. Gusfield (1986).

8. Schwadel and Ellison (2017); Schnabel and Sevell (2017). Importantly, however, views of cannabis have become more favorable among all members of the public, including evangelical Protestants.

9. There can, however, be public support for decriminalization accompanied by efforts at control and harm reduction through public health initiatives rather than harsh punishment, even if there is unlikely to be support for full legalization.

10. For historical accounts of Prohibition repeal, see Kyvig (2000); Severn (1969). On the role of women in repeal movements, see Rose (1997). On the WONPR specifically, see Neumann (1997); Thomas, Thomas, and Snow (2013).

11. Kyvig (1976).

12. "Charles H. Sabin, Banker, Dies at 65." New York Times, October 12, 1933, p. 25. Their front-page wedding announcement in the Times declared that "Mrs. Sabin, as Pauline Morton, was one of the most popular girls of her set in Washington and New York." "Chas. H. Sabin Weds Mrs. Pauline Smith." New York Times, December 29, 1916, p. 1.

13. Okrent (2010:290).

14. Okrent (2010:229).

15. Sabin (1928:254).

16. Miron (1999); Woodiwiss (1988).

17. Sabin (1928:272).

18. Sabin (1928:272).

19. Sabin (1928:272).

20. Sabin did, however, speak out against using Democratic presidential nominee Al Smith's Catholicism to foment xenophobia, saying, "I would rather see the Republican Party go down to defeat in November than to win as a result of religious intolerance." "Hilles Repudiates Support by Bigots; Stresses Dry Issue." 1929. New York Times, September 25, p. 1.

21. http://avalon.law.yale.edu/20th_century/hoover.asp.

22. Okrent (2010:316).

23. Lerner (2007:275–76, 284).

24. To be clear, Sabin continued to appear on the society pages after beginning her work with the WONPR. Articles or society page notes about Sabin's events at Bayberry Land and elsewhere are not included in the dataset for content analysis or the count of articles pertaining to the repeal movement.

25. "Mrs. Sabin Sounds Call for Wet Fight." New York Times, April 4, 1929, p. 1.

26. "Women Organize to Fight Dry Laws." New York Times, May 29, 1929, p. 3.

27. Root (1934:11–12).

28. As quoted in Root (1934:12).

29. Information is taken from Root (1934:180–211). By comparison, data from the 1930 census indicates that approximately 9 percent of women over age thirty-five were unmarried in the United States overall (Elliott et al. 2012).

30. "Mrs. Sabin to Survey Effects of Dry Law Among Wives of Workers throughout the Nation." *New York Times*, July 2, 1929, p. 12.

31. Although later dropped, charges also were brought against the same agent in 1926 for having burglary tools in his car.

32. "2 Dry Agents Seized in Rum-Running Plot." *New York Times*, July 2, 1929, pp. 1, 12.

33. Root (1934:14).

34. "Dr. Butler Scores Law Board Report." *New York Times*, January 15, 1930, p. 18.

35. Wadsworth Jr. served in the Senate from 1915 until 1927, as the first senator from New York elected by popular vote. He would later serve in the House of Representatives for the Thirty-Ninth District from 1933 until 1945, and for the Forty-First District from 1945 until 1951. See Fausold (1975).

36. "Doran Hears Wets Condemn Dry Law." *New York Times*, January 27, 1930, pp. 1, 17.

37. "Four Women Lead Attack on Dry Law." *New York Times*, February 14, 1930, p. 1.

38. "The Debate on Prohibition: A Summing Up." *New York Times*, March 30, 1930, section 9, p. 3. Sabin's father, Paul Morton, who served a five-year stint as president of the Equitable Life Insurance Company before his death in 1911, provided the contacts necessary to secure such information. In contrast to Sabin's claims, however, innovative research shows that the consumption of alcohol did in fact decline sharply at the beginning Prohibition, before rising to approximately 60 to 70 percent of pre-Prohibition levels at the time of the passage of the Twenty-First Amendment (Miron and Zwiebel 1991).

39. "Four Women Lead Attack on Dry Law." *New York Times*, February 14, 1930, p. 18.

40. "Bitter Tilts Open Jenks Bill Hearing." *New York Times*, February 20, 1930, p. 3.

41. "Says College Girls Oppose Prohibition." *New York Times*, March 20, 1930, p. 2.

42. "Women Wets Stage Mass Protest Here; Dry Act Revolt Seen." *New York Times*, April 14, 1930, p. 1.

43. "Mrs. Sabin Meets Rival in Debate." *New York Times*, April 22, 1930, p. 4.

44. Root (1934:20).

45. Root (1934:21).

46. "Women Begin Drive to End Prohibition." *New York Times*, June 4, 1930, p. 2.

47. Root (1934:xii).

48. "Women Say Repeal Is Chief 1932 Issue." *New York Times*, November 20, 1930, p. 22.

49. "Dry Leaders Drink, Mrs. Sabin Asserts." *New York Times*, February 11, 1931, p. 23. Also see "Mrs. Sabin Urges Women Wets Bolt." *New York Times*, April 13, 1931, p. 2.

50. Root (1934:43, emphasis added).

51. "Women Wets Urge Repeal on Hoover." *New York Times*, April 16, 1931, p. 1.

52. "Form 'Labor Legion' to Change Dry Law." *New York Times*, April 29, 1931, p. 21.

53. It has been said that "No other national argument ever flooded the country with so many books, pamphlets, reports, surveys, news releases and speeches" as did repeal activists (Severn 1969:159).

54. "Dry Effort Failing, Wadsworth Insists." *New York Times*, July 2, 1930, p. 2.

55. Dighe (2010).

56. "10,000 Wets Parade in Rally at Newark." *New York Times*, October 18, 1931, p. 10.

57. Root (1934:57).

58. See, for example "Women Wets Tell of Growing Power." *New York Times*, September 16, 1931, p. 14.

59. "Young Women Join in Fight on Dry Law." *New York Times*, October 18, 1931, p. 3.

60. "Mrs. Sabin Urges a Wet Amendment." *New York Times*, November 11, 1931, p. 18.

61. "Mrs. Sabin Proposes a 'Party Moratorium.'" *New York Times*, January 1, 1932, p. 26.

62. Root (1934:67).

63. McBain (1928).

64. Root (1934:69).

65. "Billion Liquor Tax Urged on Senators." *New York Times*, April 15, 1932, p. 22.

66. "Women in 41 States Open Repeal Week." *New York Times*, May 15, 1932, p. 4.

67. "Women's Parade Today Launches 'Repeal Week.'" *Chicago Tribune*, May 16, 1932, p. 6.

68. "Dry Law Foes Seek 1,000,000 Recruits." *New York Times*, May 16, 1932, p. 10.

69. Rogers ([1932] 1979:151).

70. Rogers ([1932] 2006:323–26).

71. "Chides Will Rogers as Wet Drive Critic." *New York Times*, May 21, 1932, p. 32.

72. "Mrs. Sabin Demands Apology from Dry." *New York Times*, May 24, 1932, p. 2.

73. "Wet Leaders Hold Dr. Colvin Bigoted." *New York Times*, May 25, 1932, p. 3.

74. "Repealists Score the Hoover Plank." *New York Times*, June 16, 1932, p. 14.

75. "Mrs. Sabin Assails Republican Plank." *New York Times*, August 10, 1932, p. 6.

76. "Wets Enthusiastic for Repeal Plank." *New York Times*, July 1, 1932, p. 15.

77. "Women Wet Leaders Endorse Roosevelt." 1932. *New York Times*, July 8, pp.1, 11.

78. "Charges Mills Aided Women in Wets' Revolt." *New York Times*, July 12, 1932, p. 5. At the time, Bishop Cannon had been embroiled in a number of scandals, dramatically falling from grace as a champion of public morality. This reference allowed Sabin to unify her constituency (us vs. them [dry organizations]), while also alluding to the hypocrisy of some dry activists. On the rise and fall of Bishop Cannon, see Hohner (1999).

79. "Dissension Subsides in Women's Wet Group." *New York Times*, July 14, 1932, p. 6.

80. Root (1934:103).

81. "Predicts Wet Vote in Next Congress." *New York Times*, October 10, 1932, p. 2. "Congress Nominees Found Wet by 10 to 1." *New York Times*, October 24, 1932, pp. 1, 9.

82. Root (1934:117).

83. "New Repeal Drive Urged by Mrs. Sabin." *New York Times*, November 14, 1932, p. 3.

84. "Women Wets Call for Repeal First." *New York Times*, November 29, 1932, p. 2.

85. "Dry Repeal Loses in House 272–144, Wets Short 6 as Lame Ducks Say Nay." *New York Times*, December 6, 1932, pp. 1, 16.

86. "Women to Survey Wet Legislation." *New York Times*, December 7, 1932, p. 18.

87. "Mrs. Sabin Predicts Lucky Year for Wets." *New York Times*, January 16, 1933, p. 2.

88. "Test in Committee for Repeal Today." *New York Times*, January 9, 1933, p. 40.

89. "Modified Repeal Bill Now before Senate." *New York Times*, January 10, 1933, pp. 1, 2.

90. "Repeal in Danger, Mrs. Sabin Warns." *New York Times*, February 14, 1933, p. 2.

91. "Mrs. Sabin Hailed as a Great Leader." *New York Times*, February 13, 1933, p. 12.

92. "Senate Votes Dry Repeal by Conventions in States; House Will Act Monday." *New York Times*, February 17, 1933, pp. 1, 13.

93. "Wets Shift Fight to Legislatures." *New York Times*, February 21, 1933, p. 12.

94. "House Votes Dry Law Repeal, 289–121; States Begin Move for Ratification." *New York Times*, February 21, 1933, p. 1.

95. "Women Gather for Repeal Drive." *New York Times*, April 2, 1933, p. 3.

96. "Women Complete Repeal Week Plan." *New York Times*, May 3, 1933, p. 4.

97. "State Wet Sweep Predicted Today." *New York Times*, May 23, 1933, pp. 1, 13.

98. "Repeal by 20 to 1 Is Voted in State; 6th Wet Victory." *New York Times*, May 24, 1933, pp.1–2.

99. "Repeal This Year Held Possibility." *New York Times*, June 18, 1933, p. 13.

100. "Dry Senators See Swing to Repeal." *New York Times*, June 22, 1933, p. 6.

101. "Quick Action Urged to Control Liquor." *New York Times*, September 10, 1933, section 2, p. 1.

102. Root (1934:158).

103. "Views of Smith and Others on Repeal." *New York Times*, November 9, 1933, p. 3.

104. Dioun (2018); Golan (2010); Kilmer and MacCoun (2017); Pichardo (n.d).

105. Haines-Saah et al. (2014).

106. Stryker (2003). Also see O'Callaghan and Hannon (2003).

107. Keyes et al. (2011).

108. Baker and Smith (2015). In supplemental analyses we treated years of the GSS as cases and gave them attributes using aggregated survey responses from that year. Between the years of 1991 and 2016, the correlation for the percent of a sample claiming no religion and the percent favoring marijuana legalization in each year during those 14 waves of data was r = .96!

109. On the contingencies of connections between public opinion and social policy see Burstein (2003); Erikson, Wright and McIver (1993); Manza and Cook (2002); Shapiro (2011); Sharp (1999).

110. The source of the measure for the percent of evangelical Protestants in each state—the 2007 Pew Religious Landscape Survey—used denominational affiliation as the primary classifier, following the classification scheme outlined by Steensland et al. (2000). Respondents who reported generic religious identities such as "Baptist" or "Christian" were classified based on a follow-up question about being "born again."

111. Interviews with cannabis users suggest that even when the illegal status is removed, the social stigma of marijuana use remains. Hence, some researchers have suggested that "normification" is a more apt description than full normalization, as the latter suggests that something ceases to be perceived as deviant. In contrast to full normalization, many of those with higher stakes in conventional identity continue to hide their cannabis use, even after legal restrictions have been removed (Hathaway, Comaeu, and Erickson 2011).

112. While this book was in production, Michigan legalized recreational marijuana (Proposition 1 in 2018) by popular referendum (with 56 percent of the vote).

CONCLUSION: STUDYING DEVIANCE MANAGEMENT

1. The following is a list of the twenty-six states that had court rulings in favor of same-sex marriage before the *Obergefell v. Hodges* decision and the dates of those rulings: Alabama (2/9/2015); Alaska (10/7/2014); Arizona (10/17/2014); California (6/28/2013);

Colorado (10/7/2014); Connecticut (11/12/2008); Florida (1/6/2015); Idaho (10/13/2014); Indiana (10/6/2014); Iowa (10/24/2009); Kansas (11/12/2014); Massachusetts (5/17/2004); Montana (11/19/2014); Nevada (10/9/2014); New Jersey (10/21/2013); New Mexico (12/19/2013); North Carolina (10/10/2014); Oklahoma (10/6/2014); Oregon (5/19/2014); Pennsylvania (5/20/2014); South Carolina (11/20/2014); Utah (10/6/2014); Virginia (10/6/2014); West Virginia (10/9/2014); Wisconsin (10/6/2014); Wyoming (10/21/2014).

2. Delaware (7/1/2013); Hawaii (12/2/2013); Illinois (6/1/2014); Minnesota (8/1/2013); New Hampshire (1/1/2010); New York (6/24/2011); Rhode Island (8/1/2013); Vermont (9/1/2009).

3. On resource mobilization, see Snow and McAdam (2000:56). See also McAdam (1982) and McCarthy and Zald (1977). On organization structures, see Lofland (1969:15). For an overview of the role played by political opportunity structures in the success or failure of social movements see Meyer (2004). Tarrow (1994:71–90) integrates these issues into a broader theory of social movement dynamics. Lofland (1969) calls individuals and organizations with the power to mediate or facilitate a group's normalization "normal-smiths." This term has not been championed by so-called normal-smiths enough for us to use it.

4. Studies of the framing of social movements are the most closely related to our study. See Snow et al. (1986) for a detailed discussion of the role of framing in movement mobilization processes, and Benford and Snow (2000) for an overview of research and theory on the framing of social movements (also see della Porta and Diana 1999). On the use of "collective identity" as a concept in social movement studies, see Fominaya (2010).

5. Phelps (2005).

6. Cf. Berger (1967:53–80); Weber ([1930] 2002).

7. Of the twenty members we interviewed, sixteen were college graduates and the remaining four were young members between the ages of eighteen and twenty-one, all of whom were currently enrolled in college.

8. Quotes are from taped and transcribed interviews with members of the Westboro Baptist Church.

9. Baker, Bader, and Hirsch (2014).

10. See Chen (2015) on the importance of outside friendships in the de-conversion of Megan Phelps-Roper and Grace Phelps-Roper, two of Shirley Phelps-Roper's daughters and Fred Phelps Sr.'s granddaughters.

11. Much of this results from the highly unusual image of God espoused by the WBC (Baker, Bader, and Hirsch 2014).

12. Cf. Best (2003); Dwelling, Kortarba, and Pino (2014); Miller, Wright, and Dannels (2001); Sumner (1994).

13. Goffman (1963) is an obvious exception.

APPENDIX ONE

1. This, of course, is not a novel observation. Sociologists have long noted that the likelihood of fully converting to a deviant organization, such as a religious "cult," greatly depends upon building strong relationships to current members combined within an absence of "extra-cult" attachments (Lofland and Stark 1965). Sociologists of religion have long empha-

sized the importance of friendships inside and outside of religious groups in predicting individuals' religious commitment, as well as the overall strength of religious organizations.

2. On this process, see Baker (2018).

3. For linear modeling and analyses, indexed measures of conventional and deviant identity can be used in full to preserve their variance, and the addition of a multiplicative interaction term (conventional × deviant identity) provides estimates for empirical patterns across combinations of conventional and deviant identities. This strategy maximizes the variation in the measures and provides a more informative test of how the deviant and conventional identities intersect.

4. This, of course, does not stop individuals from attempting normalization while maintaining anonymity and hiding. For the example of pedophilia, see the exploits of North American Man/Boy Love Association (deYoung 1989).

APPENDIX TWO

1. We followed Allison's (1999:66–69) formula for estimating standardized coefficients.

REFERENCES

Abbott, Andrew. 2001. *Chaos of Disciplines*. Chicago: University of Chicago Press.

Adams, Josh. 2009. "Marked Difference: Tattooing and Its Association with Deviance in the United States." *Deviant Behavior* 30 (3): 266–92.

Adler, Patricia A., and Peter Adler. 1983. "Shifts and Oscillations in Deviant Careers: The Case of Upper-Level Drug Dealers and Smugglers." *Social Problems* 31 (2): 195–207.

———. 2005. "Self-Injurers as Loners: The Social Organization of Solitary Deviance." *Deviant Behavior* 26 (4): 345–78.

———. 2007. "The Demedicalization of Self-Injury: From Psychopathology to Sociological Deviance." *Journal of Contemporary Ethnography* 36 (5): 537–70.

———. 2011. *The Tender Cut: Inside the Hidden World of Self-Injury*. New York: New York University Press.

Agnew, Robert. 1992. "Foundation for a General Strain Theory of Crime and Delinquency." *Criminology* 30 (1): 4–87.

Akerlof, George A. 2007. "The Missing Motivation in Macroeconomics." *American Economic Review* 97 (1): 5–36.

Akerlof, George A., and Rachel E. Kranton. 2000. "Economics and Identity." *Quarterly Journal of Economics* 115 (3): 715–53.

———. 2010. *Identity Economics: How Our Identities Shape Our Work, Wages, and Well-Being*. Princeton, NJ: Princeton University Press.

Alderman, Jesse H. 2006, November 4. "Bigfoot Prof Fights for Tenure." *Casper Star-Tribune*. Retrieved August 27, 2017, from http://trib.com/news/state-and-regional/bigfoot-prof-fights-for-tenure/article_4562c085-75ce-5db3-b540-0ef7969aae17.html

Allison, Paul D. 1999. Logistic Regression Using the SAS System: Theory and Application. Cary, NC: SAS Publishing.

Allport, Gordon W. 1954. *The Nature of Prejudice*. Cambridge, MA: Perseus Books.

Altemeyer, Bob. 2002. "Changes in Attitudes toward Homosexuals." *Journal of Homosexuality* 42 (2): 63–75.

Altheide, David L. 2004. "Consuming Terrorism." *Symbolic Interaction* 27 (3): 289–308.

———. 2006. *Terrorism and the Politics of Fear*. Lanham, MD: AltaMira.

The American National Election Studies (ANES). 2012. The ANES 2012 Time Series Study [dataset]. Stanford University and the University of Michigan [producers]. www.electionstudies.org.

Anderson, Elijah. 1999. *Code of the Street: Decency, Violence, and the Moral Life of the Inner City*. New York: W.W. Norton.

Aronovitch, Hilliard. 2012. "Interpreting Weber's Ideal-Types." *Philosophy of the Social Sciences*. 42 (3): 356–69.

Athens, Lonnie. 1994. "The Self as a Soliloquy." *Sociological Quarterly* 35 (3): 521–32.

———. 1995. "Dramatic Self-Change." *Sociological Quarterly* 36 (3): 571–86.

Bader, Christopher D., Joseph O. Baker, and F. Carson Mencken. 2017. *Paranormal America*. 2nd edition. New York: New York University Press.

Bahr, Stephen J., John P. Hoffman, and Xiaoyan Yang. 2005. "Parental and Peer Influences on the Risk of Adolescent Drug Use." *Journal of Primary Prevention* 26 (6): 529–51.

Baker, Joseph O. 2018. "Christian Sectarianism, Fundamentalism, and Extremism." In *Handbook on Deviance*, edited by Stephen E. Brown and Ophir Sefiha, 187–98. New York: Routledge

Baker, Joseph O., Christopher D. Bader, and Kittye Hirsch. 2015. "Desecration, Moral Boundaries, and the Movement of Law: The Case of Westboro Baptist Church." *Deviant Behavior* 35 (1): 42–67.

Baker, Joseph O., Christopher D. Bader, and F. Carson Mencken. 2016. "A Bounded Affinity Theory of Religion and the Paranormal." *Sociology of Religion* 77 (4): 334–58.

Baker, Joseph O., and Buster G. Smith. 2015. *American Secularism: Cultural Contours of Nonreligious Belief Systems*. New York: New York University Press.

Baum, Dan. 2016. "Legalize It All: How to Win the War on Drugs." *Harper's Magazine* April, 22–32.

Baumeister, Roy F., Karen Dale, and Kristin L. Sommer. 1998. "Freudian Defense Mechanisms and Empirical Findings in Modern Social Psychology: Reaction Formation, Projection, Displacement, Undoing, Isolation, Sublimation, and Denial." *Journal of Personality* 66 (6): 1081–124.

Beccaria, Cesare. (1764) 2008. *On Crimes and Punishments*. Translated by Aaron Thomas and Jeremy Parzen. Toronto: University of Toronto Press.

Beck, Fred. 1967. *I Fought the Apemen of Mt. St. Helens*. Self-published.

Becker, Howard S. 1960. "Notes on the Concept of Commitment." *American Journal of Sociology* 66 (1): 32–40.

———. (1963) 1991. *Outsiders: Studies in the Sociology of Deviance*. New York: The Free Press

———. 1967. "Whose Side Are We On?" *Social Problems* 14 (3): 239–47.

Becker, Penny E., and Phyllis Moen. 1999. "Scaling Back: Dual-Earner Couples' Work-Family Strategies." *Journal of Marriage and Family* 61 (4): 995–1007.

Ben-Yehuda, Nachman. 1985. *Deviance and Moral Boundaries: Witchcraft, the Occult, Science Fiction, Deviant Science and Scientists*. Chicago: University of Chicago Press.

———. 1990. "Positive and Negative Deviance: More Fuel for a Controversy." *Deviant Behavior* 11 (3): 221–43.

Benford, Robert D. 1993. "Frame Disputes within the Nuclear Disarmament Movement." *Social Forces* 71 (3): 677–701.

Benford, Robert D., and David A. Snow. 2000. "Framing Processes and Social Movements: An Overview and Assessment." *Annual Review of Sociology* 26: 611–36.

Berger, Peter L. 1963. *Invitation to Sociology: A Humanistic Perspective.* New York: Anchor.

———. 1967. *Sacred Canopy: Elements of a Sociological Theory of Religion.* New York: Anchor.

Bernstein, Mary. 1997. "Celebration and Suppression: The Strategic Uses of Identity by the Lesbian and Gay Movement." *American Journal of Sociology* 103 (3): 531–65.

———. 2002. "The Contradictions of Gay Ethnicity: Forging Identity in Vermont." In *Social Movements: Identity, Culture, and the State* edited by David S. Meyer, Nancy Whittier, and Belinda Robnett, 85–104. New York: Oxford University Press.

Berry, William D., Evan J. Ringquist, Richard C. Fording, and Russell L. Hanson. 1998. "Measuring Citizen and Government Ideology in the American States, 1960–93." *American Journal of Political Science* 42 (1): 327–48.

Best, Joel. 2003. "Deviance May Be Alive, but Is It Intellectually Lively? A Reaction to Goode." *Deviant Behavior* 25 (5): 483–92.

Best, Joel, and David F. Luckenbill. 1980. "The Social Organization of Deviants." *Social Problems* 28 (1): 14–31.

———. 1982. *Organizing Deviance.* Englewood Cliffs, NJ: *Prentice-Hall.*

———. 1994. *Organizing Deviance.* 2nd edition. Englewood Cliffs, NJ: Prentice-Hall.

Bianchi, Suzanne. M., and Melissa A. Milkie. 2010. "Work and Family Research in the First Decade of the 21st Century." *Journal of Marriage and Family* 72: 705–25.

Biddle, Bruce J. 1986. "Recent Developments in Role Theory." *Annual Review of Sociology* 12: 67–92.

Bindernagel, John. 1998. *North America's Great Ape: The Sasquatch—A Wildlife Biologist Looks at the Continent's Most Misunderstood Large Mammal.* Courtenay, British Columbia: Beachcomber Books.

Bluff Creek Project. (n.d.). About the Bluff Creek Project. Retrieved August 25, 2017, from http://bluffcreekproject.blogspot.com/p/blog-page.html.

Blumstein, Alfred, Jacqueline Cohen, Somnath Das, and Soumyo D. Moitra. 1988. "Specialization and Seriousness during Adult Criminal Careers." *Journal of Quantitative Criminology* 4 (4): 303–35.

Bord, Janet, and Colin Bord. 2006. *Bigfoot Casebook Updated.* Enumclaw, WA: Pine Winds Press.

Bornstein, Kate. 2014. "Open Letter to LGBT Leaders Who Are Pushing Marriage Equality," In *Against Equality: Queer Revolution Not Mere Inclusion,* edited by Ryan Conrad, 23–26. Oakland, CA: AK Press.

Boyer, Paul, and Stephen Nissenbaum. 1974. *Salem Possessed: The Social Origins of Witchcraft.* Cambridge, MA: Harvard University Press.

Bradford, Judith B., and Caitlin Ryan. 2006. *National Lesbian Health Care Survey, 1984–1985.* Ann Arbor, MI: Inter-university Consortium for Political and Social Research. https://doi.org/10.3886/ICPSR08991.v1.

————. 1988. *The National Lesbian Health Care Survey: Final Report*. Washington, D.C.: National Lesbian and Gay Health Foundation.

Bradford, Judith, Catlin Ryan, and Esther D. Rothblum. 1994. "National Lesbian Health Care Survey: Implications for Mental Health Care." *Journal of Consulting and Clinical Psychology* 62 (2): 228–42.

Brame, Robert, Edward P. Mulvey, and Alex R. Piquero. 2001. "On the Development of Different Kinds of Criminal Activity." *Sociological Methods and Research* 29 (3): 319–41.

Brekhus, Wayne. 2003. *Peacocks, Chameleons, Centaurs: Gay Suburbia and the Grammar of Social Identity*. Chicago: University of Chicago Press.

Brewer, Paul R. 2008. *Value War: Public Opinion and the Politics of Gay Rights*. Lanham, MD: Rowman & Littlefield.

Broad, K. L., Sara L. Crawley, and Lara Foley. 2004. "Doing 'Real Family Values': The Interpretive Practice of Families in the GLBT Movement." *Sociological Quarterly* 45 (3): 507–27.

Broadhead, Robert S. 1974. "A Theoretical Critique of the Societal Reaction Approach to Deviance." *Pacific Sociological Review* 17 (3): 287–312.

Buhs, Joshua B. 2009. *Bigfoot: The Life and Times of a Legend*. Chicago: Chicago University Press.

Burke, Peter J. 1991. "Identity Processes and Social Stress." *American Sociological Review* 56 (6): 836–49.

Burke, Sara E., John F. Dovidio, Julia M. Przedworski, R. R. Hardeman, S. P. Perry, S. M. Phelan, D. B. Nelson, D. J. Burgess, M. W. Yeazel, and M. van Ryn. 2015. "Do Contact and Empathy Mitigate Bias against Gay and Lesbian People among Heterosexual Medical Students? A Report from Medical Student CHANGES." *Academic Medicine* 90 (5): 645–51.

Burstein, Paul. 2003. "The Impact of Public Opinion on Public Policy: A Review and an Agenda." *Political Research Quarterly* 56 (1): 29–40.

Butler, Judith. 1990. *Gender Trouble: Feminism and the Subversion of Identity*. New York: Routledge.

Callero, Peter L. 1985. "Role-Identity Salience." *Social Psychology Quarterly* 48: 203–14.

Campbell, David E., John C. Green, and J. Quin Monson. 2014. *Seeking the Promised Land: Mormons and American Politics*. New York: Cambridge University Press.

Canter, David, Christopher Missen, and Samantha Hodge. 1996. "Are Serial Killers Special?" *Policing Today* 2 (1): 1–12.

Chen, Adrian. 2015. "Unfollow: How a Prized Daughter of the Westboro Baptist Church Came to Question Its Beliefs." *New Yorker*, November 23.

Chibnall, John T. 2017. "Physical and Social Characteristics of US States as Predictors of Reports to the Bigfoot Field Researchers Organization (BFRO)." *The Relict Hominoid Inquiry* 6: 17–32.

Chipumuro, Todne Thomas. 2014. "Pastor, Mentor, or Father? The Contested Intimacies of the Eddie Long Sex Abuse Scandal." *Journal of Africana Religions* 2 (1): 1–30.

Clark, Norman H. 1976. *Deliver Us from Evil: An Interpretation of American Prohibition*. New York: Norton.

Cohen, Albert K. 1955. *Delinquent Boys*. New York: The Free Press.

Cohen, Jacqueline. 1986. "Research on Criminal Careers: Individual Frequency Rates and Offense Seriousness." In *Criminal Careers and "Career Criminals,"* edited by Alfred

Blumstein, Jacqueline Cohen, Jeffrey A. Roth, and Christy Visher, 292–418. Washington DC: National Academy Press.

Cohen, Lawrence E., and Marcus Felson. 1979. "Social Change and Crime Rate Trends: A Routine Activity Approach." *American Sociological Review* 44 (4): 588–608.

Coleman, James W. 1994. *The Criminal Elite: The Sociology of White-Collar Crime.* New York: St. Martin's Press.

Colyer, Daryl G., Alton Higgins, Brian Brown, Kathy Strain, Michael C. Mayes, and Brad McAndrews. 2015. *The Ouachita Project,* version 1.1. http://media.texasbigfoot.com/OP_paper_media/OuachitaProjectMonograph_Version1.1_03112015.pdf

Conklin, John E. 1972. *Robbery and the Criminal Justice System.* Philadelphia: J. B. Lippincott Co.

Cooper, Joel. 2007. *Cognitive Dissonance: Fifty Years of a Classic Theory.* Thousand Oaks, CA: Sage.

Cory, Donald Webster. 1951. *The Homosexual in America: A Subjective Approach.* New York: Greenberg Press.

Costello, Barbara J., and Paul Vowell. 1999. "Testing Control Theory and Differential Association: A Reanalysis of the Richmond Youth Project Data." *Criminology* 37 (4): 815–842.

Cragg, Gerald R. (1957) 2011. *Puritanism in the Period of the Great Persecution 1660–1688.* London: Cambridge University Press.

Cragun, Ryan T., Michael Nielsen, and Heather Clingenpeel. 2011. "The Struggle for Legitimacy: Tensions between the LDS and FLDS." In *Saints under Siege: The Texas State Raid on the Fundamentalist Latter Day Saints,* edited by Stuart A. Wright and James T. Richardson, 80–103. New York: New York University Press.

Cragun, Ryan T., and Rick Phillips. 2012. *Could I Vote for a Mormon for President?* Washington DC: Strange Violin Editions.

Cruikshank, Margaret. 1992. *The Gay and Lesbian Liberation Movement.* New York: Routledge.

Dannemeyer, William. 1987. "Militant Wolves in Sheepish Drag, No Longer!" *United States of America Congressional Record: Proceedings and Debates of the 100th Congress, First Session* 133 (15): 21194–95. Washington, DC: U.S. Government Printing Office.

———. 1989. "Homosexuality." *United States of America Congressional Record: Proceedings and Debates of the 101st Congress: First Session* 135 (10): 13950–53. Washington, DC: U.S. Government Printing Office.

Daschuk, M. Douglas. 2010. "Messageboard Confessional: Online Discourse and the Production of the 'Emo Kid.'" *Berkeley Journal of Sociology* 54: 84–107.

Davis, Fred. 1964. "Deviance Disavowal: The Management of Strained Interaction by the Visibly Handicapped." In *The Other Side,* edited by Howard S. Becker, 119–38. New York: The Free Press.

DeLisi, Matt. 2005. *Career Criminals in Society.* Thousand Oaks, CA: Sage Press.

della Porta, Donatella, and Mario Diana. 1999. *Social Movements: An Introduction.* Malden, MA: Blackwell Publishing.

DeLuca, Kevin M. 1999. "Unruly Arguments: The Body Rhetoric of Earth First!, ACT UP, and Queer Nation." *Argumentation and Advocacy* 36 (1): 9–21.

Dendle, Peter. 2006. "Cryptozoology in the Medieval and Modern Worlds." *Folklore* 117 (2): 190–206.

Denzin, Norman K. 1995. "Stanley and Clifford: Undoing an Interactionist Text." *Current Sociology* 43 (2): 115–23.

deYoung, Mary. 1989. "The World According to NAMBLA: Accounting for Deviance." *Journal of Sociology & Social Welfare* 16 (1): 111–26.

Dighe, Ranjot S. 2010. "Pierre S. Du Pont, and the Making of an Anti-Prohibition Activist." *Social History of Alcohol and Drugs* 24 (2): 97–118.

Dioun, Cyrus. 2018. "Negotiating Moral Boundaries: Social Movements and the Strategic (Re)definition of the Medical in Cannabis Markets." *Research in the Sociology of Organizations* 56 (May): 53–82.

Duberman, Martin. 2002. "The 'Father' of the Homophile Movement," In *Left Out: The Politics of Exclusion: Essays 1964–2002*, 59–94. Cambridge, MA: South End Press.

Du Bois, W. E. B. 1897. "Strivings of the Negro People." *Atlantic Monthly*, August, 194–97.

Durkheim, Emile. (1893) 1997. *The Division of Labor in Society.* New York: The Free Press.

———. (1895) 1982. *The Rules of Sociological Method.* New York: The Free Press.

———. *Suicide.* (1897) 1979. Translated by John Spaulding and George Simpson. New York: The Free Press.

Dwelling, Michael, Joseph A. Kotarba, and Nathan W. Pino (eds.). 2014. *The Death and Resurrection of Deviance: Current Ideas and Research.* Basingstoke, UK: Palgrave-Macmillan.

Elliot, Andrew J., and Patricia G. Devine. 1994. "On the Motivational Nature of Cognitive Dissonance: Dissonance as Psychological Discomfort." *Journal of Personality and Social Psychology* 67 (3): 382–94.

Elliott, Diane B., Kristy Krivickas, Matthew B. Brault, and Rose M. Kreider. 2012. "Historical Marriage Trends from 1890–2010: A Focus on Race Differences." SEHSD Working Paper 2012-12. https://census.gov/content/dam/Census/library/working-papers/2012/demo/SEHSD-WP2012-12.pdf.

Ellis, Albert. 1963. "Constitutional Factors in Homosexuality: A Re-examination of the Evidence." *Archives of Sex Research* 1:161–86.

———. 1965. *Homosexuality: Its Causes and Cure.* New York: Lyle Stuart.

Emslie, Carol, Kate Hunt, and Sally Macintyre. 2004. "Gender, Work-Home Conflict, and Morbidity amongst White-Collar Bank Employees in the United Kingdom." *International Journal of Behavioral Medicine* 11 (3): 127–34.

Epstein, Steven. 1999. "Gay and Lesbian Movements in the United States: Dilemmas of Identity, Diversity, and Political Strategy," In *The Global Emergence of Gay and Lesbian Politics: National Imprints of a Worldwide Movement*, edited by Barry Adam, Jan Willem Duyvendak, and André Krouwel, 30–90. Philadelphia: Temple University Press.

Erikson, Kai T. 1966. *Wayward Puritans: A Study in the Sociology of Deviance.* New York: Macmillan.

Erikson, Robert S., Gerald R. Wright, and John P. McIver. 1993. *Statehouse Democracy: Public Opinion and Policy in the American States.* Cambridge: Cambridge University Press.

Fausold, Martin L. 1975. *James W. Wadsworth, Jr: The Gentleman from New York.* Syracuse, NY: Syracuse University Press.

Felson, Marcus. 1994. *Crime and Everyday Life: Insight and Implications for Society.* Newbury Park, CA: Pine Forge Press.

Ferrell, Jeff. 2018. *Drift: Illicit Mobility and Uncertain Knowledge.* Oakland: University of California Press.

Festinger, Leon. 1957. *A Theory of Cognitive Dissonance*. Palo Alto, CA: Stanford University Press.

Finkelstein, Katherine E. 1999. "Protests in Police Killing of Diallo Grow Larger, and More Diverse." *New York Times*, March 25.

Fisher, Cynthia D., and Richard Gitelson. 1983. "A Meta-Analysis of the Correlates of Role Conflict and Ambiguity." *Journal of Applied Psychology* 68 (2): 320–33.

Fisher, Walter R. 1987. *Human Communication as Narration: Toward a Philosophy of Reason, Value, and Action*. Columbia: University of South Carolina Press.

Flynn, Jennifer, and Eustacia Smith. 2008. "Fed Up Queers," In *That's Revolting: Queer Strategies for Resisting Assimilation*, edited by Mattilda Bernstein Sycamore, 249–67. Revised edition. Berkeley, CA: Soft Skull Press.

Flynn, Kevin. 1999. "8 Arrested Near City Hall in Protest on Police Shooting." *New York Times*, February 22.

Fominaya, Cristina F. 2010. "Collective Identity in Social Movements: Central Concepts and Debates." *Sociology Compass* 4 (6): 393–404.

Forth, Gregory. 2007. "Images of the Wildman Inside and Outside Europe." *Folklore* 118 (3): 261–81.

Foshee, Vangie, and Karl E. Bauman. 1992. "Parental and Peer Characteristics as Modifiers of the Bond-Behavior Relationship: An Elaboration of Control Theory." *Journal of Health and Social Behavior* 33 (1): 66–76.

Fox, Kathryn J. 1987. "Real Punks and Pretenders: The Social Organization of a Counterculture." *Journal of Contemporary Ethnography* 16 (3): 344–70.

Froese, Paul, and Christopher D. Bader. 2010. *America's Four Gods*. New York: Oxford University Press.

Futrell, Robert, and Pete Simi. 2004. "Free Spaces, Collective Identity, and the Persistence of U.S. White Power Activism." *Social Problems* 51 (1): 16–42.

Gagnon, John H., and William Simon. (1973) 2005. *Sexual Conduct: The Social Sources of Human Sexuality*. New Brunswick, NJ: AldineTransaction.

Galinsky, Adam D., Cynthia S. Wang, Jennifer A. Whitson, Eric M. Anicich Kurth Hugenberg, and Galen V. Bodenhausen. 2013. "The Reappropriation of Stigmatizing Labels: The Reciprocal Relationship between Power and Self-Labeling." *Psychological Science* 24 (10): 2020–29.

Galliher, John F., Wayne H. Brekhus, and David P. Keys. *Laud Humphreys: Prophet of Homosexuality and Sociology*. Madison: University of Wisconsin Press.

Gamson, Josh. 1989. "Silence, Death and the Invisible Enemy: AIDS Activism and Social Movement 'Newness.'" *Social Problems* 36 (4): 351–67.

———. 1995. "Must Identity Movements Self-Destruct? A Queer Dilemma." *Social Problems* 42 (3): 390–407.

Gamson, William A. 1968. *Power and Discontent*. Homewood, IL: The Dorsey Press.

Gelsthorpe, Loraine. 2007. "The Jack-Roller: Telling a Story." *Theoretical Criminology* 11 (4): 515–42.

Genzoli, Andrew. October 14, 1958. "Huge Footprints Hold Mystery of Friendly Bluff Creek Giant." *Humboldt Times* (Eureka, California).

Ghaziani, Amin. 2008. *The Dividends of Dissent: How Conflict and Culture Work in Lesbian and Gay Marches on Washington*. Chicago: University of Chicago Press.

———. 2014. *There Goes the Gayborhood?* Princeton, NJ: Princeton University Press.

Ghaziani, Amin, Verta Taylor, and Amy Stone. 2016. "Cycles of Sameness and Difference in LGBT Social Movements." *Annual Review of Sociology* 42:165–83.

Gipson, L. Michael. 2012. "Mattilda Bernstein Sycamore: Keeping the Pot Stirred." *Lambda Literary*, April 17. www.lambdaliterary.org/features/04/17/mattilda-bernstein-sycamore -keeping-the-pot-stirred/

Goffman, Erving. 1959. *The Presentation of Self in Everyday Life*. New York: Anchor.

———. 1961. *Encounters: Two Studies in the Sociology of Interaction*. Indianapolis: Bobbs-Merrill Company.

———. 1963. *Stigma: Notes on the Management of Spoiled Identity*. New York: Simon and Schuster.

———. 1967. *Interaction Ritual: Essays on Face-to-Face Behavior*. New York: Anchor.

———. 1969. *Strategic Interaction*. Philadelphia: University of Pennsylvania Press.

———. 1971. *Relations in Public: Microstudies of the Public Order*. New York: Basic Books.

Golan, Guy J. 2010. "Editorials, Op-Ed Columns Frame Medical Marijuana Debate." *Newspaper Research Journal* 31 (3): 50–61.

Goode, Erich. 1991. "Positive Deviance: A Viable Concept?" *Deviant Behavior* 12 (3): 289–309.

———. 2005. *Deviant Behavior*. 7th edition. Upper Saddle River, NJ: Prentice Hall.

———. 2015. *Drugs in American Society*. 9th edition. New York: McGraw-Hill.

Goodwin, Glenn A., Irving L. Horowitz, and Peter M. Nardi. 2001. "Laud Humphreys: A Pioneer in the Practice of Social Science." *Sociological Inquiry* 61 (2): 139–47.

Gordon, Stan. 2010. *Silent Invasion: The Pennsylvania UFO-Bigfoot Casebook*. Greensburg, PA: Stan Gordon Productions.

Gottfredson, Michael R., and Travis Hisrchi. 1990. *A General Theory of Crime*. Palo Alto, CA: Stanford University Press.

Gould, Deborah. 2009. *Moving Politics: Emotion and ACT UP's Fight against AIDS*. Chicago: University of Chicago Press.

Granovetter, Mark. 1978. "Threshold Models of Collective Behavior." *American Journal of Sociology* 83 (6): 1420–33.

Grattet, Ryken. 2011. "Social Reactions to Deviance." *Annual Review of Sociology* 37: 185–204.

Green, Adam I. 2007. "Queer Theory and Sociology: Locating the Subject and the Self in Sexuality Studies." *Sociological Theory* 25 (1): 26–45.

Green, John. 1973. *The Sasquatch File*. Agassiz, BC: Cheam Publishing.

———. 1978. *Sasquatch: The Apes Among Us*. Blaine, WA: Hancock House.

Grossman, Perry. 1996–1997. "Identity Crisis: The Dialectics of Rock, Punk, and Grunge." *Berkeley Journal of Sociology* 41: 19–40.

Gusfield, Joseph R. 1966. "Moral Passage: The Symbolic Process in Public Designations of Deviance." *Social Problems* 15 (2): 175–88.

———. 1986. *Symbolic Crusade: Status Politics the American Temperance Movement*. 2nd edition. Urbana-Champaign: University of Illinois Press.

Haenfler, Ross. 2010. *Goths, Gamers, & Grrrls: Deviance and Youth Subcultures*. New York: Oxford University Press.

Haines-Saah, Rebecca J., Joy L. Johnson, Robin Repta, Aleck Ostry, Mary Lynn Young, Jeannie Shoveller, Richard Sawatzky, Lorraine Greaves, and Pamela A. Ratner. 2014. "The

Privileged Normalization of Marijuana Use: An Analysis of Canadian Newspaper Reporting, 1997–2007." *Critical Public Health* 24 (1): 47–61.

Halperin, David M. 2003. "The Normalization of Queer Theory." *Journal of Homosexuality* 45 (2–4): 339–43.

Halperin, David M., and Valerie Traub (eds.). 2009. *Gay Shame.* Chicago: University of Chicago Press.

Hathaway, Andrew D. 2004. "Cannabis Users' Informal Rules for Managing Stigma and Risk." *Deviant Behavior* 25 (6): 559–77.

Hathaway, Andrew D., Natalie C. Comaeu, and Patricia G. Erickson. 2011. "Cannabis Normalization and Sigma: Contemporary Practices and Moral Regulation." *Criminology & Criminal Justice* 11 (5): 451–69.

Heckert, Alex, and Druann M. Heckert. 2002. "A New Typology of Deviance: Integrating Normative and Reactivist Definitions of Deviance." *Deviant Behavior* 23 (5): 449–79.

Hensley, Christopher, and Richard Tewksbury. 2002. "Inmate-to-Inmate Prison Sexuality: A Review of Empirical Studies." *Trauma, Violence, & Abuse* 3 (3): 226–43.

Hensley, Christopher, Richard Tewksbury, and Jeremy Wright. 2001. "Exploring the Dynamics of Masturbation and Consensual Same-Sex Activity within a Male Maximum Security Prison." *Journal of Men's Studies* 10 (1): 59–71.

Herek, Gregory M., and John P. Capitanio. 1996. "Intergroup Contact, Concealable Stigma, and Heterosexuals' Attitudes toward Gay Men and Lesbians." *Personality and Social Psychology Bulletin* 22: 412–24.

Hewitt, Hugh. 2007. *A Mormon in the White House?* Washington DC: Regnery.

Hirschi, Travis. 1969. *Causes of Delinquency.* Berkeley: University of California Press.

Hitlin, Steven. 2008. *Moral Selves, Evil Selves: The Social Psychology of Conscience.* New York: Palgrave-Macmillan.

Hochschild, Arlie R., with Anne Machung. 1989. *The Second Shift: Working Parents and the Revolution at Home.* New York: Viking Penguin.

Hodgson, Sarah. 2004. "Cutting through the Silence: A Sociological Construction of Self-Injury." *Sociological Inquiry* 74 (2): 162–79.

Hohner, Robert A. 1999. *Prohibition and Politics: The Life of Bishop James Cannon, Jr.* Columbia: University of South Carolina Press.

Horwitz, Allan V. 2004. "Revisiting an Underappreciated Classic: John Lofland's Deviance and Identity." *Sociological Forum* 19 (4): 671–73.

Humphreys, Laud. 1970. *Tearoom Trade: Impersonal Sex in Public Places.* New Brunswick, NJ: AldineTransaction Publishers.

Iannaccone, Laurence R. 1992. "Sacrifice and Stigma: Reducing Free Riding in Cults, Communes and Other Collectives." *Journal of Political Economy* 100 (2): 271–91.

———. 1994. "Why Strict Churches Are Strong." *American Journal of Sociology* 99 (5): 1180–211.

———. 1995. "Risk, Rationality and Religious Portfolios." *Economic Inquiry* 23: 285–95.

Iftikhar, Aliya. 2013. "Queer Activist Calls for a Return to 'Openness' Found in College." *University Wire* October 5.

Irwin, Katherine. 2003. "Saints and Sinners: Elite Tattoo Collectors and Tattooists as Positive and Negative Deviants." *Sociological Spectrum* 23 (1): 27–57.

Jenkins, Phillip. 1994. *Using Murder: The Social Construction of Serial Homicide.* New York: Aldine De Gruyter.

————. 1998. *Moral Panic: Changing Concepts of the Child Molester in America*. New Haven, CT: Yale University Press.

Jensen, Gary F. 2006. *The Path of the Devil: Early Modern Witch Hunts*. Lanham, MD: Rowman & Littlefield.

Jensen, Gary F., and David Brownfield. 1983. "Parents and Drugs: Specifying the Consequences of Attachment." *Criminology* 21 (4): 543–54.

Kaufman, M. J., and Katie Miles. 2014. "Queer Kids of Queer Parents Against Gay Marriage." In *Against Equality: Queer Revolution Not Mere Inclusion*, edited by Ryan Conrad, 76–86. Oakland, CA: AK Press.

Kameny, Fanklin. 2014. *Gay Is Good: The Life and Letters of Gay Rights Pioneer Franklin Kameny*, edited by Michael G. Long. Syracuse, NY: Syracuse University Press.

Kelley, Dean M. 1972. *Why Conservative Churches Are Growing*. New York: Harper & Row.

Keyes, Katherine M., John E. Schulenberg, Patrick M. O'Malley, Lloyd D. Johnston, Jerald G. Bachman, Guohua Li, and Deborah Hasin. 2011. "The Social Norms of Birth Cohorts and Adolescent Marijuana Use in the United States, 1976–2007." *Addiction* 106 (10): 1790–800.

Kilmer, Beau, and Robert J. MacCoun. 2017. "How Medical Marijuana Smoothed the Transition to Marijuana Legalization in the United States." *Annual Review of Law and Social Science* 13: 181–202.

Kirkham, George. 2000. "Homosexuality in Prison." In *Bisexuality in the United States: A Social Science Reader*, edited by Paula C. Rust, 250–66. New York: Columbia University Press.

Klockars, Carl B. 1974. *The Professional Fence*. New York: The Free Press.

Kornhauser, Ruth R. 1978. *Social Sources of Delinquency: An Appraisal of Analytic Models*. Chicago: Chicago University Press.

Kosut, Mary. 2006. "Mad Artists and Tattooed Perverts: Deviant Discourse and the Social Construction of Cultural Categories." *Deviant Behavior* 27 (1): 73–95.

Kozloski, Michael J. 2010. "Homosexual Moral Acceptance and Social Tolerance: Are the Effects of Education Changing?" *Journal of Homosexuality* 57: 1370–83.

Krantz, Grover S. 1992. *Big Footprints: A Scientific Inquiry into the Reality of Sasquatch*. Boulder, CO: Johnson Books.

Krantz, Grover, and Roderick Sprague. 1977. *The Scientist Looks at Sasquatch*. Moscow: University Press of Idaho.

Kraybill, Donald B. 2001. *The Riddle of Amish Culture*. Revised edition. Baltimore: Johns Hopkins University Press.

Kraybill, Donald B., and Marc A. Olshan (eds.). 1994. *The Amish Struggle with Modernity*. Hanover, NH: University Press of New England.

Kroska, Amy, and Sarah K. Harkness. 2006. "Stigma Sentiments and Self-Meanings: Exploring the Modified Labeling Theory of Mental Illness." *Social Psychology Quarterly* 69 (4): 325–48.

Krulos, Tea. 2015. *Monster Hunters: On the Trail with Ghost Hunters, Bigfooters, UFOlogists and Other Paranormal Investigators*. Chicago: Chicago Review Press.

Kummer, Chris. 2017, February 28. "We Have Found a Group of Them. They're There." Retrieved August 31, 2017, from https://www.dietiefe.com/?p=1441

Kunzel, Regina. 2008. *Criminal Intimacy: Prison and the Uneven History of Modern American Sexuality*. Chicago: Chicago University Press.

Kyvig, David E. 1976. "Women against Prohibition." *American Quarterly* 28 (4): 465–82.

———. 2000. *Repealing National Prohibition*. 2nd edition. Kent, OH: Kent State University Press.

Lamb, Richard H. 1982. "Young Adult Chronic Patients: The New Drifters." *Hospital & Community Psychiatry* 33 (6): 465–68.

Lamy, Philip. 1996. *Millennium Rage: Survivalists, White Supremacists, and the Doomsday Prophecy*. New York: Plenum Press.

Leggett, Mike. 2009. "Bigfoot-Togethers Are a Boring Proposition." *Austin American-Statesman*, October 4.

Lehr, Valerie. 1999. *Queer Family Values: Debunking the Myth of the Nuclear Family*. Philadelphia: Temple University Press.

LeMaster, BennyAaron. 2013. "Beyond the Binary." Interview with Mattilda Bernstein Sycamore. https://www.youtube.com/watch?v=F8zz8AXszcw&t=41s.

Lemert, Edwin M. 1972. *Human Deviance, Social Problems, and Social Control*. 2nd edition. Englewood Cliffs, NJ: Prentice-Hall

Lerner, Michael A. 2007. *Dry Manhattan: Prohibition in New York City*. Cambridge, MA: Harvard University Press.

Lévi-Strauss, Claude. (1975) 1982. *The Way of the Masks*. Translated by Sylvia Modelski. Vancouver, BC: Douglas & McIntyre.

Lewis, John. 1999. "Symbolism in Action." *New York Times*, March 30.

Lewis, Stacey. 2008. "An Interview with Mattilda Bernstein Sycamore." *City Lights*. www.citylights.com/resources/titles/8728610086118o/extras/An_Interview_With_Mattilda_Bernstein_Sycamore.pdf.

Liazos, Alexander. 1972. "The Poverty of the Sociology of Deviance: Nuts, Sluts, and Preverts." *Social Problems* 20 (1): 103–20.

Liebling, Alison. 2001. "Whose Side Are We On? Theory, Practice and Allegiances in Prisons Research." *British Journal of Criminology* 41 (3): 472–84.

Lincoln, C. Eric, and Lawrence H. Mamiya. 1990. *The Black Church in the African American Experience*. Durham, NC: Duke University Press.

Linder, Stephen N. 1982. *Survivalists: Ethnography of an Urban Millennial Cult*. PhD thesis. University of California at Los Angeles.

Lindsey, Delario. 2004. "To Build a More 'Perfect Discipline': Ideologies of the Normative and the Social Control of the Criminal Innocent in the Policing of New York City." *Critical Sociology* 30 (2): 321–53.

Link, Bruce G. 1987. "Understanding Labeling Effects in the Area of Mental Disorders: An Assessment of the Effects of Expectations of Rejection." *American Sociological Review* 52 (1): 96–112.

Link, Bruce G., Francis T. Cullen, Elmer Struening, Patrick E. Shrout, and Bruce P. Dohrenwend. 1989. "A Modified Labeling Theory Approach to Mental Disorders: An Empirical Assessment." *American Sociological Review* 54 (3): 400–423.

Link, Bruce G., and Jo C. Phelan. 2001. "Conceptualizing Stigma." *Annual Review of Sociology* 27: 363–85.

———. 2014. "Stigma Power." *Social Science & Medicine* 103: 24–32.

Lofland, John. 1969. *Deviance and Identity*. Englewood Cliffs, NJ: Prentice-Hall.

Lofland, John, and Rodney Stark. 1965. "Becoming a World-Saver: A Theory of Conversion to a Deviant Perspective." *American Sociological Review* 30 (6): 862–75.

Loftus, Jeni. 2001. "America's Liberalization in Attitudes toward Homosexuality, 1973 to 1998." *American Sociological Review* 66 (5): 762–82.

Long, Greg. 2004. *The Making of Bigfoot: The Inside Story*. New York: Prometheus.

Macy, Michael W. 1990. "Learning Theory and the Logic of Critical Mass." *American Sociological Review* 55 (6): 809–26.

———. 1991. "Chains of Cooperation: Threshold Effects in Collective Action." *American Sociological Review* 56 (6): 730–47.

Manza, Jeff, and Fay L. Cook. 2002. "A Democratic Polity? Three Views of Policy Responsiveness to Public Opinion in the United States." *American Political Research* 30 (6): 630–67.

Martin, Daniel D. 2000. "Organizational Approaches to Shame: Avowal, Management, and Contestation." *The Sociological Quarterly* 41 (1): 125–50.

Maruna, Shadd, and Amanda Matravers. 2007. "N = 1: Criminology and the Person." *Theoretical Criminology* 11 (4): 427–42.

Matsueda, Ross L. 1982. "Testing Control Theory and Differential Association: A Causal Modeling Approach." *American Sociological Review* 47 (4): 489–504.

———. 1997. "'Cultural Deviance Theory': The Remarkable Persistence of a Flawed Term." *Theoretical Criminology* 1 (4): 429–52.

Matsueda, Ross L., and Karen Heimer. 1987. "Race, Family Structure, and Delinquency: A Test of Differential Association and Social Control Theories." *American Sociological Review* 52 (6): 826–40.

Mattos, Nick. 2012. "Fabulously Revolting: Mattilda Bernstein Sycamore Dishes Assimilation, Exclusion, and the Promise of Radical Queer Community." *PQ Portland*. http://www.pqmonthly.com/fabulously-revolting-mattilda-bernstein-sycamore-dishes-about-assimilation-exclusion-and-the-promise-of-radical-queer-community/339.

Matz, David C., and Wendy Wood. 2005. "Cognitive Dissonance in Groups: The Consequences of Disagreement." *Journal of Personality and Social Psychology* 88 (1): 22–37.

Matza, David. 1964. *Delinquency and Drift*. New York: John Wiley.

McAdam, Doug. 1982. *Political Process and the Development of Black Insurgency, 1930–1970*. Chicago: University of Chicago Press.

McBain, Howard L. 1928. *Prohibition: Legal and Illegal*. New York: Macmillan.

McCarthy, John D., and Mayer N. Zald. 1977. "Resource Mobilization and Social Movements: A Partial Theory." *American Journal of Sociology* 82 (6): 1212–41.

McQueeney, Krista. 2003. "The New Religious Rite: A Symbolic Interactionist Case Study of Lesbian Commitment Rituals." *Journal of Lesbian Studies* 7 (2): 49–70.

———. 2009. "We Are God's Children, Y'all: Race, Gender, and Sexuality in Lesbian and Gay-Affirming Congregations." *Social Problems* 56 (1): 151–73.

Medhurst, Martin J. 2009. "Mitt Romney, 'Faith in America,' and the Dance of Religion and Politics in American Culture." *Rhetoric & Public Affairs* 12 (2): 195–222.

Meldrum, Jeff. n.d. *About the Relic Hominoid Inquiry*. Retrieved September 28, 2017, from http://www2.isu.edu/rhi/about.shtml

———. 2006. *Sasquatch: Legend Meets Science*. New York: Tom Doherty Associates.

Melossi, Dario. 2008. *Controlling Crime, Controlling Society*. Cambridge: Polity.

Merton, Robert K. 1938. "Social Structure and Anomie." *American Sociological Review* 3 (5): 672–82.

———. 1968. *Social Theory and Social Structure*. Revised ed. New York: The Free Press.

Meyer, David S. 2004. "Protest and Political Opportunities." *Annual Review of Sociology* 30:125–45.

Miller, J. Mitchell, Richard A. Wright, and David Dannels. 2001. "Is Deviance 'Dead'? The Decline of a Sociological Research Specialization." *American Sociologist* 32 (3): 43–59.

Miller, Walter. 1958. "Lower-Class Culture as a Generating Milieu of Gang Delinquency." *Journal of Social Issues* 14: 5–19.

Miller-Day, Michelle, Jess K. Alberts, Michael L. Hecht, Melanie R. Trost, and Robert L. Krizek. 2000. *Adolescent Relationships and Drug Use*. Mahwah, NJ: Lawrence Erlbaum Publishers.

Mingus, William, and Keri Burchfield. 2012. "From Prison to Integration: Applying Modified Labeling Theory of Sex Offenders." *Criminal Justice Studies* 25 (1): 97–109.

Minor, William W. 1981. "Techniques of Neutralization: A Reconceptualization and Empirical Examination." *Journal of Research in Crime and Delinquency* 18 (3): 295–318.

Miron, Jeffrey A. 1999. "Violence and the U.S. Prohibitions of Drugs and Alcohol." *American Law and Economics Review* 1 (1): 78–114.

Miron, Jeffrey A., and Jeffrey Zwiebel. 1991. "Alcohol Consumption During Prohibition." *The American Economic Review* 81 (2): 242–47.

Mock, Brenton. 2007. "Bishop Eddie Long." *Southern Poverty Law Center Intelligence Report*. Spring, no. 125.

Moon, Dawne. 2004. *God, Sex, and Politics: Homosexuality and Everyday Theologies*. Chicago: University of Chicago Press.

———. 2005. "Discourse, Interaction, and the Making of Selves in the U.S. Protestant Dispute over Homosexuality." *Theory and Society* 34 (5–6): 551–77.

Motta, Carlos. 2011. "An Interview with Mattilda Bernstein Sycamore." *We Who Feel Differently*. http://wewhofeeldifferently.info/interview.php?interview=110.

Mueller, Anna S., and Seth Abrutyn. 2016. "Adolescents under Pressure: A New Durkheimian Framework for Understanding Adolescent Suicide in a Cohesive Community." *American Sociological Review* 81 (5): 877–99.

Munns, William. 2014. *When Roger Met Patty*. Self-published: CreateSpace.

Munns, Bill, and Jeff Meldrum. 2013a. "Surface Anatomy and Subcutaneous Adipose Tissue Features in the Analysis of the Patterson-Gimlin Film Hominid." *The Relict Hominoid Inquiry* 2: 1–21.

———. 2013b. "Analysis Integrity of the Patterson-Gimlin Film Image." *The Relict Hominoid Inquiry* 2: 41–80.

Murphy, Christopher L. 2004. *Meet the Sasquatch*. Blaine, WA: Hancock House.

Murray, Stephen O. 2004. "Humphreys vs. Sagarin in the Study of Gay Social Movements." *International Journal of Sociology and Social Policy* 24 (3–5): 128–39.

———. 2008. "Donald Webster Cory (1913–1986)." In *Before Stonewall: Activists for Gay and Lesbian Rights in Historical Context*, edited by Vern L. Bullough, 333–43. New York: Routledge.

Musto, David F. 1991. "Opium, Cocaine and Marijuana in American History." *Scientific American* 265 (1): 40–47.

Musto, David F., and Pamela Korsmeyer. 2002. *The Quest for Drug Control: Politics and Federal Policy in a Period of Increasing Substance Abuse, 1963–1981*. New Haven, CT: Yale University Press.

Myers-Scotton, Carol. 1988. "Code Switching as Indexical of Social Negotiations." In *Codeswitching: Anthropological and Sociolinguistic Perspectives*, edited by Monica Heller, 151–86. Berlin: De Gruyter.

———. 1993. "Common and Uncommon Ground: Social and Structural Factors in Codeswitching." *Language in Society* 22 (4): 475–503.

———. 2000. "Explaining the Role of Norms and Rationality in Codeswitching." *Journal of Pragmatics* 32 (9): 1259–71.

Neumann, Caryn E. 1997. "The End of Gender Solidarity: The History of the Women's Organization for National Prohibition Reform in the United States, 1929–1933." *Journal of Women's History* 9 (2): 31–51.

North American Wood Ape Conservancy (n.d.). "What Will It Take to Prove It?" FAQs. Retrieved September 1, 2017. http://woodape.org/index.php/about-bigfoot/faqs#What will it take to prove it?

Nye, F. Ivan. 1958. *Family Relationships and Delinquent Behavior*. New York: John Wiley.

O'Callaghan, Frances V., and Terry Hannon. 2003. "Normalization of Marijuana Use: Its Effects on Adolescents' Intentions to Use Marijuana." *Substance Use & Misuse* 38 (2): 185–99.

Ohlander, Julianne, Jeanne Batalovab, and Judith Treas. 2005. "Explaining Educational Influences on Attitudes toward Homosexual Relations." *Social Science Research* 34: 781–99.

Okrent, Daniel. 2010. *Last Call: The Rise and Fall of Prohibition*. New York: Scribner.

Olympic Project. (n.d.). Welcome to the Olympic Project. Retrieved August 29, 2017, from http://www.olympicproject.com/.

Palepu, Anita, and Carol P. Herbert. 2002. "Medical Women in Academia: The Silences We Keep." *Canadian Medical Association Journal* 167 (8): 877–79.

Parsons, Talcott. 1951. *The Social System*. Glencoe, IL: Free Press.

Patterson, Roger. 1966. *Do Abominable Snowmen of America Really Exist?* Yakima, WA: Northwest Research Association.

Patterson, Roger, and Christopher Murphy. 2005. *The Bigfoot Film Controversy*. Blaine, WA: Hancock House.

Peiro, Jose M., Vicente Gonzalez-Roma, Nuria Tordera, and Miguel A. Manas. 2001. "Does Role Stress Predict Burnout over Time among Health Care Professionals?" *Psychology and Health* 16: 511–25.

Perry, Samuel L., and Andrew L. Whitehead. 2016. "Religion and Non-Traditional Families in the United States." *Sociology Compass* 10 (5): 391–403.

Peterson, Richard G. 1984. "Preparing for the Apocalypse: Survivalist Strategies." *Free Inquiry in Creative Sociology* 12 (1): 44–46.

Pettigrew, Thomas F., Linda R. Tropp, Ulrich Wagner, and Oliver Christ. 2011. "Recent Advances in Intergroup Contact Theory." *International Journal of Intercultural Relations* 35 (3): 271–80.

Pfuhl, Erdwin H. Jr. 1980. *The Deviance Process*. New York: D. Van Nostrand.

Phelps, Fred Sr. 2005. "A Message from Westboro Baptist Church (WBC) to Lawmakers on Legislation Regarding Her Counter-Demonstrations at Funerals of Dead Soldiers." http://downloads.godhatesfags.com/wpfb-file/20051212_legislation-message-pdf/.

Pichardo, Nelson. n.d. "Framing the User: Social Constructions of Marijuana Users and the Medical Marijuana Movement."

Pilichis, Dennis. 1982. *Night Siege: The Northern Ohio UFO-Creature Invasion*. Rome, OH: Self-published.

Piquero, Alex R. 2000. "Frequency, Specialization, and Violence in Offending Careers." *Journal of Research in Crime and Delinquency* 37: 392–418.

PlanetSasquatch. 2015. *Episode 44—Cloaked Deer Anomaly*. November 15. Retrieved August 29, 2017, from https://www.youtube.com/watch?v=frj_C5jst2s.

Plummer, Ken. 1999. "The Lesbian and Gay Movement in Britain: Schisms, Solidarities and Social Worlds." In *The Global Emergence of Gay and Lesbian Politics National Imprints of a Worldwide Movement*, edited by Barry D Adam, Jan Willem Duyvendak, and André Krouwel, 133–57. Philadelphia: Temple University Press.

Pomaki, Georgia, Abas Supeli, and Chris Verhoeven. 2007. "Role Conflict and Health Behaviors: Moderating Effects on Psychological Distress and Somatic Complaints." *Psychology and Health* 22 (3): 317–35.

Powell, Thom. 2015. *Edges of Science*. Oregon: Willamette City Press.

Provine, Doris Marie. 2007. *Unequal under the Law: Race in the War on Drugs*. Chicago: University of Chicago Press.

Rand, Erin J. 2014. *Reclaiming Queer: Activist & Academic Rhetorics of Resistance*. Tuscaloosa, AL: University of Alabama Press.

Ray, Bradley, and Cindy B. Dollar. 2014. "Exploring Stigmatization and Stigma Management in Mental Health Court: Assessing Modified Labeling Theory in a New Context." *Sociological Forum* 29 (3): 720–35.

Reasons, Charles. 1974. "The Politics of Drugs: An Inquiry into the Sociology of Social Problems." *The Sociological Quarterly* 15 (3): 381–404.

Reckless, Walter C. 1961. "A New Theory of Delinquency and Crime." *Federal Probation* 25: 42–46.

———. 1967. *The Crime Problem*. 4th edition. New York: Appleton-Century Crofts.

Reed, Isaac. 2007. "Why Salem Made Sense: Culture, Gender and Puritan Persecution of Witchcraft." *Cultural Sociology* 1 (2): 209–34.

Regal, Brian. 2011. *Searching for Sasquatch: Crackpots, Eggheads, and Cryptozoology*. New York: Palgrave Macmillan.

Reilly, Adam. 2006. "Take My Wives Please: Mitt Romney's Clumsy Mormon Shtick." *Slate*, April 26. Retrieved April 10, 2017, from http://www.slate.com/articles/news_and_politics/politics/2006/04/take_my_wives_please.html.

Reinarman, Craig. 1988. "The Social Construction of an Alcohol Problem: The Case of Mothers Against Drunk Driving and Social Control in the 1980s." *Theory and Society* 17 (1): 91–120.

———. 1994. "The Social Construction of Drug Scares." In *Social Constructions of Deviance*, edited by Patricia Adler and Peter Adler, 92–104. Belmont, CA: Wadsworth.

Reiss, Albert J. 1951. "Delinquency as the Failure of Personal and Social Bonds." *American Sociological Review* 16 (2): 196–207.

Renfrow, Daniel G. 2004. "The Cartography of Passing in Everyday Life." *Symbolic Interaction* 27 (4): 485–506.

Rimmerman, Craig A. 2015. *The Lesbian and Gay Movements: Assimilation or Liberation?* Boulder, CO: Westview Press.

Rios, Victor M. 2011. *Punished: Policing the Lives of Black and Latino Boys.* New York: New York University Press.

Rodriquez, Eric M., and Suzanne C. Ouellette. 2000. "Gay and Lesbian Christians: Homosexual and Religious Identity Integration in the Members and Participants of a Gay-Positive Church." *Journal for the Scientific Study of Religion* 39 (3): 333–47.

Rogers, Will. (1932) 1979. *Daily Telegrams, Vol. 3: The Hoover Years, 1931–1933*, edited by James M. Smallwood and Steven K. Gragert. Stillwater: Oklahoma State University Press

———. (1932) 2006. *The Papers of Will Rogers, Vol. 5*, edited by Steven K. Gragert and M. Jane Johansson. Norman: University of Oklahoma Press.

Romney, Mitt. 2007. "Faith in America." Retrieved from http://www.npr.org/templates /story/story.php?storyId=16969460.

"Romney's Health Care Overhaul." 2006. *Hardball*, April 13. Retrieved April 10, 2017, from http://www.nbcnews.com/id/12289524/#.WOv-Jvn1DIU.

Rooney, Kathleen. 2014. "The Brutality of Believing: Mattilda Bernstein Sycamore in Conversation with Kathleen Rooney." *Brooklyn Rail*, February 5. http://brooklynrail.org/2014/02 /books/the-brutality-of-believing-mattilda-bernstein-sycamore-in-conversation -with-kathleen-rooney.

Root, Grace C. 1934. *Women and Repeal.* New York: Harper & Brothers.

Rose, Kenneth D. 1997. *American Women and the Repeal of Prohibition.* New York: New York University Press.

Ruiz, Jason. 2008. "The Violence of Assimilation: An Interview with Mattilda aka Matt Bernstein Sycamore." *Radical History Review* 100: 236–47.

Ryan, Caitlin, and Judith Bradford. 1999. "Conducting the National Lesbian Health Care Survey: First of Its Kind." *Journal of the Gay and Lesbian Medical Association* 3 (3): 91–97.

Sabin, Pauline M. 1928. "I Change My Mind on Prohibition." *The Outlook*, June 13, 254, 272.

Sagarin, Edward. 1969. *Odd Man In: Societies of Deviants in America.* New York: Quadrangle.

———. 1973. "The Good Guys, the Bad Guys, and the Gay Guys." *Contemporary Sociology* 2 (1): 3–13.

———. 1976. "Prison Homosexuality and Its Effect on Post-Prison Behavior." *Psychiatry* 39 (3): 245–57.

———. 1985. "Positive Deviance: An Oxymoron." *Deviant Behavior* 6 (2): 169–181.

Sampson, Robert J., and John H. Laub. 1993. *Crime in the Making: Pathways and Turning Points through Life.* Cambridge, MA: Harvard University Press.

Schieman, Scott, Debra B, McBrier, and Karen Van Gundy. 2003. "Home-to-Work Conflict, Work Qualities, and Emotional Distress." *Sociological Forum* 18 (1): 137–64.

Schnabel, Landon, and Eric Sevell. 2017. "Should Mary and Jane Be Legal? Americans' Attitudes toward Marijuana and Same-Sex Marriage Legalization, 1988–2014." *Public Opinion Quarterly* 81 (1): 157–72.

Schur, Edwin. 1980. *The Politics of Deviance.* Englewood Cliffs, NJ: Prentice Hall.

———. 1984. *Labeling Women Deviant: Gender, Stigma, and Social Control.* New York: Random House.

Schwadel, Philip, and Christopher G. Ellison. 2017. "Period and Cohort Changes in Americans' Support for Marijuana Legalization: Convergence and Divergence across Social Groups." *Sociological Quarterly* 58 (3): 405–28.

Sears, James T. 2006. *Behind the Mask of the Mattachine*. New York: Harrington Park Press.

Seidman, Steven, ed. 1996. *Queer Theory/Sociology*. Malden, MA: Blackwell.

Severn, Bill. 1969. *The End of the Roaring Twenties: Prohibition and Repeal*. New York: Julian Messner.

Shactman, Tom. 2006. *Rumspringa: To Be or Not to Be Amish*. New York: North Point Press.

Shapiro, Gregg. 2013. "The End Is the Beginning: An Interview with Mattilda Bernstein Sycamore." *Chicago Pride*. http://chicago.gopride.com/news/interview.cfm/articleid/545625.

Shapiro, Robert Y. 2011. "Public Opinion and American Democracy." *Public Opinion Quarterly* 75 (5): 982–1017.

Sharp, Elaine B. 1999. *The Some Time Connection: Public Opinion and Social Policy*. Albany: State University of New York Press.

Shaw, Clifford R. 1930. *The Jack-Roller: A Delinquent Boy's Own Story*. Chicago: University of Chicago Press.

Shaw, Ian. 2009. "Rereading *The Jack-Roller*: Hidden Histories in Sociology and Social Work." *Qualitative Inquiry* 15 (7): 1241–64.

Shepard, Benjamin. 2010. *Queer Political Performance and Protest: Play, Pleasure and Social Movement*. New York: Routledge.

Skinner, Denise A. 1980. "Dual-Career Family Stress and Coping: A Literature Review." *Family Relations* 29 (4): 473–81.

Simi, Pete, Kathleen Blee, Matthew DeMichele, and Steven Windisch. 2017. "Addicted to Hate: Identity Residual among Former White Supremacists." *American Sociological Review* 86 (2): 1167–87.

Simi, Pete, and Robert Futrell. 2009. "Negotiating White Power Activist Stigma." *Social Problems* 56 (1): 89–110.

Simmons, J. L. 1969. *Deviants*. Berkeley, CA: Glendessary Press.

Simon, Jonathan. 2007. *Governing through Crime: How the War on Crime Transformed American Democracy and Created a Culture of Fear*. New York: Oxford University Press.

Simon, William, and John H. Gagnon. 1967a. "Homosexuality: The Formulation of a Sociological Perspective." *Journal of Health and Social Behavior* 8 (3): 177–85.

———. 1967b. "Femininity in the Lesbian Community." *Social Problems* 15 (2): 212–21.

Smith, Rachel A., and Thomas J. Hipper. 2010. "Label Management: Investigating How Confidants Encourage the Use of Communication Strategies to Avoid Stigmatization." *Health Communication* 25: 410–22.

Snodgrass, Jon. 1983. "*The Jack-Roller*: A Fifty-Year Follow-Up." *Urban Life* 11 (4): 440–60.

Snodgrass, Jon, and "The Jack-Roller." 1982. *The Jack-Roller at Seventy: A Fifty-Year Follow-Up*. Lexington, MA: Lexington Books.

Snow, David A., and Doug McAdam. 2000. "Identity Work Processes in the Context of Social Movements: Clarifying the Identity/Movement Nexus." In *Self, Identity and Social Movements*, edited by Sheldon Stryker, Timothy J. Owens, and Robert W. White, 41–67. Minneapolis: University of Minnesota Press.

Snow, David A., E. Burke Rochford Jr., Steven K. Wordern, and Robert D. Benford. 1986. "Frame Alignment Processes, Micromobilization, and Movement Participation." *American Sociological Review* 51 (4): 464–81.

Spector, Malcolm, and John I. Kituse. 1987. *Constructing Social Problems*. New Brunswick, NJ: Transaction.

Stack, Steven. 2000. "Suicide: A 15-Year Review of the Sociological Literature Part II: Modernization and Social Integration Perspectives." *Suicide and Life-Threatening Behavior* 30 (2): 163–76.

Stark, Rodney. 2003. "Why Religious Movements Succeed or Fail: A Revised General Model." In *Cults and New Religious Movements: A Reader*, edited by Lorne L. Dawson, 259–70. Malden, MA: Blackwell.

Stebbins, Robert A. 1971. *Commitment to Deviance: The Nonprofessional Criminal in the Community*. Westport, CT: Greenwood.

Steensland, Brian, Jerry Z. Park, Mark D. Regnerus, Lynn D. Robinson, W. Bradford Wilcox, and Robert D. Woodberry. 2000. "The Measure of American Religion: Toward Improving the State of the Art." *Social Forces* 79 (1): 291–318.

Steffensmeir, Darrell J., and Jeffrey T. Ulmer. 2005. *Confessions of a Dying Thief: Understanding Criminal Careers and Illegal Enterprise*. Piscataway, NJ: AldineTransaction.

Stets, Jan E., and Peter J. Burke. 2003. "A Sociological Approach to Self and Identity." In *Handbook of Self and Identity*, edited by Mark R. Leary and June P. Tangney, 128–52. New York: Guilford Press.

Stevick, Richard A. 2014. *Growing Up Amish: The Rumspringa Years*. 2nd edition. Baltimore, MD: Johns Hopkins University Press.

Stewart, Charles, Craig Smith, and Robert E. Denton Jr. 1984. *Persuasion and Social Movements*. Prospect Heights, IL: Waveland Press.

Stone, Jeff, and Joel Cooper. 2000. "A Self-Standards Model of Cognitive Dissonance." *Journal of Experimental Social Psychology* 37 (3): 228–43.

Streufert, Steven. 2011 "Patterson-Gimlin Film Site Rediscovered . . . and Documented. The Bluff Creek Film Site Project Reaches Preliminary Conclusions re the Location of the True PGF Site." Retrieved August 25, 2017, from http://bigfootbooksblog.blogspot .com/2011/11/patterson-gimlin-film-site-rediscovered.html.

Stryker, Jo Ellen. 2003. "Media and Marijuana: A Longitudinal Analysis of News Media Effects on Adolescents' Marijuana Use and Related Outcomes, 1977–1999." *Journal of Health Communication* 8 (4): 305–28.

Stryker, Sheldon. 1968. "Identity Salience and Role Performance: The Relevance of Symbolic Interaction Theory for Family Research." *Journal of Marriage and the Family* 30: 558–564.

———. 1980. *Symbolic Interactionism: A Social Structural Version*. Menlo Park, CA: Benjamin/Cummings.

———. 1981. "Symbolic Interactionism: Themes and Variations." In *Social Psychology: Sociological Perspectives*, edited by Morris Rosenberg and Ralph H. Turner, 3–29. New York: Basic.

———. 1987. "Identity Theory: Developments and Extensions." In *Self and Identity: Psychological Perspectives*, edited by Krysia Yardley and Terry Honess, 83–103. New York: Wiley.

———. 1989. "Further Developments in Identity Theory: Singularity versus Multiplicity of the Self." In *Sociological Theories in Progress: New Formulations*, edited by Joseph Berger, Morris Zelditch Jr., and Bo Anderson, 35–57. Newbury Park, CA: Sage.

———. 2000. "Identity Competition: Key to Differential Social Movement Involvement." In *Identity, Self, and Social Movements*, edited by Sheldon Stryker, Timothy Owens, and Roberta White, 21–40. Minneapolis: University of Minnesota Press.

————. 2007. "Identity Theory and Personality Theory: Mutual Relevance." *Journal of Personality* 75 (6): 1083–102.

————. 2008. "From Mead to a Structural Symbolic Interactionism and Beyond." *Annual Review of Sociology* 34: 15–31.

Stryker, Sheldon, and Peter J. Burke. 2000. "The Past, Present, and Future of an Identity Theory." *Social Psychology Quarterly* 63 (4): 284–97.

Stryker, Sheldon, and Ann S. Macke. 1978. "Status Inconsistency and Role Conflict." *Annual Review of Sociology* 4: 57–90.

Stryker, Sheldon, and Richard T. Serpe. 1982. "Commitment, Identity Salience, and Role Behavior: A Theory and Research Example." In *Personality, Roles and Social Behavior*, edited by William Ickes and Eric S. Knowles, 199–218. New York: Springer-Verlag.

Sumerau, J. E., Ryan Cragun, and Lain A. B. Mather. 2016. "'I Found God in the Glory Hole': The Moral Career of a Gay Christian." *Sociological Inquiry* 86 (4): 618–640.

Sumner, Colin. 1994. *The Sociology of Deviance: An Obituary*. Buckingham, UK: Open University Press.

Sutherland, Edwin H., and Donald R. Cressey. 1974. *Criminology*. 9th edition. Philadelphia: Lippincott.

Swarns, Rachel L. 1999. "Unlikely Protesters: Diallo Case Draws Diverse Group." *New York Times*, March 27.

Sycamore, Mattilda Bernstein. 2008a. "There's More to Life than Platinum," In *That's Revolting: Queer Strategies for Resisting Assimilation*, revised edition, edited by Mattilda Bernstein Sycamore, 1–10. Berkeley, CA: Soft Skull Press.

————. 2008b. "Gay Shame: From Queer Autonomous Space to Direct Action Extravaganza," In *That's Revolting: Queer Strategies for Resisting Assimilation*, revised edition, edited by Mattilda Bernstein Sycamore, 268–95. Berkeley, CA: Soft Skull Press.

————. 2014. "Why Gay Marriage IS the End of the World (or the Queer World, at Least)," In *Against Equality: Queer Revolution Not Mere Inclusion*, edited by Ryan Conrad, 87–95. Oakland, CA: AK Press.

Sykes, Gresham, and Matza, David. 1957. "Techniques of Neutralization: A Theory of Delinquency." *American Sociological Review* 22 (6): 664–67.

Szymanski, Dawn M., and Erika R. Carr. 2008. "The Roles of Gender Role Conflict and Internalized Heterosexism in Gay and Bisexual Men's Psychological Distress: Testing Two Mediation Models." *Psychology of Men & Masculinity* 9 (1): 40–54.

Tarrow, Sidney. 1994. *Power in Movement: Social Movements, Collective Action and Politics*. Cambridge: Cambridge University Press.

Taylor, Ian, Paul Walton, and Jock Young. 1983. *The New Criminology: For a Social Theory of Deviance*. New York: Harper & Row.

Taylor, Jodie. 2014. "Festivalizing Sexualities: Discourses of 'Pride', Counter-discourses of 'Shame.'" In *The Festivalisation of Culture*, edited by Andy Bennett, Jodie Taylor, and Ian Woodward, 27–48. London: Ashgate.

Thomas, Michael D., Diana W. Thomas, and Nicholas A. Snow. 2013. "Rational Irrationality and the Political Process of Repeal: The Women's Organization for National Prohibition Reform and the 21st Amendment." *Kyklos* 66 (1): 130–52.

Toby, Jackson. 1957. "Social Disorganization and Stake in Conformity: Complementary Factors in the Predatory Behavior of Hoodlums." *Journal of Criminal Law, Criminology, and Police Science* 48 (3): 12–17.

Travis, Jeremy. 2002. "Invisible Punishment: An Instrument of Social Exclusion." In *Invisible Punishment: The Collateral Consequences of Mass Imprisonment*, edited by Marc Mauer and Meda Chesney-Lind, 15–36. New York: The Free Press.

Troyer, Ronald J., and Gerald E. Markle. 1982. "Creating Deviance: A Macroscopic Model." *Sociological Quarterly* 23 (2): 157–69.

Turner, Jonathan. 2003. *The Structure of Sociological Theory*. 7th edition. Belmont, CA: Thomson Wadsworth.

Twenge, Jean M., Nathan T. Carter, and W. Keith Campbell. 2015. "Time Period, Generational, and Age Differences in Tolerance for Controversial Beliefs and Lifestyles in the United States, 1972–2012." *Social Forces* 94 (1): 379–99.

Ulmer, Jeffery T. 1994. "Revisiting Stebbins: Labeling and Commitment to Deviance." *The Sociological Quarterly* 35 (1): 135–57.

———. 2000. "Commitment, Deviance, and Social Control." *The Sociological Quarterly* 41 (3): 315–36.

Vail, D. Angus. 1999. "'Tattoos Are Like Potato Chips ... You Can't Have Just One': The Process of Becoming and Being a Collector." *Deviant Behavior* 20 (3): 253–73.

Vaisey, Stephen, and Omar Lizardo. 2010. "Can Cultural Worldviews Influence Network Composition?" *Social Forces* 88 (4): 1595–618.

Vaughn, Diane. 1996. *The Challenger Launch Decision: Risky Technology, Culture, and Deviance at NASA*. Chicago: University of Chicago Press.

Vaughn, Michael G., Christopher P. Salas-Wright, and Matt DeLisi. 2015. "Drifter: An Exploration into a Classical Criminological Construct." *American Journal of Criminal Justice* 40 (3): 560–78.

Ward, Elizabeth J. 2008. *Respectably Queer: Diversity Culture in LGBT Activist Organizations*. Nashville, TN: Vanderbilt University Press.

Weber, Max. (1930) 2002. *The Protestant Ethic and the Spirit of Capitalism*. Translated by Talcott Parsons. New York: Dover.

———. 1949. *The Methodology of the Social Sciences*. Translated by Edward Shils and Henry Finch. New York: The Free Press.

Weinstein, Netta, William S. Ryan, Cody R. DeHaan, Andrew K. Pryzbylski, Nicole Legate, and Richard M. Ryan. 2012. "Parental Autonomy Support and Discrepancies between Implicit and Explicit Sexual Identities: Dynamics of Self-Acceptance and Defense." *Journal of Personality and Social Psychology* 102 (4): 815–32.

Weiss, Margot. 2008. "Gay Shame and BDSM Pride: Neoliberalism, Privacy, and Sexual Politics." *Radical History Review* 100: 87–101.

Weiss, Margot. 2012. "Intellectual Inquiry Otherwise: An Interview with Mattilda Bernstein Sycamore." *American Quarterly* 64 (4): 833–36.

Williams, Rhys H. 2002. "From the 'Beloved Community' to 'Family Values': Religious Language, Symbolic Repertoires, and Democratic Culture." In *Social Movements: Identity, Culture, and the State*, edited by David S. Meyer, Nancy Whittier, and Belinda Robnett, 247–65. New York: Oxford University Press.

Winn-Lenetsky, Jonah A. 2015. "Common Ground: Performing Gay Shame, Solidarity and Social Change." Doctoral dissertation, University of Minnesota. http://hdl.handle.net /11299/172102.

Woodiwiss, Michael. 1988. *Crime Crusades and Corruption: Prohibition in the United States, 1900–1987*. Totowa, NJ: Barnes & Noble.

Wright, Kevin A., Travis C. Pratt, and Matt DeLisi. 2008. "Examining Offending Specialization in a Sample of Male Multiple Homicide Offenders." *Homicide Studies* 12 (4): 381–98.

Wright, Stuart, and James T. Richardson, eds. 2011. *Saints under Siege: The Texas State Raid on the Fundamentalist Latter Day Saints*. New York: New York University Press.

Zald, Mayer N., and Roberta Ash. 1966. "Social Movement Organizations: Growth, Decay and Change." *Social Forces* 44 (3): 327–41.

Zald, Mayer N., and John D. McCarthy. 1980. "Social Movement Industries: Competition and Cooperation among Movement Organizations." In *Research in Social Movements, Conflict and Change*, edited by Louis Kriesberg, 1–20. Greenwich, CT: JAI Press.

———. 1994. "Religious Groups as Crucibles of Social Movements." In *Social Movements in an Organizational Society: Collected Essays*, edited by Mayer N. Zald and John D. McCarthy, 67–95. New Brunswick, NJ: Transaction Publishers.

INDEX